21st Century RPG
/Free, ILE, and MVC

David Shirey

MC Press Online, LLC

Boise, ID 83703 USA

21st Century RPG: /Free, ILE, and MVC

David Shirey

First Edition

First Printing—June 2017

MC Press Online, LLC
Corporate Offices: 3695 W. Quail Heights Court, Boise, ID 83703-3861 USA
Sales and Customer Service: (208) 629-7275 ext. 500; service@mcpressonline.com
Permissions and Bulk/Special Orders: mcbooks@mcpressonline.com
www.mcpressonline.com • www.mc-store.com

ISBN: 978-1-58347-405-1

Acknowledgments

A few quick acknowledgments.

First, to my wife, Donna, for putting up with me for the last x number of years. I don't think I could have done it. Unfortunately, she was no help in developing this book. Yes, I have spent a great portion of the last x years acting as her full-time tech support. Why do people who have no technical expertise at all end up needing it? There goes a third of my life. But she is worth it.

Second, to Scott Palma for letting me use Arbor Solutions' IBM i. To tell the truth, as a consultant, I do a lot of things and don't always have an IBM i client. But the kind people at Arbor (Scott, Richie, Mike, and George) have always been a "swell bunch of fellas" in terms of letting me sign on to their system and test things.

Third, to the two editors I have worked with: Katie Tipton, who first encouraged me, and Anne Grubb, who put up with me during the difficult times. You guys rock.

Fourth, to Tom Snyder. No, not the 80s talk show host (I think he may be dead), but to the author and IBM i (among other things) guru who reviewed my first drafts and never indicated in any way that he thought I was crazy. Appreciate that, Tom, but I'm still not sure about your judgment.

Fifth, to Victoria Mack. Maybe Vic should be first, but I am not doing this in any kind of order. I have always wanted to write, and Vic gave me my first chance. I am reminded of the line from the movie *Clueless*: "Thanks to the staff at McDonald's for taking a chance on an unknown kid." That is what Vic did, and I will always have a soft spot in my heart for her. And for Lido, of course.

Finally, but certainly not least, to Alan Seiden and Aaron Bartell, two true gentlemen who always answered my questions. Alan does it because he is just that kind of guy (*club.alanseiden.com*). Don't really understand that myself, but I would send him an email question at 11 at night, and he would respond. I never, never respond to any email that I send myself. It just encourages me. But Alan is different. And Aaron ... he comes out only two or three times a year. Emerging from the forests of Minnesota only when he has furs to sell and needs to get the basics: mostly flour, bacon grease, and gun powder. Although if I remember correctly, Aaron has daughters, and so eventually he will need One Direction tickets if they ever come to the "big city" (Minneapolis). But they have both been instrumental, especially in chapter 27. Follow them because they are always doing something weird and useful.

And that's about it. To be honest, I did do some of this myself.

Contents

INTRODUCTION TO ILE

A brief introduction to the history of time, but mostly to ILE and what it means.

Chapter 1

A High-Level Introduction to ILE

Before we start, I want to make a few brief remarks about what to expect from this book.

First, it is about three things and pretty much three things only: free-form RPG, Integrated Language Environment (ILE), and Model-View-Controller (MVC). If anything else is covered, it was more or less an accident, and I apologize.

Second, I am going to try to make this as practical as possible, and I will expect you to participate.

I have lots of code samples and many of them actually work.

I will be expecting you to not just follow along but do coding yourself. Nothing says lovin' like something you code up yourself, so be prepared to do more than read. The **Now It's Your Turn** sections are specifically designed to make you do things that you have just read about. Read it, do it, live it.

Nor are any of these topics what I would call hard. But they do require some practice to learn and get comfortable with. Make sure you give yourself a healthy dose of playing with them.

Finally, this book is really meant for those of you who may feel that you are being left behind.

Naturally enough, many books, maybe most, are aimed at the people who are near the cutting edge. Unfortunately, when we are talking about the IBM i technical base, I believe that for every IBM i user who is on 7.whatever, there are three who are still on 5.4 or maybe even below. They do not go to COMMON (no money), they do not get regular upgrades to their system (no commitment from management), they drink mostly Miller or Bud (can't explain that when Sam Adams and Fat Tire are readily available almost everywhere), but they are still there, working on the i every day, using it to support their business, toting that barge and liftin' that bale.

Or maybe they are on 7.2. But for whatever reason, they are not being allowed to take full advantage of that. They are still using positional RPG, writing big single-module programs that will be almost impossible to modify in a timely manner for today's fast-paced IT environments.

As a nod to this group, I am going to assume no existing knowledge of /Free or ILE or MVC. And almost all the code examples are written from a 5.4 point of view. Because the truth is, you don't need to be on the latest release to be writing modern, effective RPG code.

Oh, I do cover the more up-to-date topics, like the new free-form control statements that can replace F- or D-specs, which came out in 7.1, or some of the stuff that shows up in 7.3. But I treat that as icing, not cake.

So if you feel that IBM is leaving you behind, and you have no choice but to code positional RPG in big ol' programs (BOPs), this one's for you. You don't have to do things the old way. You may not have all the bells and whistles available, but you can modernize your RPG quite effectively even on 5.4. Come on, man. Give it a whirl.

The Organization of the Book

I have given a lot of thought to where we will start and have changed my mind several times. I finally decided that the center of this is ILE; everything we are going to do depends on it, so it's a great place to start. Here is what we are going to do.

We will kick things off with two "more theory than practice" chapters on ILE, to give you a solid understanding of what it is based on and how it sort of works.

Then a couple of chapters on /Free, just in case you are not familiar with it, because all of the code we use here will be /Free (it doesn't make sense to use anything else).

This will be followed by three chapters where we spec out actual ILE programs (including a service program) using the /Free we have learned.

Then back to /Free for some oddball, semi-advanced topics that will be especially interesting to those of you who are on newer releases.

Next will be a return to ILE for really advanced topics, mostly related to your new best friend: service programs.

And then, at last, like the final glorious culmination of an epic adventure, MVC.

But enough preliminaries. Are you ready? Great. Let's get started.

What ~~Is~~ Was OPM?

Did you ever wonder how a program runs? That is, how it starts, how it stops, what rules (other than the code syntax) it follows during its brief and sometimes tragic life.

Me neither. I was always happy enough just to have it finish without my having to look in QEZDEBUG. But the truth is that every program has a "program model" that it follows and that governs just how it does what it does.

For many years, for RPG, this model was called the Original Program Model (OPM), and it did a number of things behind the scenes.

First, it figured out how to start a program. You know, find a spot in the system where it could run, give it the resources it needed, all that jazz.

Second, for OPM, it controlled the RPG cycle. That's that weird thing that I have never used that will do things (like read files) without you specifically asking it to. Freaky.

Third, it controlled how you called one program from another using the CALL or CALLB opcode.

And fourth, it told the program when to end by using the LR, and it released all resources and cleaned up the party debris.

Problems with OPM

Unfortunately, OPM had a number of built-in problems that got in the way of how we really want to program today. In a nutshell, it was designed to handle one large program at a time rather than a small, multi-module approach. As a result, OPM comes with the seeds of its own destruction sown inside.

Inefficient Calls

For one thing, even though you could call a second program from a first in OPM, something we really need to be able to do if we are going to switch from a BOP (Big Ol' Program) to smaller, more nimble modules, it didn't do it very well.

The calls were easy enough to make, but every time you called another program, it required a full startup of that new program (opening files, finding space for it, introducing it to the other program, letting them smell each other so they wouldn't fight, etc.) with no sharing of resources.

This takes a lot of time (relatively speaking), and if you end up calling the same program repeatedly from the OPM model, it can add up to some real time and therefore not provide the quick response that you need. Besides, just thinking about the lost time bothers some people immensely.

No Local Variable Support

This is the big one for me: every data element in an OPM program is a global element and can be used everywhere in the program. Lack of local variables is a major difference between RPG and Web languages and makes it very hard for you to build truly modular programs.

What's wrong with global elements? Well, by letting a given data element run wild throughout the entire program, you tend to increase the level of data coupling and so increase the chances of making it possible to change a data element in contradictory ways in several far-flung parts of the program. At the very least, it makes it much harder to track what is happening with that element if you are debugging. It is pretty much agreed by everyone that data coupling is bad—very, very bad.

What you want to do is use data elements that are local rather than global. That is, they are defined and can be used only in a small section of code. But the ability to do this is not available in OPM.

Generally, we refer to this kind of thing as *scope*—the extent or hunting ground of a particular variable. Items that have global scope can be used anywhere in the program, something that might seem convenient but which greatly increases the complexity of a program. Local scope variables can be used in one specific area, and so it is much easier to understand what is happening to that element and how it affects the program.

Scope is something that we in the RPG world don't think much about because in OPM we did not have a program model that allowed local variables. So everything naturally ended up everywhere, and therefore there was only one "scope." But when you get into Web languages, and especially object-oriented (OO) versions, scope becomes a critical concept and one that is carefully monitored.

As we shall see later, in ILE the question of whether a variable is global or local will be set by where in the program it is defined, and once that definition is made, hard and fast rules will control its use. And sometimes rules are good.

Limited Incentive to Set Up Modular Programs

For me, in the end, it's all about the fact that OPM pushes you toward a BOP. OPM just has very few tools for encouraging you to build multi-module applications.

The inefficient calls are one thing.

The lack of local variables is another.

The inability of OPM to handle true procedure-oriented programming is a third.

And the final nail in the coffin is the inability of OPM to support service programs. As we shall see, the main advantage of service programs is not so much just their ability to separately encapsulate source but rather the ability of the service program to insulate the logic in the service program and the programs that use them from changes in either of those entities.

To be honest, I like OPM. It is simple and direct. It is also an evolutionary dead end. And the future is ILE.

It may seem cruel, but in the end IBM decided that a new program model was needed, and they decided to call this new program model ILE.

Don't worry, they didn't kill OPM, and you can still run your programs in the old way if you want to. But there is a time for everything under the sun, and it seems like now is the time to use ILE and let OPM get some much-needed rest.

What Makes ILE Different (and Special)

ILE stands for Integrated Language Environment. It was designed to be just that: a single environment where you could develop and link together programs using a variety of programming languages, sort of a "one environment to find them all, one environment to bind them all" kind of thing but with no dwarves or elves or oliphants (sorry, Sam).

The new model was introduced slowly over a number of operating system releases, starting with C in V2R3 (that was actually before I was born ☺), and adding RPG, COBOL, and CL in V3R1. All of this happened back in the 90s, so you can see that ILE has been around for a while.

In order to list what ILE gives you, I can't do better than to refer to some of the points outlined by Barbara Morris in her excellent presentation, "ILE Concepts for RPG." Unfortunately, the Web link to it is no longer active, so you only have me to believe as to its contents. Very convenient, eh?

Modularity

ILE is all about little things: little programs, little pieces of code.

Little sections of code are easier to understand, they are easier to test, and they are less likely to go in the dumper for you. Plus, if you start doing anything in the Web arena, small pieces of code are what they use. Might as well start thinking that way, because most of us are going to end up doing some kind of Web coding.

Where you really see the beauty of small modules is during testing and down the road in maintenance. With less data coupling and fewer lines of code per unit to be tested, testing is faster and more straightforward. And small modules almost guarantee that you will no longer have to spend two days to get into a 20,000-line program before you even start your modifications.

I was struck by a sentence in James Martin's book, *Free-Format RPG IV, Third Edition* (MC Press, 2015) that talked about how the decision to not bring the GOTO into /Free would prevent spaghetti code. And that is certainly true, but there is also spaghetti code that is not created with a GOTO, but rather with a plethora of subroutines, all of which use the same data elements. Data spaghetti. Small modules with local variables and low data coupling are the only way to really prevent data spaghetti code. I guess ILE would be considered "ravioli code."

Control

OPM was like model railroading. You put the train on the track and you could have intricate track, but it pretty much just went around the setup. You don't have a lot of control over it, which is why you put your time into building a mountain pass and having a small plastic Bigfoot wave at the train.

But with ILE you can go off-roading. It gives you control over when things start, who hangs with whom (that is, what programs run with what other programs in a common environment), and how things end. It's totally cool. For once in your life, you call the signals. Yeah, baby, you're the man.

Reduced Data Coupling

This point is mentioned above, but it is worth stating on its own.

Because ILE supports local variables (we will see that when we look at sub-procedures), and because things tend to be done in smaller, more focused modules, the data coupling is generally not as extensive as it is in a BOP.

This makes debugging simpler and makes it easier to follow the data flow in the event you need to make mods to this app down the road.

When talking about ILE, the focus seems to get put on parameters and binding and service programs and activation groups. But it all begins with procedures, small bits of code that do stuff. If I could encourage you to do anything, it would be to use local variables as much as you can. I firmly believe that data coupling is at the root of many problems with program design. Reduce that with local variables. Seriously.

Error Handling

I don't bother too much with error handling myself. I see that as someone else's problem. Besides, my apps don't have errors. You know how it is. But it is important to a lot of programmers, so we should consider it.

With OPM, your error-handling options were limited. If an exception occurred that was not specifically handled, all the system could do was send an inquiry message to the system operator asking what to do. What a polite way to say "blow up, end of weekend."

In ILE, you can actually boil that error up to a higher-level program and have it handled. That is, with ILE if Program 1 has error handling, and it calls Program 2, which does not have error handling, if there is a problem in Program 2, it can be transferred back up to Program 1 to be handled.

Handling errors with ILE can be a whole area on its own and is one that we are not going to deal with. It's a little more detailed than I want to get into, so I suggest you look at the IBM Redbook (actually, it's a Red Paper, but a pretty long one) "RPG: Exception and Error Handling," by Jon Paris, Susan Gantner, Gary Mullen-Schultz, and Paul Tuohy. Or you might try chapter 16 of *Programming in ILE RPG* (now that's a textbook and a very good one), by Bryan Meyers and Jim Buck, from MC Press. Finally, there is the old standby from IBM, *Who Knew You Could Do That in RPG IV?* by a whole slew of very well-known people, some of whom the FBI has not caught up with yet.

API/Language Access

An added plus is the fact that ILE gives you access to many APIs, including the entire C library.

Now I know what you are thinking. The commonly held belief is that using C causes calluses on your feet and underarms. And frankly, that's probably true. But there are times when only a C API will do. I can't think of any offhand, but I also don't have any calluses on my feet or underarms. It all makes sense if you think about it.

In general, ILE makes accessing a number of other languages easier and more efficient. As we move into the future, we are going to see fewer applications that are just RPG (or CL) and more that involve other languages (including Web ones) as well. But more about that much later.

Better Performance

I am sort of obligated to say this. It is one of Barbara's bullet points, but to be honest, have you ever seen an IBM announcement that touted "slightly poorer performance than in previous releases because of the extra stuff we are doing"? So I find it hard to really get excited about "performance enhancements."

But in this case, I believe it. Mostly because a lot of it is based on vast and technologically unexplainable improvements in the speed with which calls are made. And since ILE relies heavily on calling procedures, it is right up ILE's alley.

Why Bother with ILE?

I am not talking here about why you should bother with ILE from the point of view of your company. If you are interested in that, just Google "advantages of ILE," and you will get links to dozens of articles.

No, what I am talking about here is why *you* should bother with it. You personally, that is.

After all, I am asking you to embrace a new set of tools, to give up the comfortable paths of the past and spend some time and energy learning something new. You've been doing RPG for quite some time now, probably without using any or much ILE, and things aren't going too bad. Why should you change? It's a reasonable question.

For you, of course, I can't answer. I know for myself that I just can't understand a professional outlook that says, "I am OK using a tool that is 30 or 40 years old rather than a newer one that actually works better." And I can't understand the concept of a professional who does not put learning new stuff near the top of his or her work "to do" list.

I guess I feel it is my obligation, my responsibility as a professional, to keep moving forward. To stop and just let my profession go on without me is, in my opinion, the very definition of unprofessional. But, that's just me.

ILE provides you with the tools you need to write modular code that can be efficiently accessed from other modular pieces of code. Modularity gives you a number of advantages: easier to code, easier to understand, easier to test, and easier to modify down the road in the unlikely event that becomes necessary. And efficiency is always a good thing, especially when the apps you are writing may be used not just in the green-screen world but on the Web as well. Yes, it will take a bit of time and some work to get proficient with these techniques. But that's what life is for—to learn new things. So why not ILE?

Just Keep This in Mind

But, at the same time, there is one thing I want you to keep in mind.

Anytime we adopt a new technique, we sort of automatically expect it to give us a big productivity boost right from the start. And I think that's pretty much true of /Free. But it won't happen so quickly with ILE.

Part of the problem here is how we define "productivity." For the most part, we do it from a very short time frame point of view. It is all about how many lines of code we can produce in a day or an hour. But that is not what productivity is all about.

Take this book, for example. Am I more productive if I write a chapter in two hours and then revise it 10 times before I am finished, or if I write it in six hours and only revise it twice?

Now you might say that it depends on how much time I spend on each revision, but in reality that doesn't matter. I am more productive if I have to pick a chapter up fewer times because the longer I work on it at one time, the more connected are my thoughts. If I revise it 10 times, that is 10 times I have to drop what I am doing and switch my thoughts back to that particular chapter.

And programming is similar, at least in terms of keeping your focus on one thing rather than switching it in and out all the time. ILE does not give instantaneous productivity increases, but it does so eventually. More important than productivity, however, which is always hard to measure, is the quality of the code you produce. With smaller modules that have less complicated code and do one particular thing, there are fewer bugs, and those that do crop up are easier to fix.

If you are new to ILE, it is quite possible that your first reaction is going to be "this is more work; it is not as efficient." But remember, all new things seem less efficient at first. If you return to OPM at that point, you are missing a great opportunity to grow professionally not only in terms of the tools you are familiar with but also with the quality of the code you produce. Hang in there, and it will get easier. Hang in there, and it will become more natural.

What Makes a Program ILE?

OK, finally, something practical. Here's the deal with ILE. It all starts with the compile command and the activation groups.

Both ILE and OPM use the same RPG compiler, but it has been enhanced, and some additional commands have been added to the operating system to modify how the compiler works. That is, OPM and ILE share the same compiler but *not* the same compiler commands. We are going to look at three separate compiler commands: CRTRPGPGM (Create RPG Program), CRTBNDRPG (Create Bound RPG), and the CRTRPGMOD/CRTPGM (Create RPG Module/Create Program) combo. Each is a little different in terms of how it handles OPM and ILE.

CRTRPGPGM

If you use the CRTRPGPGM command, the object that will be created is OPM. It has no ILE capability and will not work for a program that is stored in QRPGLESRC. Needless to say, we will not be using this command in this book, and you shouldn't use it either. 'Nough said.

CRTBNDRPG

If you use CRTBNDRPG, then the result may be an ILE program. Why "may be?" Because the ILE question with this compile command depends on the DFTACTGRP parameter that is present with this command but is missing from the CRTRPGPGM command mentioned previously.

If you specify DFTACTGRP to be *YES, then the system will compile that program using the default activation group, which means it will be an OPM program. Keep this firmly in mind. The default activation group belongs to OPM, and vice versa. It is not a real activation group.

But if you say *NO, then you will create an ILE program. Another field (ACTGRP) will then magically appear where you can specify the name of the activation group you want to use. The default is QILE, but we will see in the chapter on activation groups (chapter 17) how that is probably not the best choice. And you will want to pay attention to the activation group that you assign (lots more about that in chapter 17). It's very important.

CRTRPGMOD/CRTPGM

Finally, if you use the CRTRPGMOD and CRTPGM command combo, then the result will always be ILE. There is no DFTACTGRP parm in either of these commands; it is assumed that value is *NO; the command does not give you the option to change it. Then in CRTPGM you can set the specific activation group you want to use via the ACTGRP parm.

So the question is: based on the version of the software that you are on, what command comes up when you do an option 14 in Programming Development Manager (PDM) when you are in QRPGLESRC? Is it CRTRPGPGM? Well, it won't be because since this command only produces OPM objects, it is not available from QRPGLESRC.

And if you get CRTBNDRPG with an option 14, then the question is, what is the value for the DFTACTGRP command? If it is *NO, then you are all set for ILE. If not, then you will need to manually override at compile time or else use an H-spec in your program. Of course, you could always change the default value in the CRTBNDRPG command. That's what I would do.

QRPGSRC/QRPGLESRC

What about QRPGSRC and QRPGLESRC? They are nice and all, but the record length difference is not magic. Nor is the difference between program type RPG and RPGLE. You can create an RPGLE program in QRPGSRC, although I don't recommend it. And, by using source that is in QRPGLESRC and the CRTBNDRPG command with a DFTACTGRP of *YES, you can create what is essentially an OPM version of an RPGLE program.

The system does key in on the source type (RPG or RPGLE) to determine what compile command should be the default command applied (CRTRPGPGM or CRTBNDRPG). And the source type is set based on whether you are in QRPGSRC (RPG) or QRPGLESRC (RPGLE). So, that's something. Plus, we already saw that CRTRPGPGM would not run on a program stored in QRPGLESRC. The point is, however, QRPGLESRC is not magic, and there are other things you have to do, as we noted earlier. Just being in QRPGLESRC does not mean that you are doing ILE. It means you are ILE eligible. The rest is up to you. At the same time, you should put your ILE programs in QRPGLESRC, if for no other reason than the fact that it helps prevent confusion and prevent you from using CRTRPGPGM.

In the end, the *only* thing that determines whether or not your program is ILE is the value of the DFTACTGRP flag. *YES means OPM, *NO means ILE.

Also please remember that compiling your program as ILE does nothing per se, either. It does not rewrite your program in any way to take advantage of what ILE offers. All it does is open the gate. It makes using ILE functionality possible. But it will still be up to you to write your code so that you take advantage of this availability.

Now It's Your Turn

What? Do you need an invitation? Fine. Please, at this point, go out and do a "14" with a prompt and see what command and parms are attached to it. Will you do ILE by default or OPM?

While you are at it, you might as well do 15, too, and verify that it brings up CRTRPGMOD.

Of course, there is no number for CRTPGM. You have to key in all six letters of that yourself. You betcha. Your Dad was right. Life is rough.

What Ya Shoulda Learned

Not much practical so far, but we are just starting to get a feel for what ILE is. At this point, you should know a couple of things at least.

First, how the OPM model controlled how a program ran pre-ILE.

Second, what the problems were with that model and how they were at variance with the way people want to program today.

Third, how ILE uses a different program model to allow people to code in a more modern way.

Fourth, hopefully as a result of the previous three items you will feel you can explain to others the advantages of ILE and how it can help them develop even better, cleaner, more maintainable code.

And finally, we looked at the switch that turns OPM off and ILE on (the DFTACTGRP parameter on the CRTBNDRPG command) and took a look at what the defaults are for your system.

There's more that I want to say about ILE from a conceptual point of view, and by golly, I think I will. Get set for another exciting chapter.

Chapter 2

A Bit More ILE

Before we get started doing something practical (where you actually have to code), I want to dig a bit deeper into a few of the concepts on which ILE is built.

There are really two ways of thinking about ILE.

The first is in terms of how it affects your theory of programming. I know you have one. As Scott Klement said in his presentation "A Pattern for Reusable Code for RPG with ILE," which is on his website (*www.scottklement.com*), "People find it easy to learn RPG IV but hard to incorporate ILE because it requires you to change the way you think about your code."

And that is very true. We have talked a little about that already, but we will dig into it in greater detail below, and even more detail after we spend some time on /Free.

The second way to think about ILE is in terms of the different environments and tools that it uses. Instead of QRPGSRC, ILE programs are in QRPGLESRC. Instead of CRTRPGPGM, you will use CRTBNDRPG or else the combo of CRTRPGMOD/CRTPGM. OPM and ILE can both use /Free, but when it comes to compiling, there are big differences.

The truth is, at first glance it's not obvious what the difference is between an ILE and an OPM program. We naturally look at the different environments (QRPGLESRC vs. QRPGSRC) or commands (CRTBNDRPG vs. CRTRPGPGM), but the differences start at the concept level, long before things get practical. Sooo, let's start by taking a closer look at some of the concepts behind ILE.

Procedures: The Basic Building Blocks

In the ILE world, everything starts with procedures, not programs, so that is where we will begin.

Procedures. Small things that are easy to swallow. Like Hershey's Kisses. Or those little peanut butter cups. Or the cyanide pills Hydra inserts into your teeth in case you are captured (see *Captain America: The First Avenger*).

Two Types of Procedures

Now to be technically correct, I need to say that there are two types of procedures: main procedures and sub-procedures.

Everyone is already familiar with main procedures. They are just programs; they have F-, D-, maybe H-specs, some logic, either C-specs or /Free logic statements, and an *INLR at the end. A program is something that you can call and execute all by itself. Nothing really special here.

What I am mostly talking about in this book, of course, are sub-procedures. If you see just "procedures," read that as "sub-procedures" (can't catch everything in an edit).

Main procedures are coded up in a source file, compiled, and run. Not so with sub-procedures. They cannot exist just alone and on their own. They have to be in a program (main procedure) or service program. You can't just compile a naked sub-procedure and run it.

A sub-procedure is the most elemental unit of code in the ILE universe. It has a number of characteristics.

First, it's supposed to be small. Yes, technically you can write ginormous sub-procedures, but that sort of defeats the purpose, doesn't it? Keep it focused, and keep it small.

Second, it should be focused. That is, it should be designed around a single logical idea with limited data elements and a limited span of control. The idea is to encapsulate an idea or a method, not try to solve the whole world's problems.

Third, it should be composed primarily of local variables that insulate one procedure from another and limit data coupling. Try really hard to avoid global data elements. Often you can't eliminate them, but keep them to a minimum.

Fourth, it is bounded by P-specs (beginning and ending) and has prototype D-specs associated with it (more on that later). This is very important.

Fifth, you can't just run it on its own. It needs to be part of something else.

In the end, a procedure (sub-procedure) is not a small program. It is not executable on its own. It's a code set with local variables and the ability to be inserted either into a regular program or a service program, hopefully to do one and only one thing.

Is ILE OO?

Obviously, procedures end up sounding a lot like objects, and so it is natural to ask, is ILE object-oriented?

Of course not. RPG, whether positional or free, OPM or ILE, is not object-oriented.

But, in some ways, ILE gives RPG an "OO-like" orientation. Not literally, of course, but sort of. OO forces you to look at things in terms of objects rather than as a process.

A process is a lot of stuff. Thinking about a process makes you think you need a big thing to enclose it. A BOP (Big Ol' Program).

But thinking about things in terms of objects helps you think about things one at a time. It makes you think about small things, just describing that one object. And then, once you have a couple of objects, you start to think about the process, the way in which those objects will be connected.

ILE does not make RPG /Free an OO language, but we can still think that way. Start by thinking about the small things, your building blocks, then think about how to tie them together.

Modules

If procedures are the protons, neutrons, and electrons of the ILE world, then modules are the atoms.

A module is a non-executable piece of code that can either be a program or part of a program. Modules are coded up in a source member, and there is a one to one relationship between them (source members and modules). That is, you can't have two modules in the same source member. In a moment, however, we will see that you can bind one or more modules (and therefore source members) into a single program object.

As I said, modules are non-executable segments of code (like sub-procedures). You can't "run" a module. Its object type is not *PGM, but rather *MODULE. It has to be bound together in a program, probably with other modules. They are small, they are fast, and they can be bound together to create an executable program. They just can't run on their own.

At first glance, you might think that modules and sub-procedures have a lot in common. After all, they are both non-executable. But that is about where the similarities end.

A module is a program or service program that has been converted to a *MODULE object, so that it can be bound to other modules for efficiency purposes.

A sub-procedure is never bound to another program, and when it is converted into a *MODULE format, it does so as part of a service program, not as an entity in its own right.

Where do modules come from? Frankly, your parents should have had this talk with you when you were a kid, but I guess it's a little late to complain about that now. Well, you start by keying a program or service program into a source member. Then you run the CRTRPGMOD command on that, and it creates a new object type, the *MODULE object type. The command does not have a spot for the DFTACTGRP or the name of the activation group that you want to use. Why not? Because the *MODULE cannot be executed. Hence, it has no need for activation information. Come on, focus!

And how do we take the modules and make them into a program? Very simple: we gather a bunch of modules together that we want to be able to call from each other, and we use the CRTPGM command, being sure to list the modules to be bound together in the compile command.

Once you have issued the CRTPGM and have bound the *MODULEs into a program, the actual *MODULE objects can be deleted. They have already been incorporated into the program object and so are not needed. If the *MODULE objects would change (like if you modified the source and then reran CRTRPGMOD), then you would need to rebind everything together using the CRTRPGMOD/CRTPGM again. But I think you know that.

This command (CRTPGM) does have a spot for the activation group name, plus spots for both individual module names and binding directory information (which we will talk about later), so it looks sort of like the CRTBNDRPG command. But rather than dealing with a single source member, it will be working with one or more modules (*MODULE object type). It does *not* have a spot for the DFTACTGRP because it assumes this program will be ILE and automatically sets that parameter to *NO.

One thing to note is that the modules that are bound together can be different program types, not just RPG. We have mentioned it, but not stressed the fact that ILE is not just for RPG. It actually started with C and embraces all the languages that run natively on the IBM i. If you are using just CRTBNDRPG, then the source file you are dealing with must be RPG, but CRTRPGMOD/CRTPGM is more forgiving. And there are other commands to create modules for other language types (e.g., CRTCLMOD, CRTCMOD).

What Is a Program? And a Service Program?

Of course, we already know what a program is. It is a set of code instructions that has an object type of *PGM (as opposed to *MODULE) and which can be executed by the system to accomplish something. As we saw earlier, this set of instructions could either have originated in a single source member using the CRTBNDRPG command or have come from separate members that were bound together using the CRTRPGMOD/CRTPGM combo.

But what is a service program? We have all heard about it, sometimes in hushed tones of reverence or fear, but what is the essential difference between a regular program and a service program?

Essentially, a service program is a herd of sub-procedures (technically, such a group is known as a "gackle").

In other words, a service program consists of one or more sub-procedures. And of those two possibilities, more is better. That is, it makes more sense, just from a "keeping track of them" point of view, to roll as many procedures into a single service program, as makes sense.

What do I mean by "as makes sense?" What I really mean is "that are related to each other" or "that are oriented around a single logical idea group." So we might want to take all the procedures (yes, sub-procedures) that affect the product master file and put them in a single service program because they all deal with the same file. Or we might want to put all sub-procedures that are related to credit checking in the same service program because they all work on the same logical idea (i.e., deciding if you are a good risk).

There is no main procedure logic in a service program, just a list (sorry, a gackle) of sub-procedures and their associated prototype D-specs and P-specs.

Let's start by talking about what is similar between a regular "program" and a "service program."

First, uh, give me a minute ... I was sure I thought of something a while ago ... oh, yeah. They both have the word "program" in their name.

And now the differences.

First, a program is a *PGM object. A service program is a *SRVPGM object.

Second, an ILE program can be created either by the CRTRPGMOD/CRTPGM combo or the CRTBNDRPG command. A service program can only be created by the CRTRPGMOD/CRTSRVPGM combo.

Third, the service program has no main procedure. It is just a set of sub-procedures, one after another, with the *NOMAIN keyword.

Fourth, when you call the service program, you don't reference the name of that service program. Instead, you call the name of the particular sub-procedure you want to use. So if you plan on using several sub-procedures in a given service program, you will have to issue several calls to that service program.

Fifth, a program that is created by the CRTRPGMOD/CRTPGM combo does the bind when it is compiled. But a service program, in the default mode, forms the bind with the calling program when a specific sub-procedure from that service program is called. That is, the calling program-service program bind is defined in the compile, but it does not actually happen until you kick off the calling program and it calls one of the sub-procedures in the service program. Now, we will see later that you can modify this, but the default configuration is to do the bind when the sub-procedure is accessed, not compiled.

Sixth, because of the differences (between a program and a service program) in when the bind is actually created, there is a difference in how it handles the situation where one program in the sequence changes.

That is, for a program calling another program where they are bound together using the CRTRPGMOD/CRTPGM combo, if one of the programs in that group changes, then we need to recreate the *MODULE for the changed program and then redo the bind using CRTPGM or UPDPGM (Update Program).

This means that if the program that changes is one that is accessed by many calling programs, then the CRTPGM (or UPDPGM) must be done for each of those calling programs, a task that might take some time and could lead to an error (like if you forget one of them).

A service program is different, however. If the bind does not really happen until call time, you can change a sub-procedure in that service program every day and not have to issue the CRTPGM command on all the programs that access that service program. Know what I mean, Vern?

Now there are some considerations that have to be kept in mind related to this (like efficiency), but we are going to gloss over that for the moment and hold that for a later chapter. One thing at a time, friends.

The bottom line is service programs allow you to change the sub-procedures you are calling without all the rebinding that is required with a direct program to program bound call.

There's probably more stuff than that, but you get the idea. They are two different entities to be used in two different types of situations.

Creating an ILE Program: One Step or Two or Four

Reviewing quickly, OPM is about writing big, standalone programs. ILE is about writing small, nimble "things" that connect with each other. Now that we have had a look at the concept of a procedure, let's try to pull it all together and define exactly how to create ILE programs.

The good news, I guess, is that there are really three ways in which this can be done. We talked about this a bit in chapter 1, but let's dig into the various options a bit deeper.

The "Easy" Way: CRTBNDRPG

The so-called easy way is the CRTBNDRPG command. (Remember, you can't use CRTRPGPGM at all; it creates only OPM programs.)

CRTBNDRPG will take a single source member and create an RPG object from it in one step. The resultant *PGM object can be executed, and it can contain sub-procedures or call other programs (although these other programs will not be "bound in").

This command contains the DFTACTGRP parm (the default value for this depends on your version of IBM i OS). Depending on what this is set to (*NO or *YES), you will create either an ILE or OPM program, respectively. Don't assume *NO is the default; it probably isn't.

What it doesn't have is any parms related to modules or binding directories used to bind this program to something else. And the reason for that is simple: it's not module-oriented, and so you can't do binding on this type of object. It could be small, it could use sub-procedures, it could be part of an MVC design pattern, but this compile command does not let you do binding. I don't say that in the way of an indictment, but just as a statement of fact. Maybe you don't need binding language, for example, for this module.

But it is one step, and it is very easy to use, and it is ILE (assuming you use *NO as above).

The "Politically Correct" Way: CRTRPGMOD/CRTPGM

If you read enough articles on ILE, you may come to the conclusion that there are a fair number of people who do not believe that using CRTBNDRPG is ILE. Oh, they know it is technically ILE, they just don't consider it pure enough, and they tend to act as if it is not kosher.

Often, their preference is to create modules with the CRTRPGMOD command and then bind those modules together with the CRTPGM command.

Yes, it is two steps, but you get a nice tight bind that gives you great efficiency. And if you have many calls in the app, then you might not be crazy to use this two-step approach.

As I may have mentioned before, the CRTRPGMOD command does not have any parms for activation groups (because a module is not executable code), nor does it allow you to enter any names of other modules you want to bind in with it. (Those things are part of the CRTPGM command.) It does, however, let you specify a binding directory, which can be used when you issue the CRTPGM command to actually bind things together.

I guess one other thing I should mention is that any syntax or other errors you have in your source code will be identified during the CRTRPGMOD phase. It might not create a *PGM, but it does all the checking to make sure that the *MODULE you create will run when it is bound into a *PGM.

The CRTPGM command then takes the modules you list or the binding directories that you specify and creates an executable *PGM from the *MODULE objects. In addition, this command supports entries for the activation group (but not the DFTACTGRP, which is assumed to be *NO). You always create an ILE program out of this, and it only works if you have created modules via CRTRPGMOD beforehand.

The disadvantage of this method is once I have my modules bound, if I need to make a change to the called program, it requires me to rebind that module (or issue an UPDPGM command) to bring the new, changed module into the calling program-called program combo. Depending on how many times you change a called program and how many calling programs it is bound into, this can either be nothing at all or a major problem. Fortunately, service programs solve this issue.

The "Third" Way: CRTRPGMOD/CRTSRVPGM

Of course, the third way is to use service programs.

We will go over exactly what you need to do to use service programs (it's no big deal), in a couple of chapters. But basically you start by doing a CRTRPGMOD over the service program source, thus putting it in *MODULE form as well as doing the standard compile edits, then issue the CRTSRVPGM command on that module to create a full-grown service program.

We are not quite done at that point, however.

A service program is a strange and wondrous animal, similar to although completely different from dragons. And because of that, there are some special things that you have to do to any program that is going to call a service program.

You can't just use the regular CRTBNDRPG to compile a program that will call a service program because you have to set up a bind between the calling program and the called program (the service program), and this must be set up as part of the compile process. More about this in chapter 10.

For the moment, just remember that there is a bind between the calling program and the service program, and this has to be set up when you do the compile of the calling program. The actual bind may not occur until the service program is called, but the setup is done up front, so the system is sure it will work. This is unlike the regular CRTRPGMOD/CRTPGM between two non-service program modules, where the bind is actually done during the compile.

Does all that make sense? It should. If I wrote it up correctly. If not, it is probably best to just keep going and hope that it turns out all right in the end. That's what I would do, and look how I turned out.

What Ya Shoulda Learned

So, what did you learn here?

We started this chapter by taking a closer look at some of the terms we use (*procedures*, *modules*, *programs*, *service programs*) and how these different building blocks work to build our applications. Can you repeat verbatim what I said in that part of the chapter? If not, a reread might be in order.

"Casting my memory back there," let's remember first and foremost that what determines whether or not a program is ILE is the value you enter for the DFTACTGRP; *YES makes it OPM (because you are using the default activation group which is not ILE), and *NO makes it ILE and opens up a field where you can enter the value of the activation group you want to use.

We then looked at three ways in which to build ILE programs.

   The first is the one-step CRTBNDRPG command, which does allow for activation groups and binding language to bind modules at compile time.

   The second is the two-step process of creating modules (via CRTRPGMOD) and then binding those modules together to create a program with the CRTPGM command.

   The third, of course, is service programs, which can require up to four steps.

And now, just when you are getting excited about ILE (well, a little maybe), in the immortal words of Monty Python, "Now for something completely different." Naturally, we want to look at some examples of ILE programs, but since they are written using /Free and some of you may not be familiar with /Free, we are going to spend a few chapters looking at that (/Free). Then we will come back to ILE for a very practical look at things.

INTRODUCTION TO /FREE

Where you will get your feet wet with what /Free RPG is and begin to learn how to use it to create the ILE programs you will need.

Chapter 3

A First Dive into /Free

I will always remember the first time I heard of RPG.

It was early in my career. I had just gone to a new job: programming on an IBM 4300 mainframe using COBOL. And then a year in we found out that our particular group was going to be moving to an AS/400. Actually a System/38. The 400 was still a couple of years down the road. And the i wasn't even a gleam in IBM's eye. But I wasn't worried. Obviously this new machine would do COBOL. It was IBM.

Then fate intervened, and we bought an ERP package to run on the new machine. A package that was written in RPG.

RP what?

Fortunately, one of the older guys on the team had done a lot of RPG work at a previous employer. Don't worry, he said, it's a great language. Everything has to be placed in specific columns. Very neat from an up and down point of view, eh?

Everything has to be placed in specific columns? Like a punch card? Seriously?

But he was right about the columns, and I slowly learned to write code not in sentences but in a kind of abbreviated, inverted English where everything could be explained in six characters or less.

Many people in the RPG world take great pride in that. RPG is their language, a language with a rich history and its own unique syntax. And RPG is a good language—don't think that I am down on it. I have written a lot of good code in it, as have many other people. But it does have its issues.

First, it's limited to the IBM i, and the i is limited by IBM's ability to market things. I feel queasy already.

And second, if you try to explain the positional syntax to people who aren't enmeshed in that world, you will get blank stares or raised eyebrows. A few may even contact a certain government agency.

But here I am, a number of years later, still using RPG. So it can't be all bad, right?

RPG /Free

Today, RPG is fighting for validity. We, the Chosen Ones, know of its value, and perhaps that's enough. But people who truly care about the language want other people to know it is not some kind of dinosaur wandering around looking for a tar pit.

RPG is a language that can do in the business world what Java and many other Web-oriented languages can't do nearly as easily. And we want people who are doing Web development for the IBM i to know that there may be some things they would be wise to use RPG for.

Unfortunately, an RPG based on putting things in certain columns is too much of an uphill battle. You are never going to be able to convince a large number of Web coders to take it seriously. And so, IBM embarked on a program to develop a position-less version of RPG called RPG /Free.

Some people didn't see a need for it. They wished IBM would spend their time putting additional functionality into positioned RPG, but I think if IBM had done that they would have spent more of their time adding functionality to RPG that could be done more easily by using SQL or a Web language. And IBM agreed with that (although in fairness, they thought of it first and never consulted me). So /Free is here, and that is where the language is headed. As a result, that is what we are going to use in this book, just /Free. Ta-dah!

Unfortunately, it is possible that you don't know /Free. So before we get to ILE and MVC, we will spend a few chapters going over how to code in /Free so that you are comfortable with it. This is an introduction, although a pretty comprehensive one if I do say so myself, but the real book on /Free is James Martin's *Free-Format RPG IV, Third Edition* (MC Press, 2015; available at *www.mc-store.com/products/free-format-rpg-iv*). It's not one of those 800-page opuses (so it is something you could work through in your lifetime), and it has everything in it that you need to know about /Free. Buy it, read it, live it.

What Is /Free?

/Free is not a new version of the IBM i OS (although it has been a series of enhancements over a number of i OS versions).

Nor is it a new release of the RPG compiler—RPG V, for example (although it probably should have been, and certainly changes have been made in the compiler to support it).

There is not even a separate /Free compile command (CRTFREERPG). /Free programs get compiled with the regular, old RPG IV compiler, so there are no new commands or libraries that you need to get used to. How simple is that? As we saw, ILE changes how we compile; /Free does not.

The initial version of /Free (part of V5.1) only affected C-specs.

Later, under 7.1 TR7, F-specs, D-specs, H-specs, and P-specs (prototype-oriented specs introduced as part of ILE) went position-less as well. We may cover that later if I don't forget, but for now all we care about are the C-specs. Although, as we shall see, /Free does not use C-specs. But that will come in a few minutes, and I don't want to spoil the surprise.

Nothing is being done for I- or O-specs and I 'spec it won't be. Actually, starting in 2018 it will be illegal to use them. That's a joke by the way. You can still use them but only as specs.

Why /Free?

But the real question is, why should you use /Free? Certainly positional RPG is familiar to everyone in our world. Why bother to learn or use /Free? Fortunately, there are a ton of articles out there about the advantages of /Free, so I am not going to belabor it. Just search on "RPG Free advantages".

The thrust of /Free is simple: it gives you opcodes and structures that do not have to be in a given column position on the screen. And this allows you to do four things.

First, to write code that looks similar to an English sentence (that is, in straightforward order, not inverted like German), so it is more readable.

Second, it lets you have longer field names, thus giving you the ability to make them more understandable. The maximum length you can have in /Free is 4,096 characters, which I admit might be a bit too long for good communication. You probably want to shoot for something under 20 or so, but the ability to have more meaningful names is a critical feature.

Third, it allows you to indent to show structure more clearly, just as these few sentences have been indented to show they are subordinate to the paragraph above. This is huge for me.

Fourth, it removes a number of opcodes from the mix, simplifying and cleaning up the language by gently forcing you to make extensive use of IBM's built-in functions (BIFs).

So, in a nutshell, why would you want to use /Free?

With the indentation, sentence-type structure, and the ability to create longer names, the code is much more readable, which means it's much more maintainable.

Code written in /Free doesn't look outdated and quirky to outsiders the way positional RPG does, and its syntax really is not all that different from some other Web languages like C or Java. Certainly it's much closer than positional RPG is. Who cares what others think? We have to, because many times those heathen others make the decision about what platform and language we will be allowed to use. Nothing says "outdated" quite as clearly as positional requirements.

Finally, this is the direction that the language is going in. We gave up RPG III to go to IV (kicking and screaming on the part of some, I'll admit), and we should give up positional RPG now for /Free.

Who Can Use /Free?

Anyone can use /Free if they are on 5.1 or above (it really became functionally useful with 5.3), and no one can be denied access to it based on race, gender, sexual orientation, or even what sports teams they root for.

Most of what I am going to do will be using version 5.4. Yes, I know, that is an old version and a lot of people are on 6.1 or 7.*x*. But a lot is not all; as I said earlier, I believe many people are still on 5.4 (or below), captives of a management that does not recognize the benefits of upgrading, so I am going to use that version of the operating system to be sure that you can do what I can do. I will mention the additional features you have in 6.1 and 7.*x* but not require their use.

So the first thing you want to do is find out what version of the system you are on to be sure you can use /Free. If you don't know or don't know how to check, go to a command line and enter this command:

```
'dspptf'
```

See the OS version you are on at the top part of the screen.

For those of you who are on 7.1, we will be talking later about whether or not you are on TR7 because some additional /Free functionality was added at that point. To check your technical refresh level, run this command:

```
WRKPTFGRP GRP(SI99707)
```

The display that results will show you the level you are on. The level number is your TR level.

In the meantime, I will assume you are set to go. Please sign a copy of the enclosed *Permission to Code in /Free* form and hand it to the person on your right. I will pick them up later.

Permission to Code in /Free

Be it known that I,

_____

(Your Name)

a person who has absolutely no authority but rather just a grandiose and ill-founded notion of his/her own importance, hereby request permission to code in RPG /Free without ever having to use positional RPG again. The bearer of this certificate is entitled to all of the privileges, rights, and honors (that is to say, you get to code not only at work but at home in the evenings as well as on weekends, which you are probably already doing) associated with being a /Free programmer.

In addition, you are entitled to talk to your employer about an immediate 25 percent raise to compensate for the increased productivity you will have. Go on, go talk to her/him right now. Might as well get it over with (don't forget to take a copy of this certificate with you so it can be validated).

Certified by

_____ (date)

David Shirey, Chancellor, Only Coding in /Free Society (OC/FS)

Certificate Not Transferrable

What's Not in /Free

/Free was not only an attempt to do something that was more structured but also a way of simplifying the number of opcodes that are supported. Let's face it, there are a ton of them in positional RPG. I mean there are almost three dozen Move statements alone. And so, a number of tried and true RPG favorites didn't make the cut.

Like indicators on the I/O functions,

Or the ability to define variables on the fly,

And the Move opcodes (gasp ... yes, all of them),

And some others.

How could they do that?

Complete disregard for what you need to do your job? I suppose that would be one way to look at it, but in reality it was done to make things simpler. To get away with this, /Free makes extensive use of two things.

First, BIFs. You can use them in positional RPG, of course, but they are standard operating fare for /Free.

And second, some additional, simplifying functionality (for example, how record keys are handled) that is new and exclusive with /Free.

For a complete list of what RPG operators have been deprecated just do an Internet search on "deprecated RPG opcodes in /Free". Seriously. There are a couple of appendices in the James Martin book that pertain to this also. Appendix A is a brief description of every opcode that did make it into /Free, and Appendix C tells you what /Free opcodes you can use to replace the deprecated ones. I just didn't feel like doing one; I prefer to Google.

Setting Up a /Free Program

All set? Great. Now let's create a /Free program.

Probably the easiest way to do it the first time is to copy a short positional RPG program that we will modify to be a /Free model. (P.S. If you can't find a short one, which is more than likely, take a long one and just delete more C-specs.)

Once copied, delete all the C-specs. Yep, that's right, everything with a C in position 6 gets deleted. This should shorten up the model a bit. I would also delete all but one of the F-specs, and most of the D-specs, too. Oh, yeah, get rid of I- and O-specs also. This will get rid of a lot of the debris from the old program that we will not need in our model. Everyone whistle when you are done.

Now It's Your Turn

Come on now, get going. Create a copy of a short positional program that you are going to use to move to /Free.

I think it is very important as we go through this book that you code up the things we are talking about. Reading is nice, but doing cements your knowledge. Just take the time to do it. And if you don't, I can only repeat June Cleaver's final words to the two gentlemen sitting in 16A and 16B. I just can't spell them.

Once you have gone through and cleared off all the C-specs and cleaned it up a bit by removing most F- and D-specs, be sure to note the new name so you don't forget what it is. This will be the model we build all of our /Free programs from.

You don't need to compile yet, and if you do you will get errors, so just be patient.

The /Free Delimiter Tags

OK, we have created a very rough model program with essentially nothing in it. The next step is to talk about the /Free delimiter tags.

If you are on a release below 7.1 TR7, you will need to put "/Free" at the start of a section of /Free code and "/end-Free" at the end. Since we are looking at things from a 5.4 point of view, we will use the delimiters in all code examples. You can also use these delimiters if you are above 7.1 TR1, but those folks have some other options as well, which we will talk about when we discuss "advanced" /Free.

Of course, this (having beginning and ending tags) implies that you can intermix /Free and positional statements, and that is true, but we will say more about that in a minute.

For the moment, let's just look at the basic column rules for /Free with the delimiters.

- Nothing ever goes in column 6 (where the C used to go) in /Free.

- The starting and ending delimiters (/Free and /end-Free) are the only things that begin in position 7.

- Normal /Free logic statements can begin anywhere in positions 8–80.

At this point, I am going to assume you are not on 7.1, TR7 and so let's put

```
/Free
```

starting in position 7 at the beginning of where you want your /Free logic statements to start (remember, they are not C-specs in /Free). There is no C or * or anything prior to it. I know it will look weird, a naked line of RPG, and you will think you have done something wrong, something that might even be a felony in some states, but it's fine. Trust me.

Then, at the end of a section of /Free code we will put the delimiter

```
/end-Free
```

again starting in position 7. If the entire program after the /Free start tag is /Free, then you can omit the /end-Free.

What's that? Do you need to capitalize /Free and /end-Free the way I have? No. What is ya? Ignorant? RPG is not case-sensitive, and that includes the /Free tags. That's just the way I do it, and I don't even always do it that way. The same will be true for the rest of the /Free operators and code. Capitalize or not capitalize however the spirit moves you.

If you are going to intersperse C-spec code in between sections of /Free, then you will need to use the /end-Free where one /Free section ends and C-specs begin, and then a /Free at the end of the C-specs to start back up into /Free again.

The fact that you can do this (intermingle C-specs and /Free lines) may make you think that situation is normal. This is kind of an emotional issue for me, so let me take a moment to center myself before I reply.

Mixing positional with /Free is not a normal situation. I write programs to be either /Free or positional, depending on what my client wants. I never mix the two if I can help it (I am afraid of them mating).

There are situations, especially depending on what version of the operating software you are on, where you might have to switch back into positional RPG. Like if you are doing SQL and have a GOTO tag (/Free doesn't handle that). Or if you are doing an ILE sub-procedure in 5.4 and need to specify P-specs (which are not supported by 5.4 /Free).

Bottom line: as much as possible, code /Free and don't look back. Don't use C-specs as a crutch when you come to something you are not sure how to do in /Free. It looks pathetic to switch back and forth between the formats, and 99 percent of the time there really is no need to do so.

There, I think I got through that pretty well.

Now It's Your Turn

So, the next thing I want you to do is put the /Free and /end-Free into your program. They will be really close together; there should be nothing in between them but maybe a few blank lines so it doesn't look weird, but that is OK, they generally get along fine. When you have done that, just sit tight. Don't compile it yet; we have one more thing to do before this program can be compiled. But that will have to wait for the next exciting chapter.

What Ya Shoulda Learned

So, what have we done so far? We have created a /Free program by copying a positional program, removing all the C-specs, and inserting the start and end /Free tags (/Free and /End-free).

You did do that, right? I mean code along with this, not just read but do it? Very important. At least for me, it would be. I need to do something in order to really get it. And even then sometimes it's hard to tell.

Below is a summary of what you should have learned in this chapter.

This isn't required, but I think it would be nice if you could defend yourself if you are attacked by a positional RPG stalwart. You should know what the advantages of /Free are and why it is a good idea to use it. Just for your own protection, of course.

For /Free code:

- nothing is allowed in column 6,

- column 7 is reserved for the start of the /Free delimiter tags (/Free and /end-Free),

- delimiter tags are required to identify /Free code if you are below 7.1, TR7, and

- actual code (logic statements) and comments can be placed anywhere in columns 8–80.

If you are on TR7 of 7.1 or 7.2 or above, then you have additional flexibility on this kind of stuff, but we are not going to get into that now.

What is really important at this point is that you have created a model /Free program that you can use as a starting point for much of the stuff we are going to do later, because remember, when we get to ILE and MVC, all our work will be using /Free.

Chapter 4

Diving Deeper into /Free

In the last chapter, we started building a /Free program, something that we could use as a model, but we didn't get far enough to even be able to compile it. Let's fix that right now and get this baby off the ground.

It may seem that we are going very slowly here, and if you have any experience with /Free you might think we could move it along a bit. You're probably right.

But I am concerned about those people who are not yet using /Free. And I think there might be a fair number of them out there. One of the big myths we have in the IBM i world is that everyone is on a fairly recent release.

Unfortunately, I honestly don't think that is true. I think the i population is like an iceberg. I think that many i professionals are with companies that are not actively moving forward. They could, for example, still be on 5.4 or before. And they are not using /Free because regular, old, positional RPG has served them well up to this point, and they can't see a real, solid business need to change. Could be wrong, it's happened before, like the time I swore I would never pay more than $4,000 for a new car. But, I think I may be somewhat right on this one.

So I am taking it slow to start with. I want to show those people who are not on 7.2 that they can grow, too. Modern approaches are not exclusive to those whose management realizes it is important to use the new tools. It is something that almost everyone can do. But it's something you do one step at a time, and I don't want to scare off or leave anyone behind. Those of you who are already there can just either skip past or speed read through.

Now, let's continue on with developing that /Free model.

Ending a /Free Program

Please note that I am not talking here about the /end-Free tag. That ends a /Free code section but does not actually end a program. No, I am talking here about the LR indicator and how it is used in the /Free world.

In one sense, there is no change in /Free in terms of how you end a program. The need to set the LR indicator on is driven not by /Free or positional, but by the program model, OPM or ILE.

In the OPM world, we tend to write monolithic programs, or BOPs (Big Ol' Programs). When we are done, you need to close the program and reclaim all the resources.

And you can do the same in ILE, although with ILE you are hopefully writing smaller modules or using sub-procedures and service programs, which do not use the LR. Plus, with ILE you have activation groups to consider, and that will change what happens when your program ends.

That said, what has changed in /Free is the way we code up setting the LR. The SETON opcode from positional didn't make the cut into /Free, so to end a /Free program you have to code it up like this:

```
*INLR = '1';
```

Since it is a logic statement, you will start it in column 8 or beyond and before the /end-Free, if you are using one.

You may think that this violates what we said in a previous chapter about indicators and /Free. But it doesn't. Indicators are supported in /Free, although there are other ways to do things, and, except for the INLR, it is hoped you will stop using IN43 to control things. What is no longer supported, however, are indicators in I/O statements. We will talk more about that later.

VERY IMPORTANT: Every /Free statement or clause will end with a semicolon. That is what tells the compiler that one statement is finished and another is starting (because a given /Free statement might be spread out over several lines).

Now It's Your Turn

Go ahead and put your program close logic in, then try to compile your new /Free program using your normal compile procedure. At this point, I don't care if it ends up ILE or not.

If you have problems, then look at the error messages and fix it and try again. (Seriously, did I really have to say that? I mean that's the big attraction of writing a book over doing a class—I don't have to solve your problems for you.)

Comments

This section should probably have come before we talked about ending the program because comments should always come before you do any logic statements. Otherwise, they never get added. You know how it is. Fortunately, comments are easy to do in /Free.

Just set them up preceded by two slashes (//). The // can go in any two adjacent columns from 8–80. After the //, you can put whatever you want; it's comments.

```
// The following program is very likely to blow up at
// the weirdest times. Good luck.
```

You can even put the comments after the end of a valid /Free statement, but I really don't like that. Just a personal thing.

```
*inlr = '1';        // This is the end of the program.
```

Interestingly enough, you can also use the // for comments in positional RPG. I never knew that. I probably won't do it, as it seems sort of traditional to use * in positional, but then I hope I won't have too much coding using positional anyway, so it's not a big deal.

Now It's Your Turn

Take a moment and add some comments in to the program you have just created. Try some different styles (across the line or to the right of the code statement) and see what looks best to you.

Then compile the program again to make sure you haven't screwed it up. We are going to talk later about the various compile commands that there are in the i, but I don't want to worry about that now. Just compile it the way you would any ol' other program.

EVAL Statement Stuff

Now that we have a functioning shell, let's start doing things "the /Free way."

The first thing we will do is very simple. Let's add an EVAL statement to the skeleton program. Now remember, we said that some opcodes were not transferred over to /Free, and one of those was the MOVE (in all its forms). I will give you just a moment to stop hyperventilating, and then we will move on. (Get it? "Move" on. I kill myself!)

Anyway, in /Free, all value setting will be done with the EVAL opcode.

When doing an EVAL, you can specify the EVAL opcode:

```
eval name = 'Dave';
```

or else just skip the opcode entirely (which is what the cool kids do) and use this:

```
name = 'Dave';
```

where *name* is obviously a variable either from a file or a D-spec or somewhere. By itself, /Free has not changed variable-naming standards (it can't start with a number, blah, blah, blah), although you can use longer names. Neither has it changed the maximum size of a variable or the types of variables you can define. That was done separately from both /Free and ILE in various operating system releases.

One thing that is very important is that in /Free, variables cannot be spontaneously defined within the code; they must be set up prior to the execution steps.

The statement can be set up anywhere from column 8 to 80 (unless you are on 7.3), so you have the ability to stack things for easy viewing. For example:

```
name        =   'Dave';
address1    =   '1 Horton Plaza';
address 2   =   ' ';
city        =   'Salem';
state       =   'Illinois';
zipcode     =   '66666';
```

One thing to keep in mind about the EVAL is that it only allows you to relate fields that are of the same type or accept data of the same type (numeric or character oriented). That is, you can't use the EVAL to move packed data into a character field. There are ways to do that, but not by using the EVAL by itself. Later we will look at how to do that with BIFs.

Now It's Your Turn

Let's keep it nice and simple, shall we? Grab that model program we created a few minutes ago, and copy it to a new program. We want to keep the model clean.

Then, add a few lines of EVALs. Try some different formats, and see what looks easy to read. Don't forget the semicolon at the end of each line. And remember, you can either code the EVAL operator or not.

Of course, since you can't define fields spontaneously, you will have to include either a real F-spec or else create a couple of D-specs to cover the variables you are using in the EVAL.

Then compile it and see what errors you get. When you get a clean compile, stop. Come on now; everyone face forward and get to work.

EVAL Opcode Extenders

Another thing to mention is that you can use the opcode extenders—h, m, and r—with the EVAL statement (although then of course you must use the EVAL opcode and not omit it). For example:

```
EVAL(h) CM_ARBAL = AR_TOTAL;
```

All of this looks pretty simple, doesn't it? And it is. I mean that's the whole idea behind /Free, making things simpler than they were before. As we go through this book, however, we will see the EVAL can be a complex statement.

For example, later we will see that the EVAL can use not just variables, but BIFs and other complex things as elements in the equation. And, under the heading of ILE, we will see that we can even use the EVAL to call other modules—generally called a *function call*—rather than using the CALLP. So it is simple, but we will see the EVAL with but mostly without the opcode EVAL, in many places and guises.

Other EVAL Opcodes

As I mentioned, IBM did not bring the MOVE opcodes over into /Free, so you use the EVAL. But there are a few different flavors of that command.

EVAL-CORR(h/m/r)

This EVAL allows you to move a group of identically named fields from one data structure to another.

```
EVAL-CORR data_struc1 = data_struc2;
```

where data_struc1 and data_struc2 have at least some field names in common.

This opcode can be used with both /Free and positional RPG, but when you use it in /Free you can include the h/m/r extenders. No room for them in positional.

EVALR(m/r)

And this one will perform the evaluate and then right adjust. Since it is only for character fields, there is no h extender.

```
EVALR MSG = 'Function Successful';
```

If we assume the MSG field is 25 characters, then the result will be

```
'        Function Successful'.
```

You can try these if you want, but it's pretty simple. You may not even ever use them. Who knows?

What Ya Shoulda Learned

So far, we have gone pretty slowly, but don't worry, that is only because I want to lengthen the book a little and bump up my royalties. I suppose you could argue that I don't want to scare anyone away from /Free, and that is true, but frankly it's mostly the former. After this chapter, we will pick up the pace just a bit. What is really important is that as we go through things, try them. Use the model we set up to do some code and compile to make sure you have it right. Fool around with stuff. See how much you can bend the syntax. Get comfortable with it.

Below is a summary of what you should have learned in this chapter.

To end a program, the SETON opcode is no more, and you have to do an EVAL to turn the INLR on (*INLR = '1';).

Comments are indicated not by an * but by double slashes (//), which can be set up anywhere in columns 8–80.

Variables can no longer be defined on the fly in the code. They must be set up in an F-spec, D-spec, or something like that.

Especially important, MOVE and all of its mutations did not make it into /Free. EVAL is used instead. Unlike the MOVE, EVAL does not allow you to automatically mutate one data type into another (that will be handled by BIFs within the EVAL), but it does do the equivalence part.

- The EVAL opcode name is optional unless you are using the opcode extenders.

- You can only equate fields that are the same data type.

- EVAL supports the h/m/r extenders for the appropriate data types.

In addition to EVAL, the EVALR and EVAL-CORR are also supported.

Most importantly, you should have created a second model /Free program and used it to try out some of the EVAL statements. And naturally, compiling both of these cleanly is an essential part of that create process.

Chapter 5

/Free Control Statements

Now, when last we left our intrepid /Free heroes, they had just completed creating a simple but honest /Free program. Before we go on, let's take a moment to review some of the things we have learned.

There are no C-specs in /Free. /Free code has logic statements, not C-specs.

Nothing ever goes into position 6.

Position 7 is reserved for the start of the /Free and /end-Free tags, which enclose /Free code and tell the compiler to look for it.

Unless you are on 7.1 TR7 or higher, in which case the tags are not required. At that level, the compiler is smart enough to recognize /Free on its own. More on that in a subsequent chapter.

/Free code statements start anywhere from position 8–80 and end with a semicolon (;).

If you are on 7.3, then the 80-column limit is lifted, and you can go out as far as the 132-character restriction of the source file. This is nice and in line with Web languages, but I am not sure if it is really helpful. Do you enjoy reading text that goes beyond the bounds of the page you can see? If yes, you will like this; if not, maybe not.

The SETON opcode did not make it into /Free, so we must use *INLR = 1 to end a program.

Comments are delineated by // starting anywhere in columns 8–80, including after a valid logic statement.

MOVE was not brought over into /Free, and so EVAL is used to set values. This includes the use of EVAL-CORR and EVALR plus the h/m/r opcode extenders.

We also talked about how /Free makes it possible to indent code and how important that is in terms of being able to see the structure of the program at a glance. But we will see that more in this section.

And, most importantly, we all set up a model /Free program and used that to create a /Free program with a couple of EVALs in it. That was the funnest part.

Of course, if you have been programming for even a little while, you know that you can't do too much with just EVAL statements. So this chapter will look at the control statements that /Free uses: things like the IF, SELECT, and DOU/DOW opcodes that allow you to control the flow through your program. Should be pretty interesting.

IF Statement Stuff

In its simplest format, an IF statement in /Free looks like this:

```
IF ZIP_CODE = '55613';
    CITY = 'Enid';
ELSE;
    CITY = 'Unknown';
ENDIF;
```

Obviously, if there were no ELSE clause, then you wouldn't need to code it. Duh. The ENDIF, however, is required. No big surprise there. That's the way we roll in the /Free world.

The semicolon after each statement: have I mentioned that yet? If you are into PHP programming, you will notice that this is different from PHP, where only the operational statements (for example, the 'CITY =' statements) would be ended by ';'.

And, as usual, capitalization or not of the IF, ELSE, ENDIF is up to you. The semicolon should never be capitalized, of course.

The indentation of the EVAL statements? That is something you don't have to do. You could just line up every statement above as such:

```
IF ZIP_CODE = '55613';

CITY = 'Enid';

ELSE;

CITY = 'Unknown';

ENDIF;
```

But if you did, we would be forced to have the Style Police come and hit you with their tiaras. Indenting is the single biggest reason that I love /Free. It makes the code so much easier to read, and it's just wonderful. Take full advantage of it, especially for nested IF statements.

ELSEIF Construct

You also have access to the ELSEIF clause. It basically allows you to combine an ELSE and a follow-on IF into a single level and so reduce the amount of indenting required.

```
IF ZIP_CODE = '55613';

    'CITY = 'Enid';

ELSEIF ZIP_CODE = '55523';

    CITY = 'Tulsa';

ELSEIF ZIP_CODE = '55419'

    CITY = 'Oklahoma City';

ENDIF;
```

The nice thing about using the ELSEIF construct is that you don't need to figure out how many ENDIFs you have to key in. One will do it. Please note that this is not the way it is for normal nested IFs and ELSEs. There you need an ENDIF for each and every pair. Since I always miscount, using the ELSEIF saves me compile errors.

You Can't Do This

Unfortunately, there is one thing you can't do, and I always want to do this when I am coding in /Free. You cannot have multiple values for a single IF statement variable. That is, you *can't* do this:

```
IF CITY = 'Tulsa' or 'Enid' or 'Oklahoma City';

    Zip_Code > '49300';

ENDIF;
```

I repeat, you CAN'T do that. It would be nice if you could, but it doesn't work. Instead, the *correct* way to do it is as such:

```
IF CITY = 'Tulsa' or

    CITY = 'Enid'  or

    CITY = 'Oklahoma City';

    Zip_Code > '49300';

ENDIF;
```

Please note also exactly where the semicolons are placed on the IF clause for this type of example.

Now It's Your Turn

Go ahead now and add a couple of IF statements to your model program. You will probably have to add a file or some D-specs—do them the way you normally would (we will talk about the /Free versions of those specs later). Keep it simple, but do it so you get the feel. Decide about your spacing and general IF format. But do it like I did. You know. So it's cool and all.

More Complex IF Statements

But what if you want a little more complexity? What if one variable is not enough, if you follow my meaning (wink, wink, nudge, nudge)?

```
IF (CM_CUSNO  = AR_CUSNO) AND
   (CM_CCUS#  = AR_CCUS#);
   Cust_Valid = 'Y';
ELSE;
   Cust_Valid = 'N';
ENDIF;
```

The parentheses are not required. The IF would work fine without them, processing ANDs first and ORs second. I like to use them, though. Makes it easier for me to see what goes together, and makes it harder for you to make a mistake with the syntax. Please use them as well—just in case I ever have to look at your code.

Columns or Not

I have a tendency to line up the conditions in columns. You could write it all out on one line, but I like the ability to put them vertically so they are easier to read. If you have condition lengths that are different, then you can insert blanks or whatever to line things up neatly. For example:

```
IF (CM_CUSNO = AR_CUSNO) and
   (CM_CDE   = 'L'      );
   Cust_Valid = 'Y';
ELSE;
   Cust_Valid = 'N';
ENDIF;
```

Or, if you like things strung out, you can do it like this; it's up to you:

```
IF (CM_CUSNO = AR_CUSNO) and (CM_CDE = 'Y');

    Cust_Valid = 'Y';

ELSE;

'   Cust_Valid = 'N';

ENDIF;
```

Either way, you should be sure to indent. That is where /Free really shines, in helping make those big nested IFs look a little more logical.

Comparison Operators

Not everything always breaks down to an "equals" situation, of course. There is "less than," "greater than," "almost not quite less than although if seen from some angles it might be greater than," and lots of other things. And /Free makes a little change here from positional RPG.

Gone are the *LT, *EQ, *GE, and others.

Instead we go with a more mathematical syntax: >, <, =, >=, and so on. Using these, our example might look like this:

```
IF (CM_ARBAL > *zeros  )  and

   (CM_LPYMT < CM_MINPY);

    Cust_Valid = 'N';

ELSE;

    Cust_Valid = 'Y';

ENDIF;
```

It is the final triumph of Intermediate Algebra.

Negative IF Statement

It's generally always a good idea to be positive with IF statements. I mean, seriously, how many of us would say, "I don't not want to not stop speaking to you" in casual conversation. And yet, that seems to happen with distressing frequency when you read other people's code.

Good design principles encourage you to state your conditions from a positive rather than a negative point of view. Sometimes, however, it is more convenient to look at things from the negative side of the road (as in cases where you do something if the answer is negative, and do nothing if it is positive. So, how do you do that in /Free?

Well, one way is with the "not equal to" operator: <>.

```
IF CM_CUSNO <> AR_CUSNO);
    Cust_Valid = 'N';
ENDIF;
```

Or, if you want to use a more alphabetically oriented syntax, you could use a NOT operator on a condition set up as an equality. The thing to remember using this option that it is best to put the thing(s) that you are NOT-ing in parenthesis. It is not a requirement, but it certainly makes it much easier to understand what is being negated. For example:

```
IF NOT (CM_CUSNO = AR_CUSNO);
    Cust_Valid = 'N';
ENDIF;
```

Now It's Your Turn

I want you to take some time and play with the IF statements again, this time with some of the more complex conditions we have talked about in the last few pages. Things where you have to use AND/OR and parentheses. See what format looks most natural and readable to you. You can use debug to see that everything is working correctly.

Decide what kind of indenting structure you want to use.

Play with the mathematical-oriented comparison operators.

Try some NOT-oriented IFs as well, and be sure to use debug to check it out.

Just have fun with it. You know, like they tell fashion models during a shoot.

SELECT/WHEN

/Free also supports the use of a case structure, just as positional RPG does, but I think it looks more natural in /Free. I recommend using it (SELECT/WHEN) instead of nested IFs whenever you get a chance.

I like the SELECT statement; it reminds me of the Case structure command on the old IBM 8100. Anyone remember that machine? It was a kind of mainframe AS/400: simpler than CICS but with an integrated development environment and very programmer friendly. For some reason, after a fast start, it just sort of petered out. I think the release of the 4300 series might have had something to do with that. Plus, IBM was doing the marketing, so maybe it never had a chance. Great machine, though.

Anyway, the SELECT statement is great when you have a number of options for your IF, and you want something that isn't going to confuse you to death. I use it if I have more than two clauses for my IF. But I'm exceptionally easy to confuse. The format is quite simple:

```
SELECT;
     WHEN logical statement;
          imperative statement;
     WHEN logical statement;
          imperative statement;
     OTHER;
          imperative statement;
ENDSL;
```

The logical statements in the WHEN clause do not have to have anything in common. They don't need to reference the same variable (although often they do). In addition, they can be as complex as you want them to be with logical operators and parentheses and even BIFs. For example:

```
SELECT;

WHEN CM_CORP_CUST = 'Y';
     imperative statement;


WHEN (CM_CORP_CUST = 'M') or

     (CM_CORP_CUST = 'C');
     imperative statement;


WHEN (ACCEPT_ALL    = 'Y') and

     (ACCEPT_NONE    <> *BLANKS) and

     (%DATE(TRNDT)   =   %DATE());

     imperative statement;


 OTHER;
     imperative statement;

ENDSL;
```

The OTHER keyword is used alone (no conditional statement), and it is a catchall for things that don't fit into one of the previous WHENs.

And—do I even need to say it at this point?—a semicolon at the end of every statement. Please, please try to keep up.

Now It's Your Turn

Yep, you guessed it. Go back to your /Free program and pop a little SELECT/WHEN action in there, being sure to put some variety in it and then compiling to make sure you got it right.

DO Stuff

There's an old programmers' adage: "Where there's an IF, there's a DO," and darned if it isn't true.

Fortunately, most of what we said for IFs is true for DO loops.

The DO itself has been eliminated from /Free (use FOR). And the DOWGT, DOULT, and others of that ilk are out as well.

What you are left with is simpler and more straightforward: DOW and DOU with a conditional statement. The basic syntax is:

```
DOU  CM_CUSNO > MAX_CUSTNO;

    Yada, yada, yada;

ENDDO;
```

Despite the changes in syntax, these two commands operate the same way they do in positional RPG. That is, the difference is the point in the construct where the decision is made whether to continue with the loop or get out. For the DOW, it is done at the start of the loop; for DOU, it is at the end. In both cases, an ENDDO is required.

As with the IF statement, you can use parentheses and logical operators to write more complex conditions, and you can split them up on multiple lines with a semicolon only at the end-of-line group. For example:

```
DOU      (CM_CUSTNO > MAX_CUSTNO) or
   Not ((VALID_CUST = 'N') and (CM_CUSTNO = 11));
   Yada, yada, yada;
ENDDO;
```

Now, please don't think that I consider the above example a good example of coding. God help you if you end up ever having to duplicate this kind of logic. In reality, I would break this up into a couple of nested IFs, even though I hate those, too. It's just an example, not my vision of reality.

Now It's Your Turn

Time to drag out the program again, and this time put a DOU or DOW in there and see if you can get it to compile. Shouldn't be too hard since you have the IF condition stuff down.

In the code above, weird though it may look, we are saying that we want to do this loop until either the CM_CUSTNO is greater than the value of the MAX_CUSTNO—OR—the statement that the VALID_CUST flag is 'N' and the CM_CUSTNO is 11 is not true. I would set this up in a simple program, set the variables up in D-specs, and then play with the parentheses to see how they affect how the statement is interpreted.

FOR Loop

To be honest, this is one that I don't use that much. But strangely enough, right after I switched to /Free, I used it. Haven't touched it since. For some reason, using it puts me in a FORTRAN sort of mood and makes me want to drink Harvey Wallbangers. Never really liked them when they were popular, so it's a good reason to try to avoid the FOR. The Galliano bottles were cool, though.

But, sometimes you need to do a loop a given number of times, and that is what the FOR is there for.

```
FOR i = 1 to 5;
    your indented logic statements;
ENDFOR
```

(There is a syntax error in the above statement. Do you see what it is? Hint: have I mentioned the importance of the semicolon before?)

The From and To limits in the FOR can easily be variables.

One important thing to note is that the FOR statement will automatically update the i value each time the loop ends. So don't do it yourself. That would be sooooo weird.

Now It's Your Turn

Take a guess. What do you think I want you to try? Think about it.

Leaving a Loop

Sometimes you may be in an IF statement or a loop and decide you just want to get out. It can be a panic situation. You know, you feel the walls beginning to close in, and the longer the loop runs, the tighter and tighter and tighter ..., well, you get the idea. Often what we do is set a flag and fudge the structure of the loop so that when this flag is set, you can exit. Of course, back in the real olden days we would just do a GOTO and get out, but that was abused and has rightfully been banished by the Great Queen who rules Game of War.

Fortunately, /Free supports the LEAVE and ITER opcodes.

LEAVE will take you to the next statement after the end of the loop you are currently in. It truly gets you out of the loop. Ta-dah!

ITER causes you to jump to the ENDDO (or ENDFOR) and perform the normal checking that is done to see if you should get out or do another iteration. You skip any code within the loop but come back in the loop for another go-round.

In other words, LEAVE does just that: it kicks you out of the loop you are in. ITER bypasses all of the logic between you and the end of the loop, but keeps you in the loop and lets it do the normal checking to see if you should be set free or if you have another ticket to ride.

Both of these opcodes work only if you are in a DOx or FOR loop. You can code it inside a DOx or FOR loop that is in an IF or SELECT statement, but if you just put it in a standalone IF or SELECT, you will get a compile error.

CALLP

The CALL opcode was not moved over to /Free. Instead, you will use the prototyped call, CALLP.

The format for this is pretty simple:

```
CALLP DWS0001(parm1:parm2:parm3);
```

Like the EVAL opcode, however, the CALLP is optional. So you may see the call to a program set up to look more like a BIF statement:

```
DWS0001(parm1:parm2:parm3);
```

Some people consider this the only civilized way to set up a call, and they use it frequently. For my money, I prefer the first form. The main issue to me is one of clarity. I like having the CALLP there because that is a very clear visual sign that a call is being made. I suppose I should be smart enough to instantly recognize that the other is a call, but I am not. In this case it is obvious, but if I had named my PR spec AP_CREDIT_CHECK instead of DWS0001 (an obvious program name), it might not be quite so clear. And don't worry, we will talk about what PR specs are later.

It's a small thing, but to me it sometimes seems that now that we have a version of RPG that is very easy to read and understand, we are taking steps to make it more cryptic. I agree, it looks more Web-like that way, but I would hardly argue that Web languages are easy to read.

But chose whatever form seems best to you. They both work just fine. And, as we shall see later, sometimes you have to use the format without the CALLP.

Indent

While we are talking about control logic statements, I want to say just a final word about indenting your code.

Do it!

Indenting is something RPG programmers generally don't think about too much (since you can't do it in fixed-format mode). But indenting is probably the single most powerful structure tool a programmer has. Anyone who has struggled to match up IFs and ENDIFs in a big logic section has to appreciate the ability to be able to indent code and so easily see which ENDIF matches up with which IF.

So get in the habit right now. I like to indent four spaces; some people like more or fewer, but they are crazy. The important point is to start to build indenting into your coding style with /Free right away. You won't regret it.

What Ya Shoulda Learned

OK, we are a couple of chapters into /Free now, and your feet should be getting pretty wet. You already know enough to do quite a bit of damage, but we are not going to stop here. Before we go on, though, I want to quickly review what we have talked about here.

- First, you should have a good handle on setting up the IF statements.

- Second, need I mention that you have to have a semicolon after each statement?

- Use parentheses as necessary to make the whole thing easier to read and compile (that is, for the compiler to understand what you want).

- Use the new mathematical comparison operators (versus the old alphabetic abbreviations).

- If you do use not on an expression, be sure to surround the expression with parenthesis for clarity.

- In addition, we went over the SELECT/WHEN.

- And the FOR.

- Plus the DOW/DOU, which when used in conjunction with a condition statement replace the DOWEQ, etc. operators from positional RPG.

- And finally, we saw the prototyped call parm, CALLP, and its two formats.

- But most important, you have not only learned about these things but actually used them in your sample /Free program. You did try each one of these, right? I hope so.

And now we are tired; happy but tired. So let's rest for just a minute before we move on to /Free I/O.

Chapter 6

/Free I/O Statements

Again, fighting against not even close to incredible odds, our brave explorers have hacked their way through basic /Free structure and the control statements that can be used to tame it and bend it to our will.

But what about files? So far, we have not really talked about them. How cruelly unfair, as files are at the heart of everything we do. But that is about to change.

As we shall see, most of the changes are to do with RPG I/O, not the way embedded SQL is used, but we will talk about that briefly also. SQL in full is definitely another topic for another day and has very little to do with /Free per se.

Some things in /Free have not changed from fixed format, like the opcode names for the database I/O: READ, READE, READP, READPE, CHAIN, SETLL, SETGT, UPDATE, WRITE, and DELETE.

And you still have that weird thing where READ, CHAIN, and SETLL can use the file ID in the statement while UPDATE, WRITE, and DELETE must use the record format.

Of course, the basic syntax is different (from positional RPG), with the order being more English language and the semicolon at the end. And the indicators that show the outcome of the I/O operation are not supported. But you have some additional options with keys that I really like. Shall we?

Working with Keys

Speaking of keys, remember how in the olden days you had to code up C-specs with the KLIST and KFLD elements? Well, that's not supported in /Free. Can I get an Amen? Neither do you have to set up key definitions in either D- or C-specs. Instead, you may simply list the keys as arguments separated by colons (not semicolons) in the I/O statement, and the system does the rest.

```
CHAIN (keyfld1:keyfld2:keyfld3) FileID;
```

or

```
SETLL (keyfld1:keyfld2:keyfld3) FileID;
```

Where does /Free get the info to know what the proper keys are, how long they are, what data type, and so on? From the files that are specified in the F-spec, of course, with help from a little compiler magic that is what makes /Free free. I like this. I like seeing the list of keys that we are using right in the CHAIN/SETLL: it's very self-documenting.

And the keyfld fields that are specified in the I/O statement do not have to be the actual ones from the file you are reading. That is, the name used in the CHAIN/SETLL does not have to be the name of the actual key field in the file. It can be any field name as long as it currently holds the value you want to key by. Naturally, the non-file field does have to be the same size and type as the actual key field.

So, if you are picking up a field from a screen, say a product number, and want to see if it is valid, you could use the field from the screen right in the CHAIN or SETLL. No time wasted moving it to the actual key field name.

It could even be a BIF statement, like %CHAR(num_field). Don't forget that's just a variable like any other variable except that it will be transformed before it is used. Sort of like a caterpillar becoming a butterfly, which is then eaten by a bat.

Technically, if there is only one field in the key, then you don't need to put it in parenthesis, but I think it's a good way to keep things organized. Besides, what self- respecting file has only one key field? Sheesh!

Of course, if you do have a large number of key fields in the file, then the list could become pretty long and unwieldy. But since this is /Free, all you do is just stack them up vertically and keep on going.

```
CHAIN (key-fld1:
       key-fld2:
       key-fld3:
       key-fld4:
       key-fld5:
       key-fld6) FileID;
```

Another Way to Deal with Keys

Now, in fairness, I have to tell you there is another option for handling keys. I don't care for it, but that is a personal preference, so I will still cover how to use it. It's a perfectly fine method, if you like doing things that way. I guess it's up to you. Takes all kinds, don't ya know.

The other method starts with a D-spec that sets up the key format using the LikeRec keyword and the record format of the file:

```
D  KeyRec        DS      LikeRec('Recfmt':*key)
```

Then, in the /Free portion of the program, we set the values of the KeyRec fields, then issue the opcode.

```
KeyRec.field1 = Data1;
KeyRec.field2 = Data2;
KeyRec.field3 = Data3;
KeyRec.field4 = Data4;
KeyRec.field5 = Data5;
KeyRec.field6 = Data6;
Chain %kds(KeyRec)FileA;
```

It just seems like a lot of bother to me. But use whatever works best for you. You know what they say: "Even folks what prefer a paddle can make use of water-soaked branch from time to time." And I agree.

Now It's Your Turn

Let's dust off that sample program that you have been developing and do some I/O with it.

You will need to add a file (or two if you are ambitious). At this point, just put it in there with a traditional F-spec. If you are on 7.1 TR7 or later, then you can do /Free file control statements to replace that F-spec, but I don't want to screw with that now. Then try your basic I/O commands: CHAIN, SETLL/READ, etc.

Output Opcodes in /Free

Of course, you can also do WRITE, UPDATE, and DELETE in /Free.

WRITE

WRITE is pretty much what it was in positional RPG. Actually, it's exactly the same, if you ask me.

You specify the file record format, not the file ID, and that's that. It writes the entire record out at one time.

```
Write record-format;
```

UPDATE

UPDATE is also pretty much the same, using the record name versus the file ID.

The one difference is that in positional RPG, you can update only some fields in a record. To do this, you need to use the EXCEPT operator and set up O-specs to indicate what fields are being changed.

You can do the same thing in /Free (a partial update) but much more directly by using the %fields addition:

```
UPDATE record-format %fields(field1:
                             field2:
                             field3:
                             field4);
```

DELETE

The DELETE also operates on the record name.

In positional RPG, you do not have to do a CHAIN first, but if you don't, it will delete the last record read.

In /Free, you now have the option of putting a key value in the DELETE statement, which makes that read unnecessary:

```
Delete (keyfld1:keyfld2:keyfld3) file-record;
```

Workstation-Type I/O Statements

Although green screen is not anyone's "le petit chérie" for development anymore, it still does appear. And so we need to know what opcodes we can use for the display files they are built on.

EXFMT (Write, then Read)

This opcode is used for workstation input and output. Generally, it is used when we need to do both a write and a read in sequence, as when we are dealing with a subfile.

It does a write to the display file of whatever data has been moved to that file record, then reads the next display record in the sequence.

```
EXFMT display-record-name;
```

WRITE

If all we need is a write, like when we write a display file header record, then WRITE works fine.

```
WRITE display-record-name;
```

DSPLY

Finally, we have the display operator, which lets you put in free-form verbiage to show up on the screen.

```
DSPLY verbiage;
```

The DSPLY can show complex statements through the use of parentheses and quote marks to separate out the various components.

Now It's Your Turn

Again, you don't really have to try any of the stuff on the last two pages; just remember how they are similar to what is in positional. By the time we reach the end of this book, hopefully you will feel good about being ready to integrate another language into the RPG world, so that you can get a Web look and feel that is green only if those are your company colors.

Error Checking

/Free does not support the old HI, EQ, LO indicator scheme, so you can't use indicators to check the results of your I/O. Yes, let's all stand very solemnly and wave goodbye to the indicators as they drive out of sight. OK, cue the music, and let's get this party started.

Or maybe you don't feel that way. Maybe you liked using them. In which case, I am deeply and sincerely sorry for your loss. Hey, is that beer cold?

To do I/O checking in /Free, you need to rely on the built-in functions. Namely %Found for CHAIN and %EOF for SETLL, and so on. To set a "not" condition, simply code it as NOT (%Found), for example. (And yes, you are right, you could use this same technique if you are doing positional RPG.)

Remember, if you don't specify a file ID with the %EOF/%FOUND, the system will look at the last record read. To avoid that, or even just to provide additional clarity, you can include the file ID in the BIF. Either of the following ways works.

```
DOW Not(%EOF);
```

or

```
DOW Not(%EOF(MSPMP100));
```

```
IF %FOUND;
```

or

```
IF %FOUND(PSPSP100);
```

I am assuming that you already know how to use %EOF and %FOUND, but there are some other error BIFs that might come in handy. Remember, these BIFs are not part of /Free per se. They are part of RPG and can be used in fixed format as well. But you really need them in /Free.

%ERROR

To get this to activate, you need to use the "e" extender on your CHAIN or READ: CHAIN(e), for example.

It functions like the LO indicator in fixed format (returning a 0 for good read and a 1 for not so good) and is the kind of thing you want to use if you have an error-handling routine that you can call. Although maybe I need to restate that: if you use %ERROR, have error-handling logic to take advantage of it. The error branch will be executed if some sort of error is detected.

```
CHAIN(e) (key1) File1;
IF  %ERROR;
      EXSR ERROR_HDLR;

ENDIF;
```

%EQUAL

This is used with the SETLL opcode to see if we found a record whose key equals the key we are pointing at.

It can be used with multiple key field keys, and also with a partial key.

If the value returned is 0, then it means that no records were found for whatever key (full or partial) you used. If the value is 1, then you got a hit. %EQUAL can help eliminate the need to do an actual read and check the file field against some other field to see if anything's out there. You know, if you were just doing a CHAIN to verify the record exists, you could instead do a SETLL and check the value of %EQUAL. It's less overhead than a CHAIN, which actually retrieves the data field by field.

An IF %EQUAL branch would be triggered by a hit on the key value.

Now It's Your Turn

The only bad thing here is that with these BIFs, since they are like indicators, we know if there is a problem, but it doesn't tell you what the problem really is. But, it's all good.

Make sure you understand how these work, especially %ERROR and especially %EQUAL as you can use it to reduce unnecessary CHAINs by using SETLL instead. You might want try some code situations with that one just so you feel comfy and warm.

And yes, I know that these BIFs are not strictly /Free. You can use them in positional RPG, too. But you have to use them in /Free if you want to trap errors.

So, What About SQL?

Before we go on, we need to say just a word about SQL since so many people are using it as their I/O tool of choice.

The good news is that you can use SQL in /Free. No problem.

There is no new functionality per se in that, so I am not going to go through it (that would be a completely different chapter altogether). But there are some changes in the format.

Most of it involves what you don't need to do. For example, let's take a very simple positional example.

```
C/Exec SQL
C+    SELECT *
C+    FROM   mspmp100
C+    WHERE class > 100
C+    ORDER BY class, prdno
C/End-SQL
```

To do this in /Free, simply remove the C, the /, and the +. Then stick a semicolon (;) at the end—the very end, that is. What you end up with is this. I have included the /Free just to show that the Exec must start in position 8.

```
/Free
  Exec SQL
      SELECT    *
      FROM mspmp100
      WHERE class > 100
      ORDER BY class, prdno;
```

And that is it. No end clause is available. I sort of wish there was, but there isn't one so, I will just go on with my life.

Everything else about embedded SQL remains the same. The source member type is still SQLRPGLE. You still will have the SQL communications data structure automatically included in your SQLRPGLE program, and you still use a colon (:) to denote host variables in your SQL statement.

What Ya Shoulda Learned

So, everybody cool?

If you already know /Free, then this stuff should be no big deal. And even if you don't know /Free, this stuff should be pretty basic.

In this episode we learned about:

- How to structure our keys given the fact that the KLIST/KFLD are not supported

- How to selectively update only some fields on an UPDATE without using O-specs

- How the DELETE function differs from the way it acted in positional RPG

- How to do other types of I/O statements beyond the SETLL/READ/CHAIN

- How to check for errors or other I/O conditions given the fact that the indicator error structure is not supported in /Free

- In addition, we looked at how SQL is handled in /Free.

What's important is that you now have enough knowledge to be able to code 75 percent of the stuff that you need to do in /Free, 85 percent if you are good at faking it. Hell fire, I've done lots of stuff in other languages knowing a lot less than that. You're golden!

So settle back and relax. You're almost 3 percent of the way to being an expert in /Free-ILE-MVC. But now, I think it's time we let go of /Free for a minute and turn our attention back to ILE.

PRACTICAL ILE

Now that we have learned the theoretical side of ILE and gotten a bit of /Free under our belts, it's time to write some simple but actual ILE programs, including your very first service program. I know. Exciting!

Chapter 7

ILE Subroutines to Sub-Procedures

In the next three chapters, we will look at three different ways in which we can set up an ILE program.

- Using embedded sub-procedures (vice subroutines) within a program,
- Calling one ILE program from another, and
- Calling a sub-procedure within a service program.

As we do this, we will be highlighting *sub-procedures*, ILE's more advanced and powerful reply to the ordinary subroutine, and *prototyping*, ILE's method for accessing one module from another. For each option, we will look at a simple yet complete program example, using /Free, of course.

So, to kick things off, let's remind ourselves just how bad subroutines are.

Ready?

Why Subroutines Cause Blindness

In OPM, subroutines are a handy way to encapsulate code and keep from having one big, ugly mess of mainline instructions.

Technically, in ILE and /Free, you can still use subroutines. The EXSR and whatnot are supported, so there is no problem there.

Nor are subroutines totally evil. Before ILE, they were the best tool you had to take a section of code out of the mainline logic of the BOP and put it in a little spot all its own. You could execute it multiple times in your program but only have the code out there once, and if it were properly named (not easy given the length restrictions), it could help improve the readability of the program as a whole.

But for all the good, there are a number of serious drawbacks to subroutines.

First, the subroutine was still part of the BOP, and if the same logic were required in several programs, it had to be inserted into each of those programs separately.

> That is, it couldn't be set up as a separate entity and called by a number of other programs.

> In addition, if it were inserted in multiple programs, unless it were done via a /Copy, you could have minor variations in the code, which could affect the universality of the business rules the routine represented.

> And, if you made changes to it, then even if it were in a copybook, you still had to compile all the programs that used that copybook.

Second, it couldn't handle either local variables or parameters.

> A subroutine's use of global variables actually made it harder to follow how a particular data element was being used, because first it was here, on line 135, and then suddenly it dropped into line 5387 and probably other places as well.

The bottom line is: you should be using are sub-procedures, not subroutines. End of story.

Sub-Procedures

The idea behind a sub-procedure is simple: take some code lines that are doing a particular task, take them out of the mainline code, and put them in a little spot of their own. Very similar to subroutines. But there are some major differences.

First, sub-procedures can only be done in an ILE program. They cannot be done in OPM.

Second, sub-procedures are not delineated by the BEGSR/ENDSR tags, but by B and E (beginning and end) P-specs. More on P-specs in a minute or so (depending on how fast you read).

Third, and this is a big one, sub-procedures allow you to define local variables in between the B and E P-specs.

> You do this using D-specs that are listed after the B P-spec. This way, you can define any variable you want and use it in the sub-procedure. But only in the sub-procedure. Local variables cannot be used in any other part of the program. They are strictly for the sub-procedure. In fact, you could even give them the names of global variables that are used other places in the program or repeat the names of local variables from other sub-procedures. I don't recommend either of those options, but it's doable.

> I can't tell you how important I think local variables are and how dangerous global variables are to good program structure.

Fourth, while subroutines are accessed by using the EXSR operator, sub-procedures are "called" by doing a prototype call (CALLP). Even within a given program.

> You might think there is more work involved in doing a call rather than just an EXSR, but the truth is—well, actually I guess the truth is it is a bit more work. But only a bit. And it's well worth it to have the other advantages.

And fifth, while subroutine code must exist in the program that is using it, a sub-procedure can actually be set up in a separate program (a service program) that is truly called into the calling program using the CALLP prototype call. Service programs are an incredibly useful entity, and we will talk more about them in a couple of chapters.

Sub-Procedure Inside a Program Example

Let's start our ILE adventures by looking at a program that calls an embedded sub-procedure (that is, the sub-procedure is part of the program that uses it). The sub-procedure itself is very simple; it just validates a product number against a product master (MSPMP100). We will look at the whole mess, then break it down into its components for easy digestion. Give it a name to your own liking.

```
H*********************************************************
H DFTACTGRP(*NO) ACTGRP(*NEW)
H*********************************************************
F* PRODUCT MASTER
FMSPMP100  IF   E          K  DISK      PREFIX(PM_)
F*
F* Display File
FDWS0170FM CF  E               WORKSTN PREFIX(D01_)
F*********************************************************
D  VAL_PRDNO        PR
D    D01_PRDNO                    15
D    MSG                          60
D    ERROR_FLAG                    1
D*
D  ERROR_FLAG      S              1
D  MSG             S             60
D*********************************************************
 /FREE

     ERROR_FLAG = 'N';


     CALLP VAL_PRDNO(D01_PRDNO:MSG:ERROR_FLAG);

     *INLR = '1';
```

```
 /END-FREE

P*********************************************************
P  // SUBPROCEDURE - VALIDATE PRODUCT# FROM PRODUCT MSTR
P  VAL_PRDNO        B
D*********************************************************
D  VAL_PRDNO        PI
D    D01_PRDNO                    15
D    MSG                          60
D    ERROR_FLAG                    1
D*
D  SP_PRDNO         S             15
D*********************************************************
 /FREE
  //READ PRODUCT MASTER USING PRODUCT NUMBER FROM SCREEN
  //AS KEY.
    EVAL SP_PRDNO = D01_PRDNO;
    CHAIN (SP_PRDNO) MSPMP100;
    IF NOT %FOUND;
        ERROR_FLAG = 'Y';
        MSG = 'THIS IS A BAD PRODUCT NUMBER
                                  (XXX00111.01).';
    ENDIF;
 /END-FREE
P VAL_PRDNO         E
P*********************************************************
```

Now let's take that program apart and see what makes it tick. You should be able to detect hints of apricot and chocolate and ... but there I go again. Each person tastes something different, and I shouldn't try to plant suggestions.

Because I am doing this as if you are on 5.4 rather than 7.x, some things are present that may not be if you are on a more recent release of the software. Like having the F-, D-, and other specs be positional, and then having to use /Free and /End-Free to segregate the /Free from the positional code. Or the need for the H-spec to ensure this is compiled as ILE (more on that later). Sorry about that, but many of us are still back in that old era. It should not stop you from doing ILE.

Oh, and by the way, I am listing the code first, and then under it putting the discussion of that code. I would have been confused about that myself. As you go thru this section, DON'T focus on the text description. Focus on the code, devour it with your eyes, think about what you see, experience its richness and vibrancy. The text description is just to give it context, to help clarify what you are seeing. But focus on the code itself.

```
H*************************************************************
H DFTACTGRP(*NO)  ACTGRP(*NEW)
H*************************************************************
```

First, the H-spec. This is put in there because sub-procedures are an ILE construct. So they cannot be in a program that uses the default activation group (that is OPM). The H-spec makes sure that the program is compiled as ILE, but if the defaults in your compile command are set for that, then you would not need this H-spec. I am assuming you will compile this with CRTBNDRPG instead of CRTRPGMOD/CRTPGM.

```
F*
F* PRODUCT MASTER
FMSPMP100  IF  E          K DISK     PREFIX(PM_)
F*
F* Display File
FDWS0170FM CF  E              WORKSTN PREFIX(D01_)
F*************************************************************
```

This is then followed by the F-specs for this program.

Note that I am using a product master file plus a display file, and I am going to be pretending that I am picking up data entry fields from the display and editing them against the product master file for validity.

Remember, if you are on 7.1, TR7 or higher, we could set these up as file control statements. But since I am doing this book from a 5.4 perspective, we will set them up as F-specs.

```
D*
D   VAL_PRDNO          PR
D      D01_PRDNO                    15
D      MSG                          60
D      ERROR_FLAG                    1
D
D   ERROR_FLAG         S            1
D   MSG                S           60
D****************************************************************
```

Then come the D-specs. The global D-specs. We are still in our mainline program here; we haven't gotten to the sub-procedure yet. Just be patient, and quiet ... very, very quiet. We don't want to spook it.

There are two things here in the D-specs. The first is the prototype D-spec, the thing identified with the PR as the D-spec data type. This is required in the program D-specs, and it identifies what sub-procedures will be used (by the CALLP) in that program. The D-spec subfields under it for D01_PRDNO, MSG, and ERROR_FLAG are the data elements that are passed in when the sub-procedure is "called." Please note that there is no EXTPGM keyword on the PR, because we are not calling an external program, just a sub-procedure in this program.

If you had more than one sub-procedure embedded in this program, then you would need a PR prototype D-spec for each one of those sub-procedures.

Below that are two more D-specs: ERROR_FLAG and MSG.

ERROR_FLAG is a global data element, and it is used in the sub-procedure but also in the program calling the sub-procedure. Our little snippet does not show the ERROR_FLAG being used, but if there were more calls to other sub-procedures, they would be contained within an IF statement checking to see whether or not the ERROR_FLAG were set.

MSG is also a global variable, just a message field that we will set if there is an error.

What is interesting is that both of these fields are defined under the PR D-spec. So why are we defining them here again? Have I screwed up, defined them twice, and so the compile will fail? Normally, that would be a very good guess indeed, but not tonight. They are there because even though I have "defined" them in the PR above, anything listed in a PR is not really defined. It has to exist somewhere else, and so I have defined the field in a second, normal D-spec. Why aren't things in a PR really defined to the system as fields? You might as well ask why the earth is an oblate spheroid. Because. Just because that's the way it is. Deal with it.

```
/FREE

    ERROR_FLAG = 'N';

    CALLP VAL_PRDNO(D01_PRDNO:MSG:ERROR_FLAG);

    *INLR = '1';

/END-FREE
```

This is the /Free code that calls the sub-procedure.

And it's very simple. I set the ERROR_FLAG (a global variable) to 'N', then call the sub-procedure, and then end the program. If this were a real program, we would probably have more calls to other sub-procedures, each covered by an IF ERROR_FLAG clause, to edit each of the fields on the display file. Oh, I guess I did use the ERROR_FLAG, after all, to initialize it.

Note that the call to the sub-procedure VAL_PRDNO is actually a call, using CALLP (Call Prototype).

And notice that the three data fields mentioned (can't really say defined) in the VAL_PRDNO PR are sent to the sub-procedure as parms separated by a colon and surrounded by parentheses.

Just as an interesting side note, if there were no parms being sent to the sub-procedure, then nothing would be listed under the PR line in the D-specs (although we would still need the PR itself), and nothing would be included in the parenthesis on the CALLP. However, the parenthesis would still be included; they would just be empty—().

Finally, the /end-Free delimiter needs to be set because when we define the sub-procedure (next step), we will use P-specs and D-specs, which are positional RPG, not /Free. Granted, in 7.1 TR7, we can make them /Free, but that is not the version of the operating system that this book is based on.

```
P*****************************************************************
 // SUBPROCEDURE - VALIDATE PRODUCT # FROM PRODUCT MSTR.
P VAL_PRDNO        B
D*****************************************************************
D  VAL_PRDNO       PI
D    D01_PRDNO                   15
D    MSG                         60
D    ERROR_FLAG                   1
D*
D  SP_PRDNO        S             15
D*****************************************************************
```

The sub-procedure itself really starts with the P-spec that has a B in position 24. The two lines above that are just icing that I put in to make it easier to see. Note that even though I have come out of /Free (last statement on previous page), I can still use the double slash for comments. Pretty cool, eh?

Then we have D-specs for the sub-procedure. If you are on a release 6.1 or above, you can also include F-specs in here, so instead of defining the files at the global level, you can define them in the sub-procedure. (This is separate from the stuff in 7.1 TR7.) But we are at 5.4, so that option is not open to us.

Note that we have another D-spec that defines the prototype, but this one is a PI, which is called the *procedure interface*. So we have a PR in the program and a PI in the sub-procedure. Let's replay that one more time. The PR is the **pr**ototype D-spec; the PI is the **p**rocedure **i**nterface D-spec. Try to remember that.

Then, we have one more D-spec for SP_PRDNO. Technically, this field is not necessary for the functioning of this module. I could have just as easily used the global variable D01_PRDNO from the display file, but I was so excited about local variables that I just had to define one. If you tried to use this local variable (SP_PRDNO) in the mainline code above, you would get a compile error saying the data element was undefined. But you can use it in the sub-procedure code below.

Please note that the PR and PI specs are D-specs. D-specs. The P-specs are just used to denote the start and finish of the sub-procedure as a whole.

```
/FREE
    //READ PRODUCT MASTER USING PRODUCT # FROM SCREEN.
    EVAL SP_PRDNO = D01_PRDNO;
    CHAIN(E) (SP_PRDNO) MSPMP100;
    IF NOT %FOUND;
        ERROR_FLAG = 'Y';
        MSG = 'THIS IS A BAD PRODUCT NUMBER +
                            (XXX00111.01).';
    ENDIF;
/END-FREE
P VAL_PRDNO        E
P**********************************************************
```

Finally, we are into the code for the sub-procedure. As you can see, we are going back to /Free here, and the code is very simple. Like subroutines, all the sub-procedures will be listed after the *INLR = '1' in the mainline logic.

Even though I don't need it, I set the local variable equal to the value from the display file and used that to read the product master file. I could have just as easily used D01_PRDNO, which is a global variable, in the statement. There is no advantage to using the local variable here; I just wanted to showcase it. There are, however, advantages in general to using local variables.

If it doesn't get a hit, I set the ERROR_FLAG to 'Y' and throw message verbiage into the MSG field. Both of these values (the parms) are returned and can be used in the mainline code. The only thing that can't be used in the mainline is the local variable SP_PRDNO.

Finally, the very last line in the whole mess is another P-spec, this one with a E (for End). If there were other sub-procedures in the program, they would be listed below just as we list subroutines below each other at the very end of the program.

Now It's Your Turn

Think you could recreate this now from memory? Go ahead, give it a try.

What? You can't remember how the whole thing started? Hmmm, actually, I can't really remember, either. So why don't we do this.

Go back to the example I gave, and following section by section (the stuff that is in bold with the explanation), key it into a version of your master program; then compile it. Don't just read it again, key it in. The act of keying reinforces what you are learning in ways that reading can't. And in the end, you will have a coded-up example of how to use an internal sub-procedure all set to go. It's a win-win.

It won't count until you compile it, of course. If you have keyed it in correctly, there should be no errors, but I'm not a betting man. Use CRTBNDRPG but make sure (the H-spec should take care of it) that the result is ILE.

One More Thing: Debug

There is one more thing that I should probably mention.

One of the best ways to get into these methods is to run debug through the programs. But if you are using STRDBG (Start Debug) in PDM, you may be surprised when the F10 sequencing skips right over the sub-procedure.

To step into the sub-procedure, you can either set a breakpoint within the sub-procedure and use F12 to get to it or else use F22 versus F10 when you are ready to step into the sub-procedure.

What Ya Shoulda Learned

Yes, it's different from the way we do subroutines. Not completely different—there are some similarities, but different enough to be different.

But it's not bad. I mean, it's doable. Really pretty easily doable. And by the end of this episode, if you did the **Now It's Your Turn** activity, you should know how to:

- Learn about the differences between subroutines and sub-procedures.

- Code up a sub-procedure that is used internally in a program.

- Learn about the difference between global and local variables.

- Learn how to code up both the PR (prototype) D-spec, and the PI (procedure interface) D-spec.

- Learn how to use the P-specs, both the B and E versions. Also, make sure you are clear on the difference between the P-spec, and the D-specs that define the prototype, and the procedure interface—that is, the PR and the PI.

Take a minute and think how odd it is that to access the sub-procedure in the program you have to use a CALLP. But just a moment. And then smile, and say to yourself in a very calm voice, "But I think that's nice." If that doesn't work, try a double bourbon straight up. Don't sip.

Remember that this is an ILE program, so you must compile this program as ILE (that is, with the DFTACTGRP set to *NO and an ACTGRP specified in the compile). Otherwise you can expect some very weird errors in your compile. Including the H-spec will take care of this.

Even if you never go any further with ILE than doing this (using sub-procedures instead of subroutines), you will have made an important step forward in your professional development. But, of course, you will go further, especially after the subliminal messaging in this chapter kicks in. Oh, yes, you will go further.

Chapter 8

ILE: Calling One Program from Another

But maybe you don't want to just use a sub-procedure in your program. Maybe you actually want to write the sub-procedure up as a small program and then call it from another program. Granted, that is not technically a sub-procedure, but we will let that go for the moment and concentrate on the call of one program by another.

Back in the olden days, we would have used a CALL with a PARM list. But the regular, old CALL was not carried over into /Free. It wasn't efficient enough. And so the new way to call from one program to another is via the CALLP, a prototyped call.

What is a prototyped call? Well, as we have already seen, it is a structured call where the parameters are defined in both the calling and the called program. Fortunately, you have already had a look at the prototyping tools in the previous chapter. They are the PR and PI D-specs.

OK, enough titillation. Let's create a simple program that prototype calls another very simple program. Now there's a top 10 skill for me. Simple stuff.

Calling Program: DWS0996

Obviously, we will need two programs to do this, so here's the first one, the calling program, DWS0996. I am using the same basic program that I used for the previous chapter. I figure that way you at least have a feel for what I am doing. Here it is.

```
H*******************************************************
H* DWS0996 - Calling Program
H*******************************************************
H DFTACTGRP(*NO) ACTGRP(*NEW)
H*******************************************************
F* Display File
FDWS0170FM CF   E              WORKSTN PREFIX(D01_)
F*******************************************************
D*
D  DWS0997        PR                      EXTPGM('DWS0997')
D    D01_PRDNO          15
D    MSG                60
D    ERROR_FLAG          1
D
D  ERROR_FLAG    S       1
D  MSG           S      60
D
D*
 /FREE
      ERROR_FLAG = 'N';
      CALLP DWS0997(D01_PRDNO:MSG:ERROR_FLAG);


      *INLR = *ON;

 /END-FREE
```

See, pretty simple really. But let's break it down anyway.

```
H******************************************************
H* DWS0996 - Calling Program
H******************************************************
H DFTACTGRP(*NO) ACTGRP(*NEW)
H******************************************************
F* Display File
FDWS0170FM CF   E              WORKSTN PREFIX(D01_)
F******************************************************
```

We will start with the H- and F-specs. The H spec is needed to make sure this program gets compiled as ILE and that it is assigned to the activation group *NEW. If your compile command defaults to DFTACTGRP(*NO) instead of *YES, then you don't have to bother with that parm, although as we will see later, you should set the activation group (otherwise it will default to QILE). You can use CALLP with OPM programs, so it won't blow up if you don't have that in there, but since this book is about ILE—sort of seems wrong not to go that direction. It's the sub-procedures that have to be done in ILE. CALLP can be used in both ILE and OPM.

I then have only the display file, the theory being that I get my product number from that file. I know I don't have logic in the program to read that file, but that just seemed like a distraction from what we are really doing.

```
D*
D DWS0997        PR               EXTPGM('DWS0997')
D   D01_PRDNO           15
D   MSG                 60
D   ERROR_FLAG          1
D
D ERROR_FLAG     S      1
D MSG            S      60
D
D******************************************************
```

That brings up the D-specs. We have the prototype D-spec (the PR), but this time there is an additional parameter there, a keyword EXTPGM('DWS0997'), representing the program we are going to call.

Some people like to call the D-spec something other than the program name, like VAL_PRDNO or something like that. Something more English language-oriented that can easily be identified. And that is fine. It is not a sign of psychosis or anything bad. I just like using the program ID. Not very creative, I guess.

What is important is that the actual name of the program you want to call is in the EXTPGM keyword. If you fail to put in the EXTPGM keyword, the compile will fail in the binding stage. If you put in the EXTPGM keyword but use a value in it that is not a valid object, then the compile and bind will work, but the job will fail when you run it.

Then we define the ERROR_FLAG and the MSG since things aren't really defined in the PR. We saw this in chapter 7, but it is worth remembering. And, as it always has, D01_PRDNO is in the DWS0170FM and so does not need to be defined separately.

Also, please note that the calling program has a PR spec but no PI spec.

```
/FREE
    ERROR_FLAG = 'N';
    CALLP DWS0997(D01_PRDNO:MSG:ERROR_FLAG);
    *INLR = *ON;
/END-FREE
```

Then, finally, there are the actual code statements. Note that the CALLP statement is the same as the one that we used for the call to the sub-procedure in the previous chapter except that I am using the program ID now rather than VAL_PRDNO. You can do it either way, but the name of the D-spec is the one that must appear in the CALLP. So you can't really do it either way. What I meant is you have to use the name of the PR D-spec, but that name could be either DWS0997 or VAL_PRDNO. Please note there are no quote marks in this CALLP statement.

The Called Program: DWS0997

And now, the program you are calling, the program that represents the sub-procedure logic. Hang onto your hats, folks.

```
H************************************************************
H* DWS0997 - Called Program
H************************************************************
H DFTACTGRP(*NO) ACTGRP(*CALLER)
H************************************************************
F* PRODUCT MASTER
FMSPMP100  IF   E       K DISK    PREFIX(PM_)
F************************************************************
D*
D DWS0997         PR
D   D01_PRDNO                    15
D   MSG                          60
D   ERROR_FLAG                    1
D DWS0997         PI
D   D01_PRDNO                    15
D   MSG                          60
D   ERROR_FLAG                    1
D************************************************************
 /FREE

     ERROR_FLAG = 'N';

  //READ PRODUCT MASTER USING PRODUCT NUMBER FROM
  //SCREEN AS KEY.
     CHAIN(E) (D01_PRDNO) MSPMP100;
     IF NOT %FOUND;
        ERROR_FLAG = 'Y';
        MSG = 'THIS IS A BAD PRODUCT NUMBER +
                                  (XXX00111.01).';
     ENDIF;

     *INLR = *ON;
 /END-FREE
```

Now, let's take this baby apart.

```
H**********************************************************
H* DWS0997 - Called Program
H**********************************************************
H DFTACTGRP(*NO) ACTGRP(*CALLER)
H**********************************************************
F* PRODUCT MASTER
FMSPMP100  IF   E            K DISK     PREFIX(PM_)
F**********************************************************
```

No surprises here. I included an H-spec to make sure (in my outdated environment) that I end up with an ILE program. And F-specs to define the Product Master that will be used for the validation. I don't need the display file because that is in my calling program, and the value I entered there will be passed in via the prototype specs.

```
D*
D  DWS0997            PR
D    D01_PRDNO                  15
D    MSG                        60
D    ERROR_FLAG                  1
D  DWS0997            PI
D    D01_PRDNO                  15
D    MSG                        60
D    ERROR_FLAG                  1
D**********************************************************
```

Now the D-specs look a little different. For one thing, there are two of them. We start with the PR, the prototype spec, just like we had in the calling program.

To that we now add the PI, the procedure interface, which we had used in the sub-procedure D-specs in chapter 7. The name for both of these D-specs must match—each other, you know. As must the subfields that are being specified. Otherwise you will get a compile error.

I haven't included the SP_PRDNO—there's no need. Since we are not using sub-procedures here, and so there is no need to show off local variables. I will just use D01_PRDNO from the display file.

There is one more thing here. Where are the definitions for the D01_PRDNO, MSG, and ERROR_FLAG field? And the answer is, even though the PR doesn't really define a variable, the PI does. I don't know the reason for that. Never asked, don't really care. It makes no sense that one does and one doesn't, but if I insisted that everything make sense, I would still be waiting.

```
/FREE

    ERROR_FLAG = 'N';


    //READ PRODUCT MASTER USING PRODUCT NUMBER FROM
    //SCREEN AS KEY.
    CHAIN(E) (D01_PRDNO) MSPMP100;
    IF NOT %FOUND;
        ERROR_FLAG = 'Y';
        MSG = 'THIS IS A BAD PRODUCT NUMBER +
                                (XXX00111.01).';
    ENDIF;


    *INLR = *ON;

/END-FREE
```

And finally, the logic statements. They are identical to what we used in the sub-procedure except that I am just using the D01_PRDNO field and not bothering with the SP_PRDNO local variable.

Now It's Your Turn

I think you know the drill by now. Create another two programs from your model and set them up like the previous examples. Naturally you can use your own files, and you don't have to check for the product number validity; you can do whatever you would like.

Again, you will use the CRTBNDRPG command to compile both programs. And, of course, both programs must be ILE, so watch that DFTACTGRP.

As you go through this, don't be afraid to experiment. Change the sizes of the fields between the PR and PI on the called program and see what happens when you compile. Play around with it for a bit so you feel comfortable with the prototype structures. Just have fun.

What Ya Shoulda Learned

Basically, a lot of the same stuff that you should have learned in the last chapter. In fact, both program sets are almost identical, aren't they?

So which one is better?

Using the sub-procedure or the separate program, I mean?

And the answer, like most things is: it depends.

Certainly the sub-procedure is more efficient, although with the new CALLP they are both pretty quick. If you get hung up worrying about which is faster, then you really need to switch to decaf.

Obviously, there are advantages to putting the validation logic in a separate program so it can be more easily used in other situations. Although, as we will see in the next chapter, we can make a sub-procedure available to multiple programs without using a separate program call.

Also, please note that I assume you did this by compiling both programs with CRTBNDRPG. But you could have also used CRTRPGMOD on both of them and then CRTPGM to bind them together. We will talk more about the differences in these two approaches later. For now, let's keep things simple, shall we?

Before we can decide which is best, there is one more option.

Yes, you guessed it. A dark and dangerous option. An option that is spoken of only in whispers where the ragged IT people go. An option so terrifying and powerful that few mere mortals have attempted to capture and tame it.

Service Programs.

Chapter 9

ILE Service Programs

There is one more type of program structure that I want to introduce you to. And that is a service program: a program that can be called by many other programs and which basically serves as a holder for a variety of sub-procedures.

Service programs are a natural part of ILE and the culmination of what it promises.

And the drawback? Well, I guess it would be that just the idea of service programs scares some people, but there is no reason for that. To be perfectly honest, service programs are just a hair more complicated than either of the previous two options. And I am not being tongue in cheek when I say "just a hair."

The truth is, in some ways, service programs are like one of those haunted Halloween houses, all smoke and mirrors. Once you get into it and understand the basics of prototyping (which you do by now), service programs are no big deal, and even someone like you can use them extensively. And people say I have no tact. Ha!

So let's stop talking and get started.

The Service Program Scenario

This scenario consists of two programs, just like it did with the CALLP example in chapter 8.

There is the calling program: the program that would like to use the services (sub-procedures) contained in the service program.

And there is the service program itself, standing alone, cold, and aloof.

The difference between this scenario and the standard CALLP model is that we are going to actually bind the two programs together in a tighter bind than is possible with just the CALLP. This will make a call to a service program very fast. And it will also produce a bind that is more resistant to changes in the called module than if we had used the CRTRPGMOD/CRTPGM combo.

The end result will be a connection that is very fast and uses very little resources as it is processed. And that is why "time travel is not only possible but has probably already happened." Or in this case, that is why "service programs are a big deal."

The Service Program: DWS0260SRV

So far we have started with the calling program, but this time let's start with our old friend the product number validation program and set it up as a sub-procedure in a service program. Are you listening to me? This program is *not* the program that calls the service program. The program below *is* the service program. Got that? You always create the service program first, although many times it already exists when you go to use it. OK, good, here we go. Oh, and I am naming this DWS0260SRV. We will need that name when we go to bind everything together.

```
H*********************************************************
H* DWS0260SRV - Product Master Service Program
H*********************************************************
H NOMAIN
H*********************************************************
F*********************************************************
F* Product Master
```

```
FMSPMP100  UF   E              K DISK    PREFIX(PM_)
F********************************************************
P********************************************************
P****   Beginning of Procedure VAL_PRDNO ***************
P********************************************************
P VAL_PRDNO       B                       EXPORT
P*
D********************************************************
D*/COPY DSHIREY/QCPYLESRC,DWS0260SRV
D*
D VAL_PRDNO       PR
D   PRDNO                         15
D   MSG                           60
D   ERROR_FLAG                     1
D VAL_PRDNO       PI
D   PRDNO                         15
D   MSG                           60
D   ERROR_FLAG                     1
D*
 /FREE

  //Verify Product Number
     MSG = *BLANKS;
     CHAIN (PRDNO) MSPMP100;
         IF NOT %FOUND;
             MSG = 'R U KIDDING?  PRODUCT NUMBER +
                            NOT VALID (DWS0260SRV.01)';
             ERROR_FLAG = 'Y';
         ENDIF;

     CLOSE MSPMP100;
 /END-FREE
P VAL_PRDNO E
P********************************************************
```

Not really too bad. That's all there is to a service program with a single sub-procedure. Of course, most self-respecting service programs will contain more than one sub-procedure, sometimes many more than one, but this will give you the idea. In reality, for all their street rep, service programs are really just a sheath, something that goes around a group of procedures.

Where should you keep your service program source? Well, you could create another source file to put your service programs into, but that's up to you. They don't have a special source type; they are just RPGLE like everything else. The object type is different, of course: it's *SRVPGM instead of plain old *PGM. Just don't put them in QSRVSRC. You will want to keep this available for the binding language source that we will talk about later (as in chapter 20).

Now let's play.

```
H*******************************************************
H* DWS0260SRV - Product Master Service Program
H*******************************************************
H NOMAIN
H*******************************************************
```

We start with another H-spec, and this one is required. What it basically says is that there will be no main logic to this program. This wipes out the RPG cycle, but who cares. It clears the way to have a program that consists of just (gasp) sub-procedures.

Remember before when we had the sub-procedure embedded in a program, we also had mainline logic. This is not the way it works in service programs: all you have is sub-procedures, and to make this legal, you need the NOMAIN spec.

Service programs are not created through the CRTBNDRPG command and cannot be created in an OPM environment. We will look at just how we create the service program in a minute, but for now, just know that because of this we do not need the DFTACTGRP H-spec.

```
F*******************************************************
F* Product Master
FMSPMP100  UF   E           K DISK     PREFIX(PM_)
F*******************************************************
```

Next, we have our F-spec for the file we will use in the sub-procedure.

If we were at a newer level of the operating system (V6.1 or above), we could just put this in the sub-procedure that is coming up, but with antiquated 5.4 we don't have that option. Not a big deal. The advantage of putting it in the sub-procedure is that if you have several files defined in your service program, then you don't open them all when the service program starts. You will wait till you get into the sub-procedure and then open just the ones required for that.

```
P*************************************************************
P****    Beginning of Procedure VAL_PRDNO ****************
P*************************************************************
P  VAL_PRDNO        B                    EXPORT
P*
```

Then, without so much as a "have an apple," we start the first sub-procedure by having the B P-spec. Remember that everything that comes after this is part of the sub-procedure. If the service program contained several procedures (which it almost always will), then you list them one right after the other. And remember that this is not a D-spec. It is a new type of spec, the P-spec, that defines when a sub-procedure begins and ends.

We are not going to talk about exporting now (that will happen when we talk about binding language in chapter 20), but we need to put EXPORT as a keyword on the beginning P-spec. Trust me. This is very important, and nothing will work in this example if you don't do that. You'll thank me later.

```
D*************************************************************
D*/COPY DSHIREY/QCPYLESRC,DWS0260SRV
D*
D  VAL_PRDNO        PR
D    PRDNO                       15
D    MSG                         60
D    ERROR_FLAG                   1
D  VAL_PRDNO        PI
D    PRDNO                       15
D    MSG                         60
D    ERROR_FLAG                   1
D*
```

Next we have D-specs that define the prototype.

Technically you can put the PR up above in the global part of the program (that is, before the first P-spec), but I see no reason to split them up, so I put it in the sub-procedure with the PI.

The PR and the PI must be identical, and the name on the PR D-spec must be the same as the name on the associated PI D-spec. So, it's not like you can get away with one global PR, even if the subfields on the different PIs were identical. But it's up to you where you put it. I don't really care.

Often, people will use a copybook to bring the PR or PI in, and it is up to you if you like that kind of action. In fact, that is probably the default with all the cool kids. Not the first time I have bucked the trend. I have included a commented-out Copy statement, just to show you how it would replace the PR D-spec. If you use the Copy statement, then you don't need the D-spec.

```
/FREE

 //Verify Product Number
    MSG = *BLANKS;
    CHAIN (PRDNO) MSPMP100;
       IF NOT %FOUND;
          MSG = 'R U KIDDING?  PRODUCT NUMBER NOT +
                                VALID (DWS0260SRV.01)';
          ERROR_FLAG = 'Y';
       ENDIF;

    CLOSE MSPMP100;

/END-FREE
```

This is followed by the logic statements, which you should be quite familiar with now. The key for the read was passed in via the prototype, and the message is set in this code.

Also, please note that there is no *INLR logic. No need for it. There is no main procedure in the service program. I'm serious. Can you dig it?

```
P  VAL_PRDNO       E
P*******************************************************
```

Finally, here is the end P-spec to close the sub-procedure. And that's it. If there were more sub-procedures here, then we would start with another B P-spec. If this were the end of the service program, which it is in this case, then this would be the end. There is no *INLR or anything else. We don't need the *INLR because there is no main procedure to end. Neat, eh?

Compiling the Service Program

Now before we go any further, that is, before we create the program that calls the service program, we need to look at how to compile the service program because it's just a tad different from what we did before.

And this must be done before we compile the calling program, so we might as well get it out of the way now. The reason for this is that when we compile the calling program, we want to actually bind the object for the service program into the object for the calling program. So, the service program object must exist before we compile the calling program.

To create the service program object, issue the following two commands:

```
CRTRPGMOD MODULE(MyLib/'service program') SRCFILE(MyLib/QRPGLESRC)
CRTSRVPGM SRVPGM(MyLib/'service program') EXPORT(*ALL)
```

> Note: specifying EXPORT(*ALL) is important, and it is not the default. There are other values for the EXPORT parm, but right now just use *ALL and don't worry about it. We will talk about it later. And yes, that was a threat.

And that's all you need to do to create your service program object. I know it's two steps and doesn't use option 14 (for the PDM crowd), but heck fire, boy, it's not like you are going to be doing this every day. Once you get them set, you probably won't touch them. Maybe. Actually, it's pretty simple, eh? A lot of it is just what we did when we created the program with the sub-procedure. You see, it all fits together once you get your head out ... well, once you start getting into it.

Debugging? If you want to debug a service program, you have to set the DBG parm in the CRTRPGMOD command to *SOURCE when you do the CRTRPGMOD for the service program. You do not, however, do a STRDBG command for the service program module. Instead, you can do it for the program that calls the service program and then use F22 instead of F10 to step into the service program.

Now let's look at the program that calls the service program.

Now It's Your Turn

But, before we do that, I think it would be good to stop for a moment and create our service program: creating a new source physical file if you want to, putting in the source code, and going through the compile steps to get a good object.

Take your time and make sure you understand how things are structured and why. You could even set up a second sub-procedure that did something else to the file that you are screwing around with. It's up to you.

Program That Calls a Service Program

Ah, you thought we were done, didn't you? But no, we still need to define the program that calls a service program. Although, as we will see, we are really not calling the "service program," rather we are going to call a sub-procedure within the service program. This will be a stripped-down version that focuses just on the call. Remember, a normal program that calls a service program will probably have other logic in it that has nothing to do with that call.

```
F*****************************************************
F*  DWS0995
F*****************************************************
F* Display File
FDWS0170FM CF   E               WORKSTN PREFIX(D01_)
F*
D*
D  VAL_PRDNO       PR
D    D01_PRDN                  15
D    MSG                       60
D    ERROR_FLAG                 1
D*
D  MSG             S           60
D  ERROR_FLAG      S            1     INZ('N')
D*
 /FREE

  //Check Vendor Number for validity against MSVMP100.

     CALLP val_prdno(D01_PRDNO:MSG:ERROR_FLAG);

     *INLR = *ON;
 /END-FREE
```

And that's it. I know. Looks too small, doesn't it? Man, you people complain about everything, don't you?

Now, piece by piece, just like always.

First, I have not included an H-spec. We are going to tie this program to the service program and so will be using a CRTRPGMOD rather than the CRTBNDRPG. As a result, the program will by default be ILE, and the H-spec is not required. You could still use the H-spec to set the activation group we will use if you don't want to specify it in the CRTRPGMOD command. I will leave that to you.

```
F*************************************************************
F*  DWS0995
F*************************************************************
F* Display File
FDWS0170FM CF   E              WORKSTN PREFIX(D01_)
F*
```

F-specs, just like always, for the display file where we are getting the product number we need to verify.

```
D*
D  VAL_PRDNO      PR
D    D01_PRDNO            15
D    MSG                  60
D    ERROR_FLAG            1
D*
D  MSG            S        60
D  ERROR_FLAG     S         1  INZ('N')
D*
```

Then we have the D-specs. Note that this is a prototype D-spec, so we also need to define the fields to the program via a separate definition.

Also note that there are no P-specs in this program (because there are no sub-procedures, they are in the service program).

```
/FREE

//Check Vendor Number for validity against MSVMP100.

    CALLP val_prdno(D01_PRDNO:MSG:ERROR_FLAG);

    *INLR = *ON;
/END-FREE
```

Then the code. Just a simple CALLP to the service program with the parameters defined in the PR D-spec. And that's it. Pretty simple, eh? You betcha, by golly. Just be sure that you notice that we didn't CALLP DWS0996SRV, which is the actual name of the service program. Instead, we accessed the sub-procedure in that program that we needed, VAL_PRDNO. There are two theories on why it is this way.

One is that this is just the way it is, and so the service programs hate the sub-procedures they contain and who get all the publicity. IBM thus created a situation analogous to one where a caretaker is forced to care for someone they despise, a situation that almost always ends in a grisly murder.

The other, and this is probably a bit far-fetched, is that the service programs were originally created as part of a secret government project, and so their identities have to be concealed from the general public. I know, that is ridiculous. After all, if it were true then we would undoubtedly have heard about it in *X2: X-Men United* when they breached that secret government fortress. But as I have said before, some people will believe anything.

Compiling the Calling Program

Once you have the program coded that is going to call a service program, you have to compile it, and you can't use CRTBNDRPG. Because it involves something a little different (object binding), you are going to have to execute the following commands:

```
CRTRPGMOD MODULE(MyLib/'calling program') DBGVIEW(*SOURCE)
SRCFILE(MyLib/QRPGLESRC)
```

```
CRTPGM PGM(MyLib/'calling program') BNDSRVPGM('service program')
ACTGRP(*NEW)
```

You can see why the service program needs to be created first, and you can see how it is bound into the calling program where the CRTPGM command lists the calling program in the module section and the service program in the BNDSRVPGM parameter.

Now It's Your Turn

Well, what are you waiting for? Go on, get busy. Create the calling program, and compile it.

Then test the whole mess. Remember, to get to the service program in debug you will have to either set a breakpoint in the service program and move in that way from the calling program or else use F22 to step into it from the calling program.

Growing and Organizing Your Service Program Farm

Want to start a fight in a Service Program Bar? Just get people talking about how they will organize and grow their collection of service programs. There are definitely several schools of thought, and it is hard to say who is right and who is righter.

Where should you put your service programs?

Probably the best place is just in QRPGLESRC. Some folks like to put them in a separate source file, but I am not sure I see a need for that. And it may mean that you occasionally have to override a default to QRPGLESRC in the compile commands.

But it's up to you. If you like the idea of having all your service programs in a separate source file, go for it. Just don't use QSRVSRC. It will interfere with your using binding language.

Do you want to have just one service program for your whole system or many service programs?

Some people prefer one gigantic service program. Hard to argue that doesn't make it easy to find a specific sub-procedure. On the other hand, it is sort of weird to have a huge service program when everyone is hawking modular. But there's nothing really wrong with it. Not my cup of tea, though.

Most people like to have a number, perhaps even a large number of service programs, generally with each one targeting a different area. For example, you may have one that contains all the sub-procedures that update the Product Master. And another that affects inventory. You get the idea.

Neither is better than the other, probably. In the end it often boils down to your particular environment and what feels most intuitive to you. Just don't make it hard to find a particular sub-procedure. That will drive you crazy.

What is unlikely is that you will have only one sub-procedure in each service program.

One thing you should know about sub-procedures is that they are very gregarious. And they get lonely very quickly. Yes, they are needy in that way.

So it makes sense to put a bunch of them together. You get to decide how many is too many and how many is not quite enough.

Is there a particular scheme that should be used to name sub-procedures and service programs?

The name of the service program is not all that important in my mind because you don't call the service program by its name but rather by the name of the sub-procedure. If you did not have them in a separate source file, it would be good to put some sort of designation on them that identified them as service programs. Maybe. Maybe not. You could always keep a certain program ID sequence for all service programs. Or you may want to put "SRV" or "SP" or something somewhere in the name.

Sub-procedure names require a bit more thought. Some people like the fact that you can give them English language-type names like VAL_PRDNO or CHECK_CREDIT, and I do agree that is nice. This makes it a lot easier to see what the sub-procedure does than if you call it DWS00337. And yet, there is something to be said for including the name of the service program in there somewhere. Maybe SP337_VAL_PRDNO or something like that, where your service program name is DWS0337SP. Just a suggestion.

Bottom line: naming is not the most important thing, but it is close. The one thing you don't want to do is create a bunch of sub-procedures and service programs and then spend the rest of your days looking for this sub-procedure or that. Give it some thought and decide what naming convention you like. Then stick with that.

Do you really need to use service programs?

And the answer is, of course not. You don't have to use any of this stuff.

But can you give me a good reason for not using them?

Despite their street rep, service programs are not at all hard to do. Yes, there is an extra compile step or two, but good grief, you can't let that scare you away. Look at what the troops in WWI had to endure. And you think you've got it tough.

Service programs are the best way to encapsulate logic that can then be used by many programs in a very fast and efficient connection. What's not to like?

My opinion is that you should start thinking today of what logic you can convert to sub-procedures and of what service programs you can start building and incorporating into your environment. Putting this off only robs you of the benefits they bring to your system.

What Ya Shoulda Learned

OK, I have to ask.

How are ya feelin' right now? Have you dealt with service programs before? Or did you feel that you were just too butt dumb stupid to ever use them?

Well, I hope that now you realize that even someone like yourself can understand and use service programs. I mean, it's not like it's that hard. There are just a few things you need to know and do.

First, did you go through and actually create a service program and a calling program? It's really important that you do that. Remember what Han Solo said. "Look, good against remotes is one thing. Good against the living? That's something else." And the same is true for service programs (or any of this stuff). Just reading about it is cool, and all but you are not going to learn it just from reading. You have to do the code.

It is almost a certainty that even if you follow exactly what I have done, you will still have problems. Don't panic. Take a deep breath, pour out another couple of ounces of scotch or bourbon, and work through it. That's what I do. The new is always unfamiliar.

You should especially understand the compile and binding required to make the service programs work. In reality, what we have done in this chapter is just one type of service program connection (relax, there are really only two). Near the end of this book we will look at the other option.

Finally, before the frost is off the pumpkin, take some time to really think about the naming conventions and service program organization you want to use. Best to get this laid out right off the bat.

Chapter 10

A Summary of Your ILE Options

All right now, let's pick ourselves up off the floor. That's right, dust yourself off a bit. Make sure your shirt buttons are lined up straight. OK, smooth down that hair, assuming you have some. Come on, look sharp.

Before we go on and return to /Free for what might be considered "advanced" topics, let's take a minute and go back over what we have learned in the last three chapters. And let's start with that question. What have we learned here, and what do we want to be sure we remember?

Review of the Three Options

Let's start by going back to the three program examples we looked at in chapters 7, 8, and 9.

Sub-Procedures within a Program

This was what we did in chapter 7, and, as you well know, I heartily applaud the use of sub-procedures instead of subroutines (local variables, yada, yada, yada).

To be frank, though, ILE is about a lot more than just replacing subroutines with sub-procedures. True, we are using sub-procedures, but we still end up with one big program (large execution size and probably high complexity). And just putting sub-procedures into a large program is not what MVC is all about. I like what sub-procedures brings to the table, but just using them in place of subroutines is probably the least real ILE way to do things.

That said, it does work out just fine for places where you have a simple program that did have some complex and/or repetitive logic in it, but not for a bigger app.

Obviously, with this approach you want to use CRTBNDRPG to create the program.

Program to Program Call

This was the crux of chapter 8, and it gave us a good look at using the prototyped call and the associated PR and PI D-specs to go from one program to another.

This is still not hard-core ILE, but is probably a better way to go (than just doing embedded sub-procedures in a big program, that is). First, you are surely reducing the size of your program by spinning logic off into separate modules. Granted you now have more pieces to keep an eye on, but each piece should be simple and easy to understand or modify. This also sets you up to do MVC, which we will see a little later on.

Of course, much of the efficiency that is generated here will be dependent on how the modules are related. Are you going to just call them? Are you going to bind them together? Are you doing this in one step or two? What about the activation group scheme you will use? Lots of open questions, and we will grapple with some of those as we go forward.

In chapter 8 we treated each program as a separate entity, compiling both with separate CRTBNDRPG commands. But you don't have to do it that way.

For more efficiency, you could compile both as modules with CRTRPGMOD and then use CRTPGM to tie them together. Just remember that if you use CRTBNDRPG and CRTPGM to tie these separate programs together, you will get faster response, but since the bind happens when the programs are compiled, any change to one means a recreate of the whole thing. This can be an issue if the one being changed is the called program and it is used in lots of places.

Either way you compile, the decision is not a slam dunk, and you need to think about the characteristics of the relationship.

Service Programs

The final option (chapter 9) is to put our logic into sub-procedures (not standalone programs) and then organize them into one or more service programs (rather than CRTRPGMOD/CRTPGM standalone programs).

As we saw before, it is up to you how you organize your sub-procedures in the service programs. Sometimes you may want to do it around a master file. Or you might want to do it around a business issue or critical task (like credit checking and approval). It's up to you. Point is, I don't really care, but you should.

Again, you have small modules, the sub-procedures, and fast access because there is a binding between the calling program and the service program. You also get a fair degree of module independence because if you set up your service program right, you can change the sub-procedures in the service program without having to recompile the programs that access that sub-procedure. We will talk more about this later (binding language).

And the Winner Is?

So, what's the difference? How do you decide which one you would want to use?

And the answer is, it depends.

One thing I don't want you to do is look at the three previously mentioned options as some sort of hierarchy, where you start with a program that has sub-procedures but the best way to do it is with service programs. That is not the case. Although, maybe it is ....

What is best depends on what the application is like. And it also depends on when you want the binding to occur. And how likely it is that there will be changes in the modules once they are set. And that is the strength of ILE. You never had those options in OPM. Now you can decide what strategy is best for your particular situation.

So what do you think? You know your situation. Your environment. Your development needs. What is the best way for you to proceed? Not just for the three program examples but for using ILE in general.

It's easy to just give this some cursory thought and then turn the page and go on, but I want you to take a tooth-brushing "minute" (sing "Happy Birthday" three times) to give it some serious thought. Are you ready to start getting into /Free ILE?

If not, why not? What are you waiting for? What are the roadblocks in your way, and how can they be removed or mitigated?

If yes, then where shall we start? I assume you wrote the example programs that we went over, so you are ready to move forward on some real work. What do you want to start with? Service programs? Changing a subroutine over to a sub-procedure? What makes sense to you?

You have several weapons to choose from, so take a minute or two now to start an ongoing dialog with yourself and your teammates over how you want this whole thing to go down. And then get going on it. Yes, there is more to learn, but you know enough now to be more than dangerous. Don't let what you've learned remain theoretical. Get practical and hands-on as soon as possible.

A Few Thoughts

Of course, I wouldn't be surprised if right now you are a little confused. After all, with OPM you put code in a source member, compiled it, and you were done. There is a certain charm to the simplicity.

But with ILE we have procedures, modules, programs, and service programs. Plus goodness knows what I haven't told you about yet.

We already know there are three different ways in which programs can be built: embedded sub-procedures, program-to-program calls, and service programs.

Finally, on top of that there are two ways to compile: the one-step and the two-step method. (Of course, when you are dealing with service programs, it is a four-step process: two steps to create the service program and then two steps to create the calling program and bind the service program to it.)

Some people look at this and say "ILE is too complex." And that is too bad, because like the glass half empty or half full, you can look at ILE as either being too complex or providing extraordinary flexibility.

But that still leaves you with the question: how do I get my hands around this? What strategy is best for me? Please allow me to offer you some additional things to think about.

It's Not Just About Efficiency

First, too often ILE gets caught up in efficiency concerns: that it is fast, and everything has to be decided based on what the fastest connection is between two modules.

But for me, efficiency is usually a secondary concern. Most of the time, you are not calling one module 10,000 times a minute from another module. And even if you do call something a fair number of times, today's processors have power to spare. Your app is unlikely to have slow response time as its number-one problem.

Write Modular Code

I believe the essence of ILE is modularity. The essence of ILE is about creating small, easily understandable modules, and then combining them in whatever way seems to make the most sense given how often the modules might change and how fast you realistically need the connection to be. Know what I mean, Vern?

Bottom line: if you really want to participate in the ILE revolution, start writing modular code. We will emphasize this when we talk about MVC later on, but that's not the only game in town, and there are many patterns you can follow in writing modular code.

Embrace Binding

Too often in the IBM i world, we think of programs as being solitary things that live alone, like rogue bull elephants.

But togetherness is a hallmark of ILE, and so you want to always consider binding modules together when you are building an app.

There are a couple of ways to do this: using CRTRPGMOD/CRTPGM at compile time and via a service program at run time—and the one that works best for you is the one that most closely resembles your app.

Use Common Sense in Putting Things Together

Once you do that, then you can use common sense to put the modules together.

Is one module going to change frequently? If so, you might want to avoid a binding that happens at compile time.

Is the sub-procedure you are building a one-of-a-kind thing that will never be used anywhere else (I know never say never, but sometimes you can be pretty sure, and you have to draw some lines somewhere)? If so, then do you really want to bother with a service program? You want to use a sub-procedure because of the modularity it provides, but there are worse things than just including those sub-procedures in the program where they are used.

Is ILE Too Complicated?

It's a fair question. Especially after all the options that we have seen so far, ILE looks kind of complex, doesn't it?

And to that I say, uh, yeah, maybe. What's your point?

If you look closely at ILE, there are some things that probably could have been designed to be less surprising by IBM. But they didn't. And that is all there is to it. Time to move on.

Seriously though, when you think about it, and compare it to some of the things that go on in other languages (like PHP or Ruby or Java), it's seriously not that bad. I mean anyone who looks at ILE and says, "Oh, it's just too complex for me" is probably not giving themselves enough credit.

Yes, there is some complexity there, but most of it is born out of the fact that it's not the one-size-fits-all world of OPM. Instead, you have the flexibility to do things a variety of ways, and it is up to you to choose the way that works best for you and your situation.

What Ya Shoulda Learned

Granted, this chapter has mostly been review, but there is still plenty to think about.

- Describe, to yourself or to anyone who will listen, perhaps a loved one who has no choice, the three ILE structures that we outlined in the chapters previous to this.

- Think about the requirements you currently have facing you. How many would be good candidates for using ILE? Be honest now. Don't just say that nothing fits because your needs are special. ILE techniques can fit into a wide variety of situations. Frankly, everything is a candidate for ILE.

- For each situation you can think of, what is the best ILE approach to use?

- Lay out a plan, at least in your mind, for how you will get from where you are to where you are using those ILE options.

Seriously, think about it. The next move is up to you.

SECTION 4

ADVANCED /FREE

Even though we have used /Free to build some ILE programs, there are still a few more tricks for you to learn about the latest iteration of RPG.

Chapter 11

Function Calls and Return Values

Okie, dokie. Time to change things up a bit. We have spent some time with ILE, but before we go any deeper, I want to go back to /Free and look at a few more things. Ready to shift gears?

We are going to start by talking about two related topics: function calls and return variables.

The first thing I want to say is that this is a technique that can only be used to call a sub-procedure that is embedded in a service program *or* that is embedded in the module you are doing the function call from. Remember before how we did that with a CALLP? Well this is another way to do that without the CALLP. But the function call cannot be used to call one program from another; that must still be done with a CALLP. It only works when calling a sub-procedure.

The second thing I want to say is these two things (function calls and return values) go together. You can't do one without the other.

What Are "These Things"?

The *function call* allows you to dispense with the CALLP opcode and just express the "call or prototype" as an equality between a variable and a function, similar to the way you would in PHP or another Web language. It's kind of freaky, and I have a certain tendency toward vertigo when I use it, but it is very popular in Web languages, will get more common in RPG as we move into the future, and is way cheaper than Ecstasy.

Return values deal with getting something back from the called program, something that is not one of the parameters that is passed with the prototype. That is, we have already seen how you can send parameters along with the call and then get them back when the CALLP is over. But what if you want to have other variables returned from the sub-procedure or program beyond what is in the parameters? That is where return values come in. And a function call (as opposed to CALLP) is the only way you can work return values into the mix.

But remember, this type of call only works when you are calling a sub-procedure (either in a service program or one embedded in the program you issue the call from). You cannot use it to call an independent program.

Compile Notes

I really shouldn't bother you with this because it's pretty obvious if you think about it, but—well, sometimes we don't think unless we are told to, so let me just mention this.

If you are doing the function call/return values thing from a program to a service program, then remember that both programs will have to be compiled first with CRTRPGMOD (instead of CRTBNDRPG). Because of this, you won't need the H-spec for DFTACTGRP in either program (because CRTRPGMOD assumes you are going to be ILE). But you can include an H-spec giving the ACTGRP that you want to use (more on what those activation groups are later). Then you will need to do the CRTSRVPGM for the called program (the service program) and the CRTPGM for the calling program.

If you are doing the function call/return values thing from a program that actually contains the embedded sub-procedure, then you can use the DFTACTGRP H-spec and just compile the program as CRTBNDRPG.

Function Call/Return Values: The Details

Let's start with the function call. What is that again?

It is something that is actually very Web language-like: the ability to call a procedure through an evaluate statement. Hold it. Wait a minute! Where are you going?? Come back. It's not hard to do. Honest! See, it doesn't look scary. A little weird maybe.

```
DESCP = VAL_PRDNO(PRDNO);
```

That is, we call the sub-procedure, VAL_PRDNO, by equating it to a variable DESCP, which is defined in the sub-procedure. It has to be defined in the calling program as well; my point here is that it is coming from the sub-procedure and so needs to be valid in there as well.

This sub-procedure could be held in a service program whose name I could give a rip about because when dealing with service programs you never call the service program, just the sub-procedure (VAL_PRDNO).

Or the sub-procedure could be embedded in the program that we are in. What is important is that we are doing the call by doing an evaluate to a variable, DESCP.

Why DESCP? Because that is the variable (a description field) whose value we want to return from the sub-procedure. That is, DESCP is the "return value" of the "function call." We pick what it is. As long as it is described in the program we are calling.

Please notice that DESCP is not a parm in the prototype that is defined for the VAL_PRDNO sub-procedure. But by using the function call and a few modifications to our calling and called program, we let the compiler know that we will be returning whatever variable is on the left side of an equality involving the sub-procedure. And yes, you are right. This is as close to black magic as you can get without actually having to drink blood.

As you can see, return values are inextricably linked to the function call. What happens if you do the function call but you don't set things up to return a value? It doesn't work. The compile fails because function calls and return variables go together like Beckett and Captain Hammer.

Similarly, if you want to do a return value, then you have to use the function call. That is, if you want to return a value outside of the parms listed in the prototype that is still required for the function call, then the only way to do it is to set up a function call and put the value variable you want returned equal to the sub-procedure name and parms.

So, given that, let's look at both the calling and the called program to see what changes are required to make the return values and function call work. First, the calling program.

Calling Program

Let's start this process by taking a look at the program where the function call is issued and see what changes have to be made to accommodate it and the return value.

```
F*******************************************************
F* Display File
FDWS0170FM CF   E              WORKSTN PREFIX(D01_)
F*******************************************************
D*******************************************************
D* Prototype D-spec
D  VAL_PRDNO      PR              30
D    D01_PRDN                     15
D
D  DESCP          S               30
D*******************************************************
 /FREE
  //Check Product Number for validity against MSPMP100.

  //   CALLP VAL_PRDNO(D01_PRDNO);
       DESCP = VAL_PRDNO(D01_PRDNO);

       *INLR = *ON;
 /END-FREE
```

And now, once again, this time dissecting the program. Remember, this is the program that calls the sub-procedure held in the service program.

```
F*****************************************************************
F* Display File
FDWS0170FM CF   E                WORKSTN PREFIX(D01_)
F*****************************************************************
```

First, we don't need an H-spec to make this program ILE (because we will need to compile it using CRTRPGMOD since it is calling a service program, although we could use one to set the activation group) so we go right to the F-spec for the display file where I have defined the PRDNO value. And again, I have not included the logic to actually pick up that value in an effort to keep this simple.

```
D*****************************************************************
D   VAL_PRDNO       PR             30
D     D01_PRDNO                    15
D*
D   DESCP           S              30
D*****************************************************************
```

Then come the D-specs, which includes the PR. You might be tempted to think that with return values and a function call you wouldn't need the PR, but that is not true. You always prototype to access another module in ILE. In this case, there is one subfield under that PR because that is how the sub-procedure is written. The D01_PRDNO value will be returned automatically if it is changed in the sub-procedure. Note that DESCP is not referenced at all in the prototype; return values variables are not part of the PR D-spec.

What is different is that the VAL_PRDNO PR D-spec has a length of 30 on it. Had you noticed that? So far we have not put a length on the PR line and with good reason. According to the Treaty of Versailles, the international symbol for "I got a return value coming back on this puppy" is a length on the PR line.

This is not the overall length of the parms in the PR (that is only 15) but rather the size of the field we want to get back in the return value (DESCP). You need to put that length here so that a pipeline is established to get that value returned. Without it, the return values and the function call will fail in the compile.

```
/FREE
 //Check Product Number for validity against MSPMP100.

  //   CALLP VAL_PRDNO(D01_PRDNO);
       DESCP = VAL_PRDNO(D01_PRDNO);

     *INLR = *ON;
/END-FREE
```

Then the logic statements. Notice that instead of a CALLP to VAL_PRDNO(D01_PRDNO), we are using an evaluate statement. I have put the CALLP in there and commented it out just so you can see it.

When the sub-procedure is accessed, the value for the DESCP field will then be returned to the DESCP field in this program.

Soooooo, to summarize, in the calling program we need to:

- Put the length of the return values field on the PR, and

- Use the function call, setting it equal to the field we want passed back.

- Then, that field will not appear directly in the prototype subfields.

Called Program

And now, on to the called program. I have decided to make the call to a service program. Remember, it could also have been done to a sub-procedure that is embedded in the calling program. It cannot be done to an independent program (that call has to be done via a CALLP).

```
H*********************************************************
H NOMAIN
H*********************************************************
F*********************************************************
F* Product Master
FMSPMP100 UF   E          K DISK     PREFIX(PM_)
F*********************************************************
D*********************************************************
D  VAL_PRDNO       PR              30
D    PRDNO                         15
D*COPY DSHIREY/QCPYLESRC,DWS0260SRV
D*********************************************************
P  VAL_PRDNO       B                         EXPORT
P*
D  VAL_PRDNO       PI              30
D    PRDNO                         15
D*********************************************************
 /FREE

   //Verify Product Number
   CHAIN (PRDNO) MSPMP100;
   IF %FOUND;
      RETURN PM_DESCP;
   ELSE
      RETURN -1;
   ENDIF;

   close MSPMP100;

 /END-FREE

P  VAL_PRDNO       E
```

Seriously, I am sorry if I am belaboring some of this, but I want you to get very familiar with looking at sub-procedures and service programs. The more you do that, the less likely you will be to fear and detest them, and the more likely you will be to consider them friends and compatriots in your fight against uh, whatever you are fighting against. Yourself most likely, I would guess.

```
H*******************************************************
H NOMAIN
H*******************************************************
```

We start with the standard NOMAIN that is required for every service program.

```
F*******************************************************
F* Product Master
FMSPMP100  UF   E           K DISK      PREFIX(PM_)
F*******************************************************
```

Followed by the F-specs for the file we will use to do the validation. Remember, if you are on 6.1 or above, this F-spec could go in the actual sub-procedure.

```
D*******************************************************
D   VAL_PRDNO       PR            30
D      PRDNO                      15
D*COPY DSHIREY/QCPYLESRC,DWS0260SRV
D*******************************************************
```

Then the global D-spec for the prototype (the PR). If we had put this in with a copybook, then we would be using the COPY statement that is commented out. Note that we set a length for the PR line (30), the length of the field we are going to be passing back via the return value. This is required. We will see the same thing on the PI below because they must match.

What you might have not noticed is while PRDNO is the same on both the PR and PI here, we actually named the subfield D01_PRDNO in the calling program. Is this OK? Yes, it is. The names must match within a module, but they can be different between the calling and called programs. Not sure why you would want to do this, but it could come up. Anyway, carry on.

```
P  VAL_PRDNO      B                    EXPORT
P*
```

Then the start of the sub-procedure. We include the EXPORT keyword because we are calling this sub-procedure outside of this service program. We will talk more about this keyword and exporting later.

```
D  VAL_PRDNO      PI              30
D    PRDNO                        15
D*****************************************************
```

Followed by the D-specs for the sub-procedure including the prototype interface (PI). Again, please notice the length on the PI line indicating that a return value is to be set. Remember, the PR D-spec that we had outside of the P-spec could just as well have been set up inside here. And, if this service program had other sub-procedures that had different prototype subfields beyond just PRDNO, we would have had to set it up in here because a single PR would not work.

```
/FREE

  //Verify Product Number
  CHAIN (PRDNO) MSPMP100;
     IF %FOUND;
          RETURN PM_DESCP;
       ELSE
          RETURN -1;
     ENDIF;

  close MSPMP100;

/END-FREE
```

Finally, we get to the logic. This example will be different from the ones we have used so far because the RETURN opcode is used only for specific situations. In this case, we are going to pick up a field from the MSPMP100 record that we read—here it's the description (DESCP)—and return that. If no record exists, we return a -1, which is sort of standard for function calls that fail. Note that PM_DESCP is not specified in a PR or PI, but it is defined in the F-spec for that file.

If you indicate you are going to do a return value (by putting a spec on the PI line), then you must actually execute the RETURN opcode (so that is why we have two branches on the IF above), or else an exception will be issued.

```
P   VAL_PRDNO        E
```

And then finally, the end to the sub-procedure and, in this case, the service program.

Now It's Your Turn

Guess it should be pretty obvious what I want here. Take the program call example that we did in chapter 10 and convert it to a function call, as we did above.

Not that you will have a choice, but play around with the return values variable, making sure you get a value back and that you really know how this works.

Maybe most of all, just get used to the fact that something that looks like an evaluate is really a way of accessing another module. Learn to use the PR entries as tips to what is being called.

And One More Thing

There is one more thing that I should mention, and that is that you can use the function call without having any return values.

In other words, so far we have used the function call in concert with a return value, so that the code looked like:

```
DESCP = VAL_PRDNO(D01_PRDNO);
```

But if there is no return value that you want to have sent back, if you're just concerned with the call and its associated parms, you can dispense with the return value, and the result looks like this:

```
VAL_PRDNO(D01_PRDNO);
```

This format is wildly popular with a lot of people. It does look Web-like, and I have nothing really against it except, as I have said before, I used the CALLP as a visual clue that I was calling a module at this point in the program. But it's pretty obvious that you are doing that. I guess. Anyway, expect to see this format a lot in the future.

Does It Matter?

Does it matter whether you use a CALLP or the evaluate method to access the sub-procedure? Well, like most things, the answer is not clear-cut.

I have seen a number of articles praising this option. Some people seem to use it almost exclusively. And there might be times when you want to take advantage of it.

For example, the word on the street is that using the function prototype is more efficient than using CALLP. I am sure it is true. And it is also probably true that in most cases, that is not going to make a whole lot of difference in your response time. But if you are doing a call many, many times in your program, it might make really good sense to use the function call instead of the CALLP.

Plus, the function call-return value approach is a very Web-looking thing. That is the way it is done in PHP, and you know what I think about that. (Actually, I wish PHP had a call function like CALLP, but let's not go there.) Of course, if PHP is going to jump off a bridge, does that mean you are going to do it, too?

But it is possible that being able to say that we can do this kind of thing in RPG is one step to making our language look a little less stuffy to Web types. And perception is important.

But on the whole, for me, there are a number of things that make me say that for general use, it wouldn't be my choice.

First, it doesn't allow you to eliminate the PR and PI stuff. If it did, then that would be a real plus (maybe), but it doesn't.

Second, it doesn't allow you to return more than one parm. Granted, you could return a data structure and then break that down, but that is extra steps and extra code on top of the already-existing PR.

Nor do you want to think of this as an emergency way to get anything you want out of the sub-procedure without changing the parms.

That is, today you need the DESCP returned (which is a 30-character text), and tomorrow you will need the opening inventory balance for this month (which is an 11,3 packed thingy). You can't get both by using the same sub-procedure with return values because you have to put the parm length at the PR and PI top level in the sub-procedure. I suppose you could frog around with a default length on the PR and PI, then convert it when you got back to the calling program, but even then you would have to set it up within the sub-procedure, and that would require changes.

Plus, while the return values field is not in the prototype D-specs, you do reference the field name in both the calling and the called program, meaning you would need to modify them both if you changed the field you were having returned.

Fourth, and this is a big thing for me, it sort of hides the call. If a module is going to access another one, I like something that really stands out, like a CALLP. I agree, I still have the PR in my calling program, but using the eval versus a CALLP just hides it a bit as to where the access is occurring. I know a lot of people don't have that hang-up, but what can you do? I am what I am.

In the end, the function call-return values combo is a valid alternative to the CALLP. However, except for the efficiency improvement, there are not enough positives to recommend it to me as my go-to access method. It's OK, though, if you feel differently. What's important, even if you don't use it yourself, is that you can recognize it and understand how it works.

What Ya Shoulda Learned

In the end, there is a fair amount of stuff here, lots of rules, but there are really only a few things you want to make sure that you memorize. Other things can be looked up as needed.

- First, understand the relationship between function calls and return values. That is, they are like a Reese's Peanut Butter Cup: you don't get one without the other (chocolate and peanut butter—gee, do I have to explain everything?).

- Second, you need to know that you can only do the RETURN on one field. So if you need two fields returned, this approach by itself won't work (it results in a compile error).

- Third, you should have learned how to set up the caller and sub-procedure to return a variable other than a parm.

- You should also know how to set up a call to a sub-procedure as a function rather than by using the CALLP.

I am assuming there are other things you need to know, but I cannot relate any of them to function calls or return values.

Chapter 12

The Importance of BIFs

As I may or may not have mentioned, some of the opcodes from positional RPG did not quite make the cut into /Free. Never fear, though, because over the past few releases (like the last 10 years) IBM has been developing a set of built-in functions (BIFs) that really do what some of the old opcodes did but with less screwing around.

BIFs are not technically part of /Free. You can use them in RPG IV positional. But they are so much more necessary in /Free that it only makes sense for us to look at some of the most common ones and see how they are used.

BIFs are very, very useful. They replace the RPG tradition of moving things from one field representation to another until you get what you want. But they are not trivial. You have to look closely at what a BIF is doing, and that is particularly true if the BIF is working on another BIF. It can get complex, and you have to be very clear what you are trying to accomplish. A good source of information on BIFs and how to use them is Rafael Victória-Pereira's excellent RPG Academy BIF series at *mcpressonline.com*.

Why bother with BIFs? There are a couple of reasons in my book.

First, BIFs tend to be clear and self-documenting. The BIF contains keywords (e.g., NUMERIC, SUBSTRING, DATE) that help you see at a glance what is being done.

Second, if you are using various fields and MOVEs, you need to look two places to see what is going on: the code and the D-specs where these various fields are defined. There is nothing in the MOVE statement to tell you that you are going from a 10-character string to an 11-digit packed field with three decimal places. With a BIF statement, you can see all the parameters that are affecting this statement in one spot. Again, it's clearer and more self-documenting than non-BIF code.

Third, as we shall see shortly, a BIF can operate on either a variable or another BIF (a function), meaning that you can piggyback statements and do a very complex thing in one spot.

Of course, like all heroes, BIFs have a dark side as well, something that is an inevitable outcome of the ability of one BIF to operate on another. We will touch on that as we get toward the end of this chapter, but it is not enough to make you hesitate to use BIFs.

BIF Essentials

Let's start by taking a few minutes to look at a couple of things that make BIFs *BIFs*.

BIFs and Expressions

One thing you should know about BIFs is that they generally are written up to operate on a field. You know, you have a numeric field from a file, and you use a BIF to convert it to a character field. In this case, *x* is a string field that will carry the character representation of the numeric order number, which is the argument of the BIF.

```
x = %CHAR(ORDNO);
```

But the cool thing about BIFs is that they can also work on functions or even other BIFs. That is, instead of putting a field name in the BIF, you can use a function. Like maybe you have a function that returns today's date, and then you convert that date to a character format. Like this:

```
x = %CHAR(%DATE());
```

That's just a simple example. You can get real complex, believe me. And what do you want to remember when you do something like that? That's right, get the parentheses straight. Parentheses are fundamental to organizing BIFs, and it's important to make sure they stay balanced. And spaces are important, too. So, remember that you can embed spaces into a BIF and it is fine. It just might make it easier to read. For example, which do you prefer?

```
x = %XLATE(-:/:%CHAR(DATE()));
```

or

```
x = $XLATE( - : / : $char(Date()) );
```

Parentheses and spaces. They are the programmer's best friend. Because six months from now, it may be pretty hard to recognize at a glance exactly what you meant to do there.

Parentheses

And speaking of parentheses, almost all BIFs use parentheses. I would look to see if there are any that don't, but I just don't feel like it. I don't think there are.

The parentheses enclose the parameters that are required to make the BIF work. That is, to provide the data the BIF needs to do its thing.

You can either have the left parenthesis right after the last character in the BIF name or skip a space (or several). That is, you can either do %DATE() ; or %DATE   () ; and it makes no difference to the system.

But parentheses also surround BIFs within a BIF, and you will see plenty of that later.

Hate to repeat, but as I said above, you have to make sure the parentheses are balanced. Iin some very complicated BIFs, that requires some careful scrutiny.

Colon

The second thing to keep in mind about BIFs is that while many use just one parm, most of them are going to have multiple parms that need to (or can be) passed within the parentheses.

The colon is the default character to separate these parameters. We will see this portrayed in shocking detail over the next few pages. There can either be spaces before and after the colon or not, depending on what you like to see.

Oh, and for the people who are like me, if you have four parms in the BIF and only specify three of them, then you only use two colons. You don't need to put colons in to indicate missing parms.

Semicolon

When using the BIF in /Free (it can be used in /Free or positional), you have to end the statement with a semicolon.

Now, because I have to fill up this chapter somehow, let's look at some of the more common BIFs.

Numeric to Character

We are not going to go through every BIF—far from it. For a more in-depth and clinical look at the BIF world, I would suggest chapter 4 of Bob Cozzi's book *The Modern RPG Language* (MC Press, 2006) or chapter 6 of Rafael Victória-Pereira's book *Evolve your RPG Coding* (MC Press, 2015). I just want to take a gander at a couple of the more commonly used ones and give you a flavor for how a BIF is structured and used. Let's start our limited journey by converting some sort of numeric field or function to a character string.

%CHAR(numeric value or expression);

The first BIF we will look at is the one that converts from numeric to character representation. It's a simple one. No colons. Or an appendix, so you never have to worry about having to remove that on a weekend.

In this format, the operator can be either a numeric value or an expression (such as another BIF).

The key to this one is that when the conversion is done, the BIF will bring over periods and commas, but will truncate any leading zeros.

So, if the numeric value is 53.46 and we are going to convert that into a six-position alphanumeric field, then it will appear in that field as 53.46, rather than 053.46.

%CHAR(date-time value : format);

There is one more format of the %CHAR BIF that we should look at because it differs in one important aspect. And this is if we use a date-time value or expression in the %CHAR BIF.

In this case, there is one additional parm: the format of the character string we want returned. That is, ISO, MDY, whatever valid date-time format we want to use.

If you do not specify a format, then it defaults to ISO. Just keep that in mind.

Convert to Decimal

Oh, yeah, baby. What goes around comes around. We don't just convert from numeric to character. That coin has two sides, Mama. And now it's time to flip that sucker over and see what comes up.

%DEC() and %DECH()

I am going to deal with these two simultaneously because they are roughly the same thing, except that %DECH throws in the half adjust to round the result.

These may be used in a couple of situations, although the general thrust is to convert to a numeric (that is, packed) format.

The first is to convert either a numeric expression or a character string to a packed field. This can be done by either %DEC and %DECH. The format is:

```
%DEC(input string : [length : decimal-positions];
```

Length and decimal positions cannot be an expression (like a BIF) but must be a literal or named constant. The reason for using these two parms is simply to format and restrict the length of the output field. If you don't care, then you don't need them. Screw 'em. Unless you are using the %DECH BIF. Then you need the length and decimal positions in order to know how to do the rounding. If you are converting from a character string, then the length and decimal positions are required.

When I say "numeric value" going into the conversion, there are some limitations.

First, it can't be floating point. You need to use %FLOAT for that.

Second, it can't contain thousands separators (,).

Third, it can have a plus (+) or minus (–) sign either before or after the value, a decimal point, and blanks at any point in the field.

You can also use the %DEC to convert dates or times to a numeric (packed) representation. That is, it converts a value from a date-type field to a non-date numeric field.

The result can be either a six-digit or an eight-digit field. How do you determine which? If you set a six-digit field to be the recipient of the BIF, you get six digits. If you use an eight-digit field, you get eight. Seems pretty clear to me.

An optional parameter that can be used is the date format that you want the non-date numeric field to come out in. If you don't specify anything, then it uses *ISO (YY-MM-DD or YYMMDD).

The same is true for times, except that the output is always six positions and the default is *USA.

See how simple BIFs are? No smart talk now. It wasn't that simple when you used the MOVE and a hundred intermediate fields.

Other Conversion BIFs

The only problem with the %CHAR BIF is that it brings over the period and commas and removes any leading zeros. And sometimes that is not what you want. Fortunately, there are a couple of other BIFs that you can use.

%EDITC (Edit with Edit Code)

This BIF also allows you to specify a numeric value or expression and return a character string. Why would you use this when you can use the %CHAR? Flexibility. You have more options here than you do with the straight %CHAR.

There are really four parms involved: two required and two optional.

```
%EDITC(numeric : edit code : [*ASTFIL] : [*CURSYM])
```

Numeric is the numeric value or expression that you are going to screw around with.

Edit code is the RPG edit code that you want to use. It must be one of the valid RPG edit codes that I can never remember, and it has to be enclosed in quotes.

*ASTFIL is optional and, if specified, will left-fill any leading zeros with asterisks.

*CURSYM is optional and allows you to specify a currency symbol that will be placed to the left of the first significant digit.

What will the resultant field look like? Sort of depends on the edit code that is used. Pick the one that shows the format the way you want it to look.

%EDITW (EDIT with Edit Word)

The last character-conversion BIF we will look at is similar to %EDITC except that now you are using an edit word, not an edit code.

```
%EDITW (numeric : 'edit word');
```

There are a couple of things to remember here. First, this baby won't work if you have a floating point representation. In that case, you would have to use %DEC to convert the floating point to packed and then go from there. But, remember that since the BIF will allow you to specify another BIF as an operand, you can do it within this function.

The edit word parm must then be a valid edit word. It has to be enclosed in quotes and have valid edit word formats. Again, what the result looks like will depend on the edit mask that you use. But it will be character.

%EDITFLT (Edit with Floating Point)

Just for the heck of it, I am going to do one more, although you probably won't use this that much. This BIF converts any numeric value (including floating point) into a 23-position character value, the international standard for a floating-point field.

```
%EDITFLT(numeric value or expression);
```

Not much to say. Use it if you need it.

Date and Time Stuff

The most useful BIFs for me are the date-oriented ones. There are a number of formats available, so let's go through this one at a time.

%Date();

%Time();

This format, sans parameters, will give you today's date or time. The default is *ISO and *USA, and if you want another format when using the ( ) parm, too bad, you can't have it. To do that, you have to use the format below.

%DATE(value or function : date-format-code);

The second option will convert a value or function into a date-type field.

This value can be either numeric or character. If you are using a character field, then you can also stipulate a separator value. That is not allowed if you use a numeric value.

So, if we did want to pick up today's date in a format other than *ISO, we could simply specify:

```
x = %date(%date():*MDY);
```

This is the real power of the BIFs: the fact that they can be used in lieu of variables in another BIF statement.

Dates can get very complicated, and switching between the different formats can be challenging. I am a big fan of the cheat sheet found here: *search400.techtarget.com/tip/RPG-free-format-date-conversion-cheat-sheet*. It has helped me on more than one occasion.

SCAN, REPLACE, XLATE

There are a number of BIFs that allow you to operate on character strings and either replace whole sections of the string or else specific characters within the string.

%REPLACE

Often you need to modify a character string, and there are several ways to do this. The first is the replace, which allows you to replace part of one character string with another.

```
%REPLACE(new string : old string : start position : length);
```

Remember that %REPLACE operates at the string level. It only replaces those characters that match the replacement string value.

%SCAN

%REPLACE is often used in tandem with %SCAN, where the %SCAN is issued first and is used to determine the starting position for a replace operation.

```
%SCAN(pattern : data to be scanned : start position);
```

In this case, the %SCAN will return a value that shows the position in a string (data to be scanned) where the pattern we are looking for first appears.

%CHECK

The mirror-image companion to %SCAN is %CHECK. This BIF will also go through a character string, but instead of finding a character that is in a pattern as %SCAN does, it looks for the first character in the string that is *not* in the pattern and returns its position.

```
%CHECK(pattern : data to be checked : start position);
```

Nominally, this function goes from left to right in the character string, but there is also a %CHECKR that goes upstream, if that is your preference.

Remember, it is not looking to see if the whole pattern is in the data; rather it looks to find a character in that data that is not in the pattern set.

%XLATE

The %XLATE function is similar in that it replaces characters, but this is on a more selective basis.

```
%XLATE(from-pattern : to-pattern : initial-value : start
position);
```

The function uses two patterns, rather than straight character strings. The patterns show what should be substituted for what. For example, if we had a date field and we wanted to change the separation characters, we could do this. Note that here we are assuming we will start in the first position, so it is not specified.

```
%XLATE(- : / : '2015-03-02')
```

and it would be translated to 2015/03/02.

The thing that you have to remember about %XLATE is that it is not operating on a character string. It is operating on individual characters within that string. As a result, if you set up a BIF such as

```
%XLATE('AB' : '12' : input) where input = 'ABAA1136B'
```

then this will be translated as 121111362, not as 121136B because the function is not operating on AB, but on A and B separately.

Trim

Finally, we will go over the trim functions, again dealing with character strings. There are three of these.

%TRIM

%TRIMR

%TRIML

The descriptions of these three BIFs are pretty self-explanatory: remove leading and trailing characters (not just spaces), remove trailing characters, and remove leading characters.

```
%TRIM( base value : trim characters);
```

The trim character is optional and, if left off, then is assumed to represent blanks. If there are multiple characters to be trimmed, they can just be listed in a line with no separation characters. So, for example:

```
%TRIM(address  : '.,');
```

will remove both periods and commas from the address.

To remove blanks when you specify characters, simply include a blank in the character string to be removed.

Now It's Your Turn

Frankly, I think you should try all of these and play around with them. But it's quite possible that even if you haven't done ILE, you have used some of these BIFs in positional RPG.

You know what my philosophy is? A BIF a week. I try to get used to a new BIF every week. Eventually I will get to the end of them.

Why Personal Responsibility Matters

BIFs are great tools, but, like most things, they must be used responsibly.

The fact that a BIF can act on another BIF seems to have given some people the license to pile BIF on BIF in a single statement until it takes an IT lawyer to separate out who did what to whom. You end up with BIFs operating on BIFs, which are the results of other BIFs. In some cases, this is the only way to do things, but in others it is just showmanship.

And I guess there are different levels of understanding in the IBM i community. Most of us like things bite-wise, one step at a time. But some people, and often they are the ones writing articles, move faster and can digest more in one step.

I am not one of those people. I need things set up in a logical order. And so, in case I ever have to look at your code, I recommend that rather than writing five BIFs in one, that you break them down a bit. It may require some intermediary fields, but I think that will be overshadowed by the step-by-step progression of the separate BIFs.

Just my opinion. Everyone may be smarter than me, and I would not be surprised. Follow your heart on this one.

What Ya Shoulda Learned

There are a few things I want to be sure that you take away from this.

First, get away from the old RPG III way of converting data from one format to another (by using MOVEs and a bunch of work fields). Similarly, get away from reviewing text strings by putting them in an array and using a loop. Instead, start using BIFs to do this kind of processing. It is cleaner, involves fewer lines of code, and is quite similar to the PHP way of handling things through functions.

Second, there are quite a few BIFs, and you should be familiar with most of them, at least as far as knowing they exist and what they do. For more information about what you can do with BIFs, I would start with the two references I mentioned earlier.

Third, you should know that one of the big strengths of BIFs is that they can be used in tandem. That is, since a BIF is a function that returns a value, you can easily use a BIF as an argument for another BIF. A good example is if you want to get a date and then convert that to a straight character string. Sometimes the most difficult thing is reading compound BIFs, and for that I would recommend spending some time poring over the examples in the *search400* reference I mentioned.

Fourth, you need to set aside some time to play with these things. Don't just assume they will work the way you think they will. I mean, how many other things in your life have worked out that way? No reason it should start now. BIFs are a serious way to save time and make your coding less confusing (although a few comments sometimes when you have multiple BIFs in a function is not a bad idea).

Chapter 13

H and F Position-less Specs

As we said earlier in this book, /Free began thousands of years ago with just C-specs. But starting with Technology Refresh (TR) 7 in 7.1, /Free-ness has been expanded to H-specs, F-specs, D-specs, and P-specs, replacing them with *control statements*.

That's right, P-specs. Since these are intimately connected with ILE, it is kind of surprising that they would not have been covered by /Free earlier, and those folks who did a lot of ILE prior to 7.1 were required to switch back and forth between positional and /Free to accommodate the P-specs. But that's just tough, ain't it, and now it's only a forgotten piece of our history. Unless you're not on 7.1.

So what does that look like? The position-less specs, that is. How different is an F-spec in /Free? Well, the first difference for F-specs, and H-specs, and the others is that in /Free the F-spec does not just look a little different, it doesn't exist!

Remember? /Free does not have specs. It has control statements. We have not stressed this with the logic control statements (C-specs), but we will with the replacements for the other specs. Even so, unless the editors for this book are very good, you may find me referring to a "file control statement" as an F-spec. Old habits die hard.

/Free Delimiters

We said previously that /Free is processed by the same compiler as regular RPG, and so there needs to be something that tells the compiler what is /Free and what is positional. The rules on this vary depending on what release of i/OS you are on.

Up to TR7 of Release 7.1

That is, if you are on 5.4 or 6.1 or don't have TR7, then that something was a set of delimiter tags, specifically, /Free, which indicates the start of a section of /Free code, and /end-Free, which indicates the end of that section. Both of these tags will start in column 7.

Above TR7 of 7.1 or on 7.2

If you are above that level, like on 7.2, for example, the compiler is smart enough to differentiate /Free logic statements from C-specs without any special delimiters. You would think they could have done that from the beginning, but they didn't. And it's possible the original delimiters were used more to highlight what was /Free and what wasn't. What's important is that at TR7 or above, you don't need the /Free and /end-Free delimiters.

At 7.3 or TR3 of 7.2 or TR9 of 7.1

If you are at this level, then you get two new options.

First, you have more options in terms of the degree of "Free-ness" of your program.

You can continue to do things the way we have been describing them, using the delimiters (if you just like them) or not using the delimiters, intermingling /Free and positional code as the spirit moves you.

Or, you can lock down your program and force it to be /Free, preventing you from using any positional code at all. This is what is new at this level.

To do this (lock out positional), put **Free starting in position 1 at the top of your program (that is, line 1, not the first line of the logic statements). Then just code using /Free code, no positional, and it will be fine. If you do need to include positional code, you can do it with a /Copy. Of course, this would ability to use F- and D-specs; you would have to use the new control statements, but that's what you should be doing anyway.

Second, this level of /Free eliminates the old 8–80 column limit. That is, you can put your code anywhere on the line, and you are not limited on either end. All in all, it's just one more restriction removed, restrictions that other languages do not have, and so that is a good thing.

H-specs

OK. On to the control statements. Might as well start at the top, and the first thing we will run into are the H-specs.

The /Free replacement is called an *option control statement*, and it starts with ctl-opt and ends with a semicolon. That is something we should probably point out right at the start. These control statements are /Free statements, and, just as the logic control statements do, they also need to end with a semicolon.

Between the ctl-opt identifier and the semicolon, you may have one or more keywords.

As with the logic control statements in /Free, you have a lot of flexibility in how you write up these statements. For example, some people like to put related keywords (like maybe the keywords related to debugging) on the same ctl-opt. Or others might have multiple ctl-opt statements with just a single keyword on each line.

Similarly, if you do have multiple keywords on a control statement, you can either list them horizontally or vertically, as we did with IF statements. I will try to show various examples of this, but you will want to decide what seems best (most readable or clear) to you and standardize on that. Consistency is probably more important than picking one format over another.

Multiple parameters on a keyword are separated by colons (:), and the whole set of parameters for the keyword is surrounded by parentheses.

In its simplest form, the /Free form of the H-spec is:

```
ctl-opt;
```

If you specify just the statement keyword with no parameters, then all it accomplishes is to keep the compiler from looking for a control specification data area.

Most of the time, however, you will probably want to include some parameters with the keyword. Some of the more common keywords and parameters you might use include this for some of your debug options:

```
ctl-opt option (*srcstmt : *noiodebug);
```

Or, you might want to set up your activation group information depending on what the default in your compile command is. Note that like many /Free things, you can either list them horizontally or vertically. Remember, the end of the statement is not the end of the line but where the semicolon is. You gotta love the flexibility.

```
ctl-opt    dftactgrp(*NO):
           actgrp(*NEW);
```

One interesting thing to note is that you don't need the DFTACTGRP(*NO) if there is at least one option for ACTGRP, BNDDIR, or STGMDL, all of which require the DFTACTGRP to be *NO. See how much time you are saving with /Free?

Some of the other parameter keywords that you might use include the following:

```
ccsid(*char:*jobrun)
alwnull(*usrctl)
datfmt(*iso)
timfmt(*iso)
```

Any questions? Great. If there are, reread this section.

Now It's Your Turn

I think you know the drill. Assuming you are on 7.2 (or have TR7 installed on 7.1), you can try this. If not, then you can't.

Start by taking a program and putting an H-spec ... oops, option control statement into the program and get it to compile. Don't forget the semicolon at the end.

File Control Statements: Basic Format

And now, on to the F-specs. Oops, I mean file control statements.

Like the option control statements, the *file control statements* (FCS) starts with a statement keyword (dcl-f), then the name of the file, and finally whatever other descriptive keywords might be required. For example:

```
dcl-f MSPMP100 DISK;
```

Of course, being free form, you can write it in sentence format like this or put a few spaces in there, so it's easier to read, such as:

```
dcl-f       MSPMP100          DISK;
DCL-F       pspsp100          DISK;
```

or however you want it to look.

Now let's look at it in a little more detail. But before we do, we need to notice that while the H-spec replacement starts with ctl-opt, the F-spec replacement starts with dcl-f. All of the /Free specs start with a "dcl-something" *except* for the H-spec. I have no idea why. That's just the way it is.

FCS: Details

Unfortunately, unlike option control statements, there are a lot more options to work out here. Let's run through a few things.

What types of files can you define here?

Full procedural and output files only.

You cannot define table, record address, or cycle files with this statement. So what do you do if you just can't live without one of those files? Simple: fall back on the F-spec. Remember, you can use either the F-spec or the file control statements and even mix them together with no problem (unless you have locked the program using **FREE). The same is true of other specs and control statements. And remember, you must be on TR7 7.1 or higher, otherwise you can't do any of this.

If you do use specs with your control statements, you do not need to put a /Free and /end-Free delimiter around the /Free stuff. The compiler will know what is what.

How long can the name be?

You can use names longer than 10 digits as long as you use the EXTFILE and EXTDESC keywords. The EXTFILE must have a value of *EXTDESC, and the EXTDESC keyword will contain the 10-digit name of the file.

And if you were a fan of using ellipses here, you can't do that anymore.

It should also be noted that you can't use any of George Carlin's "Seven words you can't say on television" in the filename, although most people under 35 use them constantly in casual conversation. Actually, I use most of them pretty routinely as well. But hardly ever in filenames.

```
dcl-f Product_Master_File  Disk    EXTFILE(*EXTDESC)
                                   EXTDESC('MSPMP100');
```

Is there some sort of order you need to list all of this stuff in?

Of course, what kind of world do you think we live in? Naturally, you start with the dcl-f keyword.

Then comes the filename.

Then the first keyword you need to specify is either the device keyword (DISK, PRINTER, SEQ, SPECIAL, or WRKSTN) *or* the LIKEFILE keyword.

After that, it's a free for all. And speaking of the device keyword, here's some more stuff.

FCS: DEVICE Keyword

In case you have forgotten over the last 28 words, the third thing you need to specify is the DEVICE keyword value (or else the LIKEFILE keyword). This is required.

And the values this DEVICE keyword can have are DISK, PRINTER, SEQ, SPECIAL, or WRKSTN. To be clear, what you enter in the file control option statement is DISK or PRINTER or whatever, not DEVICE(DISK), etc. As we will see in a moment, the DISK or PRINTER or whatever value can have a parenthesis-enclosed modifier of its own.

DISK is the default, and if you don't put anything in, it will default to that (that is, if you don't specify the DEVICE keyword at all). I know: if it's required, but doesn't really require you to enter a value, is it really required?

If the file is externally described, you can put the EXT value in parenthesis with the device keyword: DISK(*EXT) or PRINTER(*EXT). But that value is the default so, again, you can ignore it.

If we are dealing with a program-defined file, then you need to specify the length of the record along with the file type: PRINTER(132) or DISK(256). Is there a better reason for not using program-defined files?

So, for example, something like this might happen:

```
dcl-f year_end_report  printer(132) oflind(overflow)
                                     extdesc('XXXXX')
                                     extfile(*extdesc);
```

Again, note that I have listed the three keywords in a vertical format, but that is not required, and there is no particular column that these have to start in. But I like to list the keywords in a vertical format, and so do most cool people. It's up to you, though.

One thing that should be re-mentioned here is that because this is free format, you need to end each statement with a semicolon. The question is, does this mean a semicolon on every line? And the answer is, no, just on the final line of a given control statement. Good grief, what do you think this is? A police state?

FCS: KEYED Keyword

Remember the K flag to indicate a file was keyed? That has been replaced by the KEYED keyword. And if you have a keyed file, you need to use this.

For an externally described file, there is no value attached to this keyword; it will pick it up from the file definition.

```
dcl-f      MSPMP100      DISK      Keyed;
```

For a program-described file, you can indicate a value of *CHAR:len where len is the length of the key (duh). Unfortunately, I guess, only *CHAR keys are supported right now. But then again, I don't dig program-described files. Why not define it externally? Are you ashamed of it? Whatever. In the example below, we have a program-defined file with a length of 120 and an eight-character key.

```
dcl-f      Prog_File     Disk(120)    Keyed(*CHAR:8);
```

What if you have a packed key? Well, then you make it an externally described file. Or, if you insist, either through willfulness or the same type of behavior that has been strongly linked to juvenile delinquency and drug abuse, you can define the key as *CHAR in your file control statement (almost said "spec") and then lay that out in a data structure, like so:

```
dcl-f   prog_file      DISK(519)      KEYED(*CHAR:7);
// you don't put ds name in the file control stmt
dcl-ds      key           len(7) qualified;
            order_number    packed(12);
end-ds;
```

And the nice thing about this is that it shows how you can mix dcl-f statements and dcl-ds statements so they are next to each other. That is, the end-ds statement could be followed by another dcl-f. Free-form.

FCS: USAGE Keyword

The USAGE keyword replaces the file type (I, O, U) and the file addition (A) flags in the F-spec—à la USAGE(*INPUT).

You can specify more than one usage, like *UPDATE and *OUTPUT or *INPUT and *OUTPUT. If you're listing more than one usage value, use a colon to separate them: USAGE(*UPDATE:*DELETE).

In F-specs, a U can be update and/or delete, but in /Free *DELETE is its own man and must be specified if you want to do a delete.

The default for DISK is INPUT, for PRINTER is OUTPUT, for WRKSTN is (*INPUT:*OUTPUT), and for SEQ and SPECIAL is *INPUT.

Of course, the old hierarchy still holds. So *UPDATE implies *INPUT, and *DELETE implies *UPDATE and *INPUT. We aren't changing everything. All we are doing is making things more visible, more obvious.

Fortunately, most keywords currently used in F-specs can still be used for file control statements. This includes things like the RENAME or the PREFIX. But for a full view of what is still supported you should check out the *ILE RPG Reference* (*http://www-01.ibm.com/support/knowledgecenter/#!/ssw_ibm_i_71/books/ sc092508a.pdf*). What you need to look at here are the lines with a "|" next to them. This shows things that are new in the 7.1 PTF and cover the new free-form control statement details.

Now It's Your Turn

Again, if you are on 7.2 or 7.1 TR7, you can do this. Go back to your program that has an F-spec and replace it with a file control statement. Play around with the keywords and get a good feel for things.

What Ya Shoulda Learned

First, you need to know that if you are on a release of the IBM i OS that is below 7.1, TR7, then you do not have the ability to use any of the control statements we have discussed. Refer to the WRKPTFGRP instructions in chapter 2 to see how to check your TR level. If you are not on 7.1 TR7 or above, then none of this will work for you, and everything (except for C-specs) must be set up as specs.

Second, if you are above the 7.1 TR7 line, then you can use either specs or control statements for H-, F-, D-, and P-specs.

Third, H-specs are being replaced by ctl-opt control statements.

Fourth, F-specs are being replaced by dcl-f control statements, with a variety of keywords replacing the old positional codes.

Fifth, for all control statements the format is more or less the same:

The control statement will begin anywhere in column 8 to 80.

There will be no F or H or D or whatever in column 6.

The format is /Free, so that amount of space you leave between different keywords is up to you.

It starts with a dcl-?? (for F-, D-, and P-specs) and opt=?? for H-specs.

Then at the end there is a semicolon.

Sixth, the following rules also apply:

The compiler is smart enough to know what is /Free and what is positional, and no tags are required.

You can mix /Free with positional like some sort of pagan warrior, and there are no consequences. Sure, go ahead, be lawless.

Seventh, if you are on 7.3 or higher, then both of the above rules apply. Plus, you get two more things. I know, confusing, isn't it?

First, you can force your source to be just /Free by using the **FREE tag in position 1 on the very first line of the source. Now you can't use any positional code (include F-, D-, or other specs, which have a /Free version). And definitely no I- or O-specs since they do not have a /Free format.

Second, if you are at this level, then you can put your /Free code anywhere starting with column 1 and go past the normal 80-column limit depending on just how large your source record is.

Chapter 14

D and P Position-less Specs

Good news! There are more control statements to look at. I just didn't want to make the last chapter too long. I know. You are thankful I am so considerate. It is my great weakness. "I am a martyr to my own generosity."

So here's the /Free scoop on D- (including PR and PI) specs and P-specs.

D-specs

If you have read the previous chapter, you can guess that things start not with a D in column 7 but with the data structure control keyword (DCS), `dcl-ds`, somewhere in columns 8–80.

This will then be followed by the data structure name, and whatever keywords that might be required.

```
dcl-ds Product_rec likerec(PMP100);
```

or if you like to leave a bit of space:

```
dcl-ds       Product_rec                likerec(PMP100);
```

As with the file control statement, use of ellipses is not supported.

Something else that is different from the control statements we have seen so far is that there are several types of data structure keywords, each one representing a different type of data structure.

We have already seen one of those, the `dcl-ds`, which is used for straight data structures, as shown above. But there are other types of data structures, and each has its own format.

DCS: Named Constants

The first thing that you can define are *named constants*, fields that can be set and then referred to by their name rather than their value. That is, if you have a field:

```
Cust_Code = '15';
```

what does that really mean? If you are a data junkie, then you know this is a customer who is "retail with a national base," but for me, it is meaningless. If you use a named constant, however:

```
Cust_Code = Retail_Nat;
```

then it is much clearer what you are talking about.

In positional RPG, this was done by using a C in the definition type of the D-spec.

In /Free data structure control statements, however, we use the dcl-c keyword. The use of the CONST keyword is optional; the statement works the same with or without it. Once the constant is defined, you can use it in your program. And I honestly don't know why I said that. Sort of stands to reason, doesn't it?

```
dcl-c        Initial_Date     D'2010-01-01';
```

Or, if you like using the CONST keyword as a special reminder that it is a named constant field:

```
dcl-c        Initial_Date CONST(D'2010-01-01');
```

DCS: Standalone Field

You can also define standalone fields, single fields that stand on their own rather than being part of a larger structure.

As you might expect, it starts with a dcl-s and ends with a semicolon.

This is followed by the name of the standalone field.

That is followed by any keywords you want to specify. The first keyword must either be LIKE or the data type and length. Following are some examples. If you use LIKE, then no other keywords may be specified, although you may enter a length adjustment.

```
dcl-s name LIKE(other_name);
dcl-s order_number packed(6:0)inz(0);
dcl-s order_code            char(6);
dcl-s order_number          packed(6:0)
                                  inz(0);
dcl-s next_order_number LIKE(order_number: +1);
dcl-s next_order_number     Like(order_number: +1);
```

DCS: Data Structures

The data structure formulation is just a bit more verbose, but I definitely like the structure it imposes.

It starts with a `dcl-ds`. This is followed by a name. Or not. Data structures may either be named or unnamed (in which case a `*N` is put where the name would be). Then come zero or more keywords to describe the data structure. And finally the semicolon.

```
dcl-ds      Customer_Address;
dcl-ds      Product_Record      Likerec(MSPMP100);
dcl-ds      Print_Record        Len(132);
```

If we are dealing with a program-defined data structure (that is, one where there are subfields under the main control statement), then we need to add an `end-ds` with an optional name field.

If the field is unnamed, then obviously, when you code the `end-ds`, you cannot put the name of the data structure in parentheses; you just use `end-ds`. End-ds is not used if you have the `LIKE` keyword on the top level because then you are unable to define subfields.

```
dcl-ds      Zip_Code;
            Postal_Code         X(5);
            The_Rest            X(4);
end-ds;

dcl-ds      Zip_Code;
            Postal_Code         X(5);
            The_Rest            X(4);
end-ds(Zip_Code);

dcl-ds      *N;
            Postal_Cod          X(5);
            The_Rest            X(4);
end-ds;
```

If you are defining subfields, you can also use the dcl-subf thing to identify what the subfields are. Please note that this is optional. Most of the time it should be pretty obvious, and for me it just gives something else to look at and confuse your visual receptors. The only time you have to use it is if the name of the subfield is the same as an RPG operator (e.g., WRITE).

```
dcl-ds      Zip_Code;
  dcl-subf  Postal_Cod      X(5);
  dcl-subf  The_Rest        X(4);
end-ds;
```

DCS: Overlay

This is a small point but an important one, and it deserves a section of its own. Ready? Brace yourselves. The Overlay keyword is now only supported in specific situations.

Specifically, you can only use it to overlay subfields. It cannot be used to overlay the entire data structure.

Now remember, this is only when you are using the data structure control statements. And there is no support at all for the Overlay(ds:*next) because that means there is no set position—just put it after the last field in the data structure, which is meaningless. It amounts to no overlay functionality.

Since you can intermix the new control statements with the old D-specs, you could still use the Overlay on the D-spec. What replaces Overlay for the free-format specs is POS(999), where you can specify the position in the data structure that a particular field is going to start in.

Now It's Your Turn

I feel kind of guilty about this, turning things over to you after we have done five or six pages' worth of stuff, but the alternative was to type one of these on each page. I wasn't going to do that. I care about you, but there is a limit.

I guess the best bet is to grab your test program(s) and replace some D-specs with the data control statements. Remember, this includes the PR and PI D-specs.

Of course, this only applies if you are on 7.1 TR7 or 7.2. Otherwise it is just interesting information but not something you can try. Want to try to convince your manager to upgrade? Yeah, I thought so.

PR and PI D-Specs

Yes, the PR and PI structures are D-specs, but because they are very special D-specs they get their own control statements. Fortunately, things for the PI and PR specs are done pretty much the same way as normal data control statements are. And the end-pi/end-pr is not required, but I like it.

```
dcl-pr dws0176 extpgm;
      parm1 char(256);
      parm2 packed(10:3);
end-pr;



dcl-pi           dws0170;
            parm1 char(256);
            parm2 packed(10:3);
end-pi;
```

If you have a return value coming back, and you use a keyword to set the data type, then that must be indicated on the PR line of the complex.

```
dcl-pr dws0176  Packed(11:3);
        parm1 char(256);
        parm2 packed(10:3);
end-pr;
```

As with data structures, if a subfield associated with a P-spec is the name of an RPG opcode, then you have to use the dcl_parm thing on the front of the subfield definition.

```
dcl-pr  Procedure1;
            CNAME        char(256);
            dcl-parm     WRITE        packed(10:3);
end-pr;
```

If there is no name for the group, then you can use *N just as you could for data structures.

```
dcl-pr *N;
        parm1 char(256);
        parm2 packed(10:3);
end-pr;
```

On the PR, the extpgm keyword is optional; if you don't code it, the compiler will default to using the name of the PR group as the program name being called. But this is only if the program name is 10 characters or less, otherwise it will initiate the Star Trek "Frank Gorshin" destruct sequence.

Also on the PR group, if the program you are calling has a mixed-case name, then you need to use the extproc keyword.

```
dcl-pr          EL3write            extproc('EL3write');
```

Or you could use the *dclcase to avoid retyping the name.

```
dcl-pr          EL3write            extproc(*dclcase);
```

This can sometimes help prevent typo errors if you have several programs you are calling that have similar names, and you copy lines but forget to change the name in the extproc keyword. Or, you can stop using mixed-case, weirdo names that you can easily screw up. Your choice.

Now It's Your Turn

OK, you know the drill. Give it a try.

P-Specs

Finally, we get to the procedures syntax in free format. In spec language, these are defined by a P-spec, but using the new free-form format, it starts with a dcl-proc with a procedure name and keywords and ends with the end-proc (the procedure name on the end-proc is optional). This end-proc is required.

```
dcl-proc        procedure-name      keywords;
end-proc        procedure-name;
```

I know by now you are all set with simple examples, so here is one that is a little more complex. But I think you can see that the basic principles are the same.

```
dcl-proc GetCurUser export;
        parm1               varchar(15) CONST;
        parm2               packed(7:1);
end-proc GetCurUser;
```

Now It's Your Turn

Ditto.

If/Then/Else in a Control Statement

I know. This is really weird. But with the 7.1 TR7 you can actually imbed If/Then/Else commands within the position-less control statements.

Now I know what you are thinking: why? Right?

Well, maybe you want to vary the keywords that are associated with a file. Or a data structure.

Or maybe you just like to make things very complicated. There are a lot of people who like to do that. I have read many of their articles.

To be honest, it doesn't really matter why you would want to do this; what's important is you can.

And seriously, sometimes it might be helpful to be able to assign file control statement keywords based on some external thingy. Like suppose you had a flag that was set based on a user profile value, and it indicated a level of trust: either an input-only or update state. You could control that with code like this built right into where your F-specs would go now. And don't confuse the slash in front of the IF with the // that indicates a comment. These are not comments.

```
/IF flag1 = 'I';
dcl-f product_master Usage(*input) Keyed;
/ELSE;
/IF flag1 = 'U';
dcl-f        product_master       Usage(*Update)       Keyed;
/ENDIF;
/ENDIF;
```

Now It's Your Turn

Now this is a bit interesting, isn't it? Sit quietly for a few minutes with your hands folded in your lap and try to think of some situations in programs you have right now that could use this kind of functionality.

Then let your thoughts drift off to a quiet meadow on a warm summer day. You can hear the sound of insects softly buzzing and smell the wild flowers that are growing around you. A young woman/man with long blonde/dark hair appears in the distance. She/he smiles at you, the kind of smile you have waited all your life to see, and then suddenly begins to run. Unfortunately, you don't quite notice the hungry grizzly bear that comes out of the woods right behind her/him.

Not sure where this is going, but it was kind of diverting. And that is life in a microcosm, isn't it?

Mixing File and Data Control Statements

Historically, we keep F- and D-specs apart because that is just the way things are done. You don't mix whiskey and vodka, do you? No normal person would do that, would they? No. But if you have a recipe that does so, I would be curious, just from an intellectual point of view, of course. But I digress.

Some of it is just how you think. I like seeing all the file control statements at one point, but some people may prefer to see everything associated with one file in one spot. I can see advantages to that actually, and maybe I should rethink how I do things. But the chances of that are small. Anyway, you could have the file control statement, followed by all the data control statements related to that file before the next file control statement. I have to admit, I may eventually like that. But I doubt it.

Another use would be if you want to define a non-character key for a file. If we go back a chapter, we saw that key fields defined on the file control statement had to be character-type fields. But now you could embed a data control statement in there and set up a data structure for the character field that was packed, for example:

```
dcl-f File1 disk(256)       Keyed(*Char:10);

dcl-ds file1_key len(10)   qualified;
           key_field       packed(18:0);
end-ds;
```

The point is, you now have a lot more flexibility in how you do things, and eventually you will find ways to use that flexibility.

Now It's Your Turn

I'm going to make a big assumption here, namely that you somehow got away from the bear and are calm enough to consider this functionality and how you might use it.

What Ya Shoulda Learned

There is a lot of detail in here, and I am not going to go back through it and list every single fact we covered. I guess the salient points are the basic structure of the control statements and what the keywords and options are for each one. Obviously, it will take some practice for you to feel as comfortable with them as you do with our old friends the F/D/H/P-specs.

But moving forward is a part of life, and I think this is an important part of your RPG life. If you are on a release that supports this, take a couple of programs, just for practice to start with, and convert them to the appropriate control statements.

In the end, this is something you practice and get good with, rather than just memorizing.

ADVANCED ILE

We have looked at several different examples of ILE programs, but now it is time to dig a little deeper and look at some features that are important and more advanced. That is, the kinds of stuff that scares most people. But not you. Oh, no. You ain't scared of nothing, are you? Yeah, I used to be that way.

Chapter 15

Prototyping Primer

I want to return now to ILE and cover a number of topics that are probably best described as "advanced." It's not that they are really that difficult, it's just that they are—uh, well, the truth is ... yeah, some of them are kind of difficult.

No, just kidding, they are not that hard. Just misunderstood. Sure, misunderstood. So we will try to understand them a little better. That should do it.

So what's on deck first? Well, we are going to start with something easy. We will start by taking a more detailed look at prototyping.

We have thrown this word around pretty casually, and we have used them (prototypes) to create actual programs, but we haven't really talked about them in an organized way. What does it require, and what does it do for us? Some of this will be review, but what's wrong with that?

What Is Prototyping?

Prototyping is a term that describes how modules are accessed within the ILE environment.

The word *prototype* also refers to a particular D-spec structure that is required to support this call or access.

As a result, the word prototype can function as both a verb and a noun. It can be the process of calling another module as well as the specific data structures required to do that call.

And by modules, I do not mean *MODULES, the formal object type that is the output of the CRTRPGMOD command, but just any code structure, be it a program or a sub-procedure or whatever. In the old OPM world, we might have referred to this as a "call." You can use prototypes to access (or call) RPG programs, sub-procedures, CL, C, Cobol, and even Java classes.

So far, we have seen examples of how to prototype with both the CALLP and the function call-return values combo.

You can even use prototypes to call OPM positional programs. That is, if you have an old program with an *ENTRY opcode, you can call it from an ILE program using prototyping in the ILE program. Of course, what you should do is rewrite the old program, but whatever. But now, let's get into some detail.

What Is a Prototype?

A prototype is a set of special D-specs with a declaration type of either PR or PI.

We will get to the differences between those two in a minute. What's important to remember now is that the prototype structure is just a new type of D-spec. In fact, if you go back to the /Free control option statements in the last chapter, we even had specific operators for the PR and PI D-specs (dcl-pr and dcl-pi).

Prototypes are *not* P-specs. Those are also used in ILE, but are different and simply delineate the beginning and end of a sub-procedure. Prototypes are D-specs. P-specs are not D-specs.

The prototype structures will be found in both the calling and the called program and will look something like this:

```
D  VAL_PRDNO       PR
```

PR and PI

As we said a moment ago, there are two types of prototype D-specs.

The PR D-spec is the "prototype" D-spec. It is in the calling and the called program.

The PI D-spec is the "procedure interface" D-spec. It is in the called program only.

You will want to remember those names because we will be using them frequently as we go forward.

PR Details

The PR (prototype) D-spec will appear in both the calling and the called program. Have I mentioned that before?

The good thing about the PR in the calling program is that it makes it very clear what parms belong to what call (because each call to a different module will have its own unique PR D-spec).

On the other hand, the PR does not actually define the fields to the program (yep, they have to be defined separately somewhere else in the program). How weird is that?

Because the PR does not formally define the fields to the program, every subfield that is going to be passed will have two representations in the calling program: one in the PR D-spec and one where the field is actually defined (in a file or another D-spec). The names of the two field representations have to be the same (otherwise it wouldn't be defined in the PR field, would it?). Similarly, the field types must be the same. What doesn't have to match are the field lengths. Go figure. We will talk more in the next chapter about what to do if the lengths are not the same.

When ILE first came out and I read some of the early articles, I actually drew the conclusion that using the PR formed some sort of magical bond between the calling and the called program, so that when you did the compile it would recognize any parm differences on the call rather than just blowing up when you ran it. That is not the case.

What those articles were actually referring to was that you could set up the PR as a copybook and then use the copybook in both the calling and the called program. This gives you the same PR in both, and since the compile of the called program will identify differences between the PR and PI D-specs (that is, generate an error on the compile), it becomes impossible to have parameter mismatches between your calling and the called program.

PI Details

The PI (procedure interface) D-spec is where the actual parameters are defined; it is used in receiving those parameters into the called program. As a result, the subfields on the PI do not actually have to be defined in the called program; the PI does it for you. Ain't that sweet?

The PI is found only in the called program.

Since the called program has both a PR and a PI D-spec, the compiler will compare the two specs. The field names of the corresponding fields do not have to match, but if they don't, the one in the PR D-spec must be defined elsewhere in the program. The field types and lengths do have to match, however, as do any keywords. In other words, in the called program, the PR and PI D-specs must be identical (except for that name thing). But you want them to be identical, otherwise you are just trolling for trouble.

Subfields on the Prototype

A prototype does not have to have subfields (parameters) associated with it.

```
D  VAL_PRDNO      PR
```

There is nothing wrong with calling a program or sub-procedure and not passing any subfields (like the example above), but you still need to define a prototype structure (it just won't have any subfields associated with the PR/PI D-spec).

Most of the time, however, you are going to be passing parms into your called program, and with subfields, the prototype would look like this:

```
D   VAL_PRDNO        PR
D      PRDNO                  15
D      MSG1                   60
```

And please remember that if you are on a release of RPG that supports the control statements, then you could set things up that way rather than using D-specs. That is, the above spec example would look like this with control statements.

```
dcl-pr   VAL_PRDNO;
    PRDNO       Char(15);
    MSG1        Char(60);
end-pr;
```

More PR and PI

There are some interesting relationships involving the size and type of the fields in both the PR and the PI.

OK, fine, I'll say it. For prototyping, size matters. There, are you happy? Bunch of sickos.

For one thing, in the *called* program where we have both a PR and a PI, the subfields must match size- and type-wise in both D-specs. So, if you have parms that are 10,0 and 3 in the PR, they have to be the same parms in the PI. That is, within the calling program.

Strangely enough, the names of the two fields whose lengths must match do not have to be the same. That is, it could be Field1 in the PR and Field11 in the PI. But at the same time, remember that if they are different (and I have no idea why you would want to do that, doesn't sound like a good idea), then you have to have the field from the PR D-spec defined somewhere else because the differently named field in the PI won't be backing it up. Know what I mean? Just make them the same, and don't go looking for trouble.

On the other hand, if you are in the *calling* program and you have a PR that has two parms, 10,0 and 3, then the actual fields in that program where those two fields are defined can have different lengths. I know, so weird. There are rules about just how different they can be, but I want to hold off on discussing that until the next chapter because I just like to put off unpleasant things.

And if that isn't weird enough, the lengths and types of the PR subfields in the calling program do not have to match the length and type of the subfields in the called program. That is, the compiles will work fine. There may be problems when you run the program, so it is not something that I recommend, but the system won't stop you. And, it is even possible that if you are passing large amounts of data, like if you are processing XML documents, you might want the lengths to be different.

And I guess that's the basics of prototyping. But I know what you are probably wondering right now.

Why are both a PR and a PI required? They look essentially identical, except for the R and the I. And we already saw that the PR is primarily documentation. So why do we need both? And the answer is simple.

Because.

Yep, that's it. Just because. Because that's the way it is. Because that's the way IBM designed it. Because if you don't do it that way, it won't work. In a nutshell, it's because that's the way we say it is, and there ain't nothing you can do about it because you don't really know who "we" are. So there!

But, as I said above, it is a story that is evolving, and so in 7.1 there are some types of programs where the prototype (that is, PR D-spec) may be left off in the called program. Those are cases where the program being called is an exit program or one that calls a command, one that is not called by another RPG program (although it can be called by a PHP or another language script), and where the sub-procedures being called are not "exported" from the program. We will talk more about exporting later. Just keep in mind that this is not a wholesale removal of the need for PR; it's just making it optional in certain circumstances. And also remember that is only for 7.1 and above.

OK, enough complaining. On to some important stuff. We will spend most of the rest of the chapter talking about keywords that are associated with the PR and PI D-specs.

Now It's Your Turn

Before continuing, are you at a point where you really feel comfortable with prototypes?

We have actually gone over the information a number of times, but feeling comfortable with the prototype structure is key to feeling comfortable with ILE. So, if you don't feel comfortable with it, take a moment and ask yourself why? Was it the explanation? Not clear enough? Too repetitious? Or maybe you are just dumb? I am not talking here about confused or a little distracted, but just flat out butt-dumb? Might be good to just admit it. I know that works for me. Takes the pressure off, you know.

Either way, you might possibly want to reread the section above. I realize that if you are really confused that may not help much, but—it's the best I can do. Good luck.

PR- and PI-specific Keywords: Top-Level Keywords

And now, on to a different topic. I think you should have a fair dinkum handle on prototypes, so let's move on.

As I may have said before, prototype (PR) and procedure interface (PI) D-specs are special and different from a regular D-spec data structure, so they have some special keywords that apply only to them.

The first set of keywords that we can look at apply to the top level of the PR/PI D-spec. This would be things like

```
EXTPGM('DWS0001')
```

This tells the prototype what program ID is being accessed with this prototype structure. It is used on the PR in the calling program. It is not used in the called program since it already knows who it is.

This keyword is required if you are using the CRTBNDRPG compile command.

The keyword is not required using CRTRPGMOD/CRTPGM option where they are bound together if the name of the PR D-spec is the same as the module being called.

One thing to note is that you cannot use this keyword if you are doing a function call and have a length on the top level of the PR. Which means a program doing a function call must use the program name as the name of the PR D-spec, *and* it must be compiled using CRTRPGMOD/CRTPGM. You cannot do it using CRBNDRPG because that requires the EXTPGM keyword.

There, see. What could be simpler than that?

EXTPROC

This keyword indicates the name of a sub-procedure that is being accessed by the prototype. It is used on the PR.

Since this is calling a sub-procedure (EXTPGM calls a program), the program must be compiled with CRTRPGMOD/CRTPGM, and so this keyword is optional as long as the name of the PR D-spec is the same as the name of the sub-procedure being called. That is why we did not need to specify it on our service program example in chapter 10.

OPDESC

This keyword passes operational descriptors (length and character type) to the called module. It is mostly used for APIs and requires the keyword on both the PR and the PI.

Even though I will probably be sorry that I do this, I want to also mention the EXPORT keyword that is used in service programs.

This is used on the prototyping P-specs for sub-procedures in a service program to indicate if a given sub-procedure can be used outside of that service program. It is *not* placed on the PR or PI D-specs.

Early on, I would get confused and think that this keyword went on the PR or PI associated with that sub-procedure. It does not. I thought you might get confused, too, so I mentioned this now. Now you will probably get confused because of what I have said. Can't win.

PR and PI-specific Keywords: Subfield Keywords

The first thing I want to stress is that all the keywords that you could normally apply to a D-spec can be applied here. That includes things like LIKE (which lets you relate a field on a D-spec, even a PR or PI D-spec) to a field that is already defined in the program), LIKEDS (which lets you define a data structure in the prototype), and so on.

The other keywords that we are going to look at are applied to the subfields within the PR or PI D-spec and are specific to ILE. The rest of this chapter and the next will pretty much be devoted to these subfield-level keywords.

Each particular subfield can have multiple keywords applied to it, so don't let that throw you if you see it.

Of course, subfields can also use the other keywords that you apply to regular, more normal D-specs; often people get confused about what has been introduced for ILE and what was there all along. For example, you will often see the VARYING keyword involved in a discussion of prototyping keywords, but that is (in the opinion of some experts) really a data type with special characteristics (even though it is a keyword) and is not confined to prototyping. Against my better judgment, we will talk about this keyword a bit more in the next chapter.

Options(*NOPASS)

Let's start with the easy one, the OPTIONS keyword and most of its family of parameters.

The first parm is *NOPASS, which lets you decide if the passing of a parm is required or optional. Specifying *NOPASS makes it optional; otherwise it is required.

This is pretty simple, but keep one thing in mind. If you have multiple parms on the prototype, then you must list them so that the required parms (not *NOPASS) are listed first. This is because once you code one parm to be *NOPASS, then every parm after that must be *NOPASS (that is, optional). Can you dig what I'm sayin'?

```
D*
D   VAL_PRDNO       PR
D      PRDNO              15
D      MSG1               60
D      MSG2               60        OPTIONS(*NOPASS)
D      MSG3               60        OPTIONS(*NOPASS)
D      MSG4               60        OPTIONS(*NOPASS)
D*
```

Remember that *NOPASS is not the same as omitting something. *NOPASS simply means that you don't have to include that parameter, that it is not required. I know that sounds weird, but keep reading.

In fact, skipping parms is not allowed when you use *NOPASS. That is, in the example above, you can't skip MSG2 and expect to send MSG3 and MSG4. You can really only skip working your way backward from the end of the parms. That is, you could decide not to send MSG3 and therefore MSG4 but send MSG2. What's important is that your parameter string is contiguous. There can't be any holes because when using *NOPASS the system can't tell what is missing. In essence, *NOPASS allows you to skip the rest of the parameter list.

While it sounds like a good idea (to be able to not send parms), just be careful in the called program. If you would reference one of those *NOPASS parms then, as IBM puts it, "unpredictable results will occur." Sometimes, just because you can do something, doesn't mean you should. Know what I mean, Vern?

Skipping Parms: OPTIONS(*OMIT)

Hey, didn't I just say that you can't skip parms?

Well, yes, but, baby, I can explain! What I said is you can't skip parms by using the *NOPASS. But there is a way to do it.

I'm talking about the *OMIT parm on the OPTIONS keyword. By using that and *NOPASS, you make the parm optional and allow it to be skipped. For example:

```
D*
D  VAL_PRDNO      PR
D     PRDNO               15
D     MSG2                60
D     MSG3                60   OPTIONS(*NOPASS:*OMIT)
D     MSG4                60   OPTIONS(*NOPASS)
D     MSG5                60   OPTIONS(*NOPASS)
D*
```

Now in this case, we can call the sub-procedure and omit MSG3 while still passing MSG4 (but not MSG5 because we don't need to this time, and it is optional).

```
CALL VAL_PRDNO(PRDNO:MSG2:*OMIT:MSG4);
```

Please note that when we do the call, we will use the *OMIT in place of the parm being skipped.

Now, if you're a smart aleck, you may be wondering how to tell in your logic in the called program which parms have been skipped. It's pretty easy, actually. If you think that a skip is possible, check to see how many parms there are and then start working backward from the end to see which ones are null.

```
if %parms() > 2;
    if %addr(MSG2) <> Null
     // a value for the MSG2 has been specified.
else;
// a value wasn't sent.
    endif;
end-if;
```

Obviously, there is a bit of fooling around you have to do if you skip parms, but it's up to you. I would just always send the parms, but people rarely ask me what I think, so who cares? And, equally obviously, if your parms are ginormous, you may have good reason to not send them if they are not needed.

Now It's Your Turn

At this point, I think you should try the *NOPASS and *OMIT keywords on one of your test programs. Use Debug to follow it through and see what the impacts of those keywords are.

Don't forget to use the %parms and %addr BIFs in your called program to help you see what is coming through.

And I know what you are thinking. You are thinking: "I have done a lot of these lab things. I am going to skip this one." Well, you're an adult, I can't stop you. But let me ask you: will you tell your mother you skipped this exercise? Let that be your guide.

Oddball Keywords

Just so no one feels left out and I don't get angry texts from IBM keywords, here are a couple more.

Options(*STRING)

This will stick an x'00' value onto the end of the string you are dealing with. This is for use with UNIX-oriented APIs.

Options(*RIGHTADJ)

Can't figure out what this one does. Oh, wait a minute. Just a wild guess, but—right-adjust the parameter?

I did happen to notice, though, in one of Scott Klement's presentations that he mentions that he has never found a use for this option. Seriously? If Scott hasn't found a use, I really doubt any of us will.

Options(*TRIM)

This keyword will trim blanks off of the front and back of the field. This one could really be useful, saving you the trouble of doing it with a BIF in your program.

Options(*NULLIND)

This keyword indicates that you are going to pass null-capable data. You know where that comes in, right? Yep, SQL databases. Freaks. You have to use the %NULLIND BIF in your RPG program to determine what is in the field you pass, but it all starts with the Options keyword.

What Ya Shoulda Learned

Soooo, how is everyone? Having fun? Hmmmmm. Well, guess that's all for now. Keep reading, though. I don't get paid unless you read every page. It's a new thing for authors these days.

In the meantime, this is what you should have picked up from this chapter:

First, we spent quite a bit of time talking about prototyping: what it means, what it does, what it looks like, etc.

At the same time, we talked a great deal about the PR and PI D-specs that are used to define the prototype, how they are similar, how they are different, and how they feel about that.

We then took a look at the PR- and PI-level keywords that could be used: EXTPGM, EXTPROC, and OPDESC.

This was followed by a review of some of the keywords that can be applied to the subfields in the prototype D-specs. Basically, we looked only at the *OPTIONS() keyword and its variations. We will continue this in the next chapter, so keep an open mind about this one.

But enough of this nonsense. It is time for other nonsense, like just how size does matter to the prototype subfields.

Chapter 16

More Prototyping Stuff

I know, it's unusual for me to keep to the same topic for two chapters in a row, but it had to happen sometime. Actually, it's just that I find the whole domain of prototyping keywords so very interesting. Or something. Anyway, in this second act, I want to look at two things.

First, let's finish up with the keywords that we can apply to the prototype subfields. This will primarily be the CONST keyword.

And second, I want to take a closer look at the various cases involving the lengths of those subfields and how the relationship between the different lengths can affect the data being passed.

CONST

The CONST keyword is not a parameter of the OPTIONS keyword, like *OMIT or *VALUES; rather, it is a true keyword in its own right.

It has two different uses, depending on where it is found: in the called or the calling module. In both cases, this keyword is applied to the subfield level of the D-spec, not at the top level, so one field in a PR can be labeled CONST, and the others cannot, and it is OK.

In addition, the CONST keyword can only be used on a prototype D-spec subfield. You can't apply it to a regular D-spec (or dcl-ds) field.

Using CONST in the Called Program

If you put the keyword on both the PR and the PI D-specs in the *called* module, then it will prevent the field from being modified in the called program. Remember, those two D-specs must be identical, so you have to put the keyword on the same subfield in both of them.

How does it do that? It causes an error in the compile if the compiler sees the CONST keyword and a logic statement that affects the value of that particular variable in the called program.

You can modify the variable all you want in the calling program. But not in the called program.

Why would you want to do this? How should I know? No telling what you are liable to do when you are on your own. Guess you just want to make sure you or someone else never adds a statement to that called program that affects the parameter value. There is some relationship to speed involved (it's more efficient to pass CONST fields than regular parms), but seriously, how much processing time can that trim if you have a POWER8 with more computing power than the entire country of Liechtenstein? We'll talk more about efficiency later.

It's also possible that, for audit purposes, you might want to ensure that a value can't be changed. This is how you would do it.

Or you may just view it as a convenient documentation tool—don't worry about these parms when you look at the program, they can't change. I can dig it.

In addition to keeping the field from being modified in the called program, it also allows you to pass a literal constant (the system will create a variable to facilitate this) or a function (you know, like a BIF).

The truth is a lot of people use CONST on a pretty regular basis for all the reasons I've mentioned, so just be aware of the fact that you might see it.

Oh, and you may actually use it yourself.

Now It's Your Turn

I want you to take a minute and go out to your program example from chapter 8 where one program called another and set it up for testing this. It's really simple.

Calling program: you don't need to do anything here; it's good to go the way it is.

Called program: put the CONST keyword on a subfield of the PR and PI D-specs, then add in a line that just sets that particular field equal to itself (no sense being too creative here). The system will see that as proof that you were going to modify that field, and when you compile the program (with either CRTBNDRPG or CRTRPGMOD), it will fail.

Then go out to the called program, remove the CONST keyword, and see that now the compile works.

Using CONST in the <u>Calling</u> Program

The result of using CONST in the calling program is very different from what we saw in the previous section.

Instead of controlling whether you can or can't update the parm it is applied to, CONST affects the relationship between the length of a parm in the calling program PR D-spec and the length of it wherever else in the calling program it is defined. Remember, the calling program has a PR but no PI, and the fields listed in the PR are not really defined in the system (although they carry a size and type), so you have to define them elsewhere in the D- or F-specs. Normally, we would expect these two fields to look identical: same type and size. But that is not necessarily the case.

Without using the CONST keyword in the calling program, the field where the parm is defined can actually be larger than the value in the PR D-spec. Yeah, seriously. It has to be the same type, but the length can be larger.

That is, if the length of the field in the PR is 15 and elsewhere in the calling program it is defined as 20, then that is OK; no keyword is required, and no compiler error is generated. The impact on the data in those fields is something else, and we will get to that in a minute.

If, on the other hand, the field in the PR is 15 and elsewhere it is defined as 10, then when you compile this program, you will get an error. You see, the system is always thinking, and it knows that since the length of 10 is the real definition of the field, it will never be able to pass a value with more than 10 characters. And so, it is worried about what will be in those extra five characters of the PR when it is passed but not initialized. Remember, this field doesn't really exist, and so it is not initialized by default.

So, in this situation, you will get an error, unless—unless you put the CONST keyword on that field in the PR. Then the system would be fine with the fact that the field in the PR is bigger than the field where it is really defined.

Of course, we are still curious what happens to those extra five digits. And the answer is that the data is left-justified and something is filled in on the right-hand side. The question is, what is that "something?"

Now It's Your Turn

Much of this will be covered in the next section, so hang on.

A Series of Facts About Parameter Size

I want to spend a little more time on parameter size issues before we go any further. And to kick that off, let's review some facts about the prototype D-specs that you should already know from earlier chapters or a previous life.

Called Program Prototype Facts

The subfields on a PR and PI must be identical—the same size and same data type. Actually, the name can be different, but you have to make sure that you have the name used in the PR defined separately somewhere in the program.

The same is true for any keywords that are applied to those subfields. They must be applied the same to both the PR and the PI.

So far, so good: everything is the same.

Calling Program Prototype Facts

First, remember that even though the calling program only has a PR and no PI, there are still two representations of each PR subfield: the subfield itself on the PR and the real field in the D or F-specs where it is formally defined.

Both of these fields must have the same name and be of the same type (for example, alphanumeric or packed) and name.

But, the two fields (the PR subfield and the defining field) do not have to be the same size. Generally, they will be, but there's no law forcing it, and so size differences could happen. The question is, what impact does it have? Let's take a look at a few examples (I won't promise I have them all covered).

And while I am thinking of it, the keywords on both fields (PR and defining) do not have to be, often are not, and sometimes can't be, the same.

What Happens If the Field Sizes Do Not Match?

As we go through this exercise, I am going to make one assumption: namely, that the size of a field in the PR of the called program is identical to the size of the field in the PR of the calling program.

That is, I am assuming we have a situation where the PR in both programs is represented by a copybook and so is identical. And if the PR field size in the called program is *x* characters, then the PI field size in the called program must match it or there would be a compile error. Everybody with me on this? OK, so the only variable is the size of the real field in the calling program relative to the size of the PR field in that program.

Calling Program: Real Field Larger Than PR Field

If the real field is larger than the PR field, then the real field length (not the length in the PR) is the length that will be sent out by the calling program and received by the called program.

This will happen naturally; no special keywords need to be used.

So, if the real field is 10 digits and the PR subfield is 6 digits and we move '123456789012' to that field, then '1234567890' is what will be sent to the called program.

If your field in the called program is 6 digits also (that is, if it matches the PR), then what you will receive into the called program is '123456'.

If your field in the called program matches the calling programs real definition (10 digits), then you will get '1234567890' in the called program.

If your field in the called program is larger than the real field in the calling program, say 12 digits, then you will get the 10 digits from the real field and, because the field in the called program is defined by the PI with two spaces at the end.

As it turns out, if the real field is larger than the PR field, then everything stays very civilized.

Calling Program: Real Field Smaller Than PR Field

If, however, the situation is reversed, if the real field is 6 digits and the PR version of it is 10 and we move '123456789012' to the real field, then we will send out the digits from the real field, '123456'. The question then becomes, what is received on the called program side where we have a 10-digit PR field waiting for it? But, before we get to that, there are two very important caveats we need to point out.

First, you will need to specify either CONST or OPTIONS(*VARSIZE) as the keyword on the PR subfield in the calling program, otherwise the compile of the calling program will fail. That was mentioned earlier, but I was afraid you had forgotten. Or weren't paying attention. Or maybe I didn't mention it, I can't remember.

Second, and this is kind of complicated, so hang on: what is transferred over will depend on which keyword is used: CONST or OPTIONS(*VARSIZE). In both cases, we will only bring over as many real digits as specified in the real field definition regardless of how big the PR field is. The difference lies in how the extra characters between the real field and the PR field length when it arrives at the called program are formatted.

> If you specify CONST on the PR subfield, then what will be received at the called program are the number of digits in the real field plus spaces for any digits up to the larger PR field. So, in our example above, CONST would send '123456   ' plus four spaces.

> If you specify OPTIONS(*VARSIZE) on the PR subfield, then what will be received at the called program will be the significant digits from the real field plus undefined characters (not spaces) for the length of the PR subfield. Using the same example as above, we would receive '123456????' in at the called program.

The problem I have is deciding which keyword to use. Oh, it's sooooo hard to choose between them: spaces versus undefined characters. I know I should go for the spaces, but I do love surprises. I am going to let you make the call here. Just be aware of what you are getting yourself into.

All seriousness aside, however, you should not need to worry about this for most normal parameters. You will just set the lengths equal (real field and PR subfield in the calling program) and go on with your life. Where this will come into play is on very large parameters, like if you are passing in several KB or more. Maybe you are screwing around with XML. Although in that case, it can be argued that you deserve what happens to you. Then you might have to define a PR field that is very large to handle a wide variety of occurrences but pass in a varying, potentially smaller, amount. Obviously, if you find yourself in this type of situation, I suggest you do some serious testing.

Now It's Your Turn

I know that all of this stuff is pretty weird, but the fact is no matter how much you might promise yourself you will never set up a program with parm values of different lengths, eventually it is going to be forced on you. Sooooo, you might as well get used to it.

Take your sample calling and called programs and set up some conditions as I have described in the previous sections. After all, you have no guarantee that I haven't made all that stuff up. I mean it's messy enough that most people aren't going to bother to check it out. So I could just make stuff up and call it good. If you think that is not possible, then you don't know me very well. You'd better make sure that I am correct.

Options(*VARSIZE) and VARYING

No discussion of subfield keywords would be complete without at least mentioning OPTIONS(*VARSIZE) and VARYING. They are not new, and they are *not* specifically designed for ILE, so part of me doesn't want to talk about them at all. But I believe there is a certain amount of confusion related to them, and I feel I deserve a chance to make it worse.

OPTIONS(*VARSIZE) is the older of the two, with VARYING having been added in version 4. Like most IBM things, they are similar and yet different, but basically, they "define" the field to which they are attached as a variable-length field where you can store anything from 0 to the maximum number of digits allowed by the length of that field.

Why would we want to use varying-length fields? For a long time, I assumed it was just a desire on the part of some programmers to be difficult, but there is a real reason for it. Almost every opcode in RPG is optimized to be more efficient when dealing with variable-length fields than fixed-length fields. That sounds almost counterintuitive to me, but they say it's true, and IBM has never lied to me yet. This is not a big deal if you have a 10-digit customer number that may range from 4 to 10 digits, but if you are dealing with very large fields, say 10K or more, then the efficiency savings can indeed build up.

Plus, and this will sound a little like an *X-Files* conspiracy thing, but—there seems to be a movement toward using variable fields across the board. I don't know if it's because of the efficiency, or if General Ripper was right and it's in the drinking water, or if it is the very first sign of the coming Zombie Apocalypse, but I see variable-length fields popping up everywhere. Is it possible that I am just a hair paranoid? I actually recently watched *Zombieland* and *Shaun of the Dead*, so I am a bit more on guard than usual. (Those are about the scariest movies I can watch. I still have nightmares from having accidentally seen *The Ring* five years ago.)

The difference between the two keywords is this:

> VARYING will store the current length of the data being held in the field (that is, the length of the current value, not the max length of the field) in the first two digits on the field. You can then use the %LEN BIF to retrieve this length, so that you know how much data you are actually dealing with.

OPTIONS(*VARSIZE) does not do that; you have to figure it out on your own. There are probably other even more esoteric differences between the two, but I don't feel it's my place to point them out. Generally, you will see VARYING more often than OPTIONS(*VARSIZE).

A Quick Review

OK, let's everyone take a deep breath and get our feet back on the ground. If you remember, this all started with a discussion of prototyping and what it means. So let's step back and see what ground we have covered.

First, let's look at the calling program.

We know we will have a PR D-spec with the parms that we are going to send, set up as subfields in the spec.

These fields will also have to be defined somewhere else in the program, be it in another, real D-spec, a file, or whatnot. The PR looks real, but it does not really define a field as an entity.

In the simplest case, the length of a subfield in the PR will be equal to the length in reality.

If the real length of the field is greater than the length specified in the PR subfield, then things will work fine except that the actual data transferred may be truncated when it gets to the called program. But remember that the amount sent will depend on the length of the real field definition, not the length of the subfield in the PR of the calling program.

If the real length of the field is less than the length specified in the PR subfield, then we need to use the CONST keyword on the PR subfield to prevent a problem from occurring. This is the use of the CONST keyword in the calling program.

And then the called program.

We are going to have both a PR and a PI D-spec, and they must match each other in every way (keywords, number/type/length of subfields).

The PI D-spec takes care of defining the parms, so they don't need to be defined anywhere else in the program.

If the CONST keyword is used on any of the subfields, that field may not be modified within the called program, and any instructions that do so will result in compiler errors.

If the length of a subfield in the PR/PI is less than the length in the calling program, there is no problem.

If the length of a subfield in the PR/PI is greater than in the calling program, you will probably have to use the VARYING keyword on the subfields involved to prevent garbage from being transferred in.

What Ya Shoulda Learned

First, we talked about using the CONST keyword on the prototype D-specs.

> If we used this in the called program, then it would prevent us from making any changes to the field carrying that keyword. But at the same time, if the field was very large, it resulted in greater transfer efficiencies.

> If we used this in the calling program, then it let us have an imbalance in the length of the subfield on the PR D-spec and the real representation of that field in the program.

Then, we looked at some general things that we could say about prototype subfield lengths: when they have to be equal, when they don't, and what kinds of problems could arise from these differences. As part of this, we took a moderately detailed look at what happens if the field lengths are not the same, an exercise that you should repeat just so you are clear.

And finally, we looked at the VARYING and OPTIONS(*VARSIZE) keywords and how they can be used if we do end up transferring data of variable lengths. You will definitely want to play around with these in order to get comfortable with them.

Chapter 17

ILE Activation Groups

Several times so far we have mentioned that one of the reasons for going to ILE is to have more control over the application and how it runs. And nothing exemplifies this more than the use of activation groups.

The activation group is nothing more than a sub-environment in which an application runs. It defines a set of resources that support a program app. Things that run in the same activation group share the same resources (e.g., files that are open, overrides).

You can also look at the activation group as a process that occurs when you kick off a program. This process sets up the environment, opens files, opens SQL cursors, defines static variables, and binds service program modules to applications associated with the activation group.

Basic Activation Group Facts

In the OPM world, every program that is invoked runs in its own little environment. If it needs a file, or an override, the program has to open that on its own. Plus, if the same program runs and finishes and then runs again later, that is two times that the run environment has to be set up. Can you spell "overhead"?

ILE programs use activation groups as their run environment, and every ILE program must have an activation group (environment) to run in. What separates ILE from OPM is the ability of ILE programs to share activation groups and to keep an activation group open even though a program ends, so that it can be used over again if that program restarts. That is, the goal of ILE activation groups is twofold.

First, to minimize the amount of time and resources spent creating and destroying run environments. Or at least to give you the control to make intelligent decisions about when that happens.

Second, to run related programs together in the same activation group (keep thinking "environment"), like BFFs, sharing resources and stuff like some sort of '60s hippie commune. Except for the sex and drugs part. And that is both good and bad (the sharing part, not the sex and drugs; RPG programmers don't go for that kind of stuff).

The good part is that sharing is good. Whether it is file opens, overrides, storage space, whatever, it helps the system be more productive overall.

And how could that be bad? Seriously, dude. Is there anything that we can develop that someone can't screw up?

Even though OPM was not very imaginative, it was consistent. A program started, an environment was created. A program ended, an environment was deleted.

But things are not always so simple with ILE. Initially that flexibility gave ILE kind of a bad name with some folks. The activation group gives you more control, which means it also gives you more opportunities to screw yourself over. Below, we will talk about several types of activation groups. Not all of them just go away automatically when the program ends, so be sure to pay attention to that because if you chose those alternatives (and you very well might for good reasons), then you will have to clear off those environments periodically.

And that's the bad news: you will actually have to think about what you are doing and the relationships between your modules, so that you do not create a bunch of unnecessary activation groups that linger after the original program is done.

The other thing that activation groups do is draw boundaries. If we think of file overrides or file cursor settings (SQL cursors, that is), then if there are multiple programs using the same override or cursor, we could actually have one program changing a cursor that is being used in others. By using named activation groups for each of these applications, we are able to set a boundary between the two apps and keep them from hurting each other.

In some ways, this is a slight shift in the way we think about resources. In OPM, the resources seem to be associated with the program. Programs have open files, and so on. But with ILE, the resources clearly belong to the activation group. Programs can come and go and depending on how things are defined; the activation group, and the resources associated with it, can keep on keeping on.

Activation groups may sound intimidating, but they really aren't all that bad. Let's take a look at them.

Default Activation Group Parm (DFTACTGRP)

The starting point for activation groups is the *DFTACTGRP parm on the compile commands. We have already talked about this, but a review is always nice.

If you are in a pure OPM environment (using RPG object-type source modules, QRPGSRC source files, and CRTRPGPGM), then you will not find this parameter on the compile command. OPM doesn't give you the option; it doesn't use activation groups, and "that's the fact, Jack."

ILE uses them, but it does not force you to use a complex activation group. So, if you are using an RPGLE object type, and the CRTBNDRPG command, you will see the DFTACTGRP parm. There are two potential values for this command.

If you specify *YES, that is bad, because that means you are using the default activation group, which is what OPM uses, so there is no chance of you sharing resources or doing other stuff. In essence, you have an "ILE" program that operates just like an OPM program. A lot of people are doing this (especially if they are on an older release of the system) and don't even realize it. They probably think they are doing ILE because they have RPGLE modules. But if you say *YES to this parm, you are totally doing OPM.

If, on the other hand, you say *NO, then you are saying you don't want to use the default activation group—that is, you want to use a real activation group, and so you are going to have a program that is true ILE. And that is what we want you to do.

It is fair at this point to wonder why IBM set this up backwards. I mean, they want you to use ILE. And normally if you want to use something, you answer in the affirmative. But they set this up so that you had to say *NO to get the ILE stuff. But I want you to think about this for a moment. This is IBM, the people who have had 20 years to turn the 400/IBM i into the default operating system for the known universe. 'Nough said.

Now It's Your Turn

I may have asked you to do this before, but it is worth doing again. What compile command are you using to create your programs? Is it CRTBNDRPG? If so, prompt it and see what the default is for the DFTACTGRP parm.

Is it *NO, so that you are automatically doing ILE? Or is it *YES, so that a default compile produces an OPM program? If it is *YES, what strategy do you want to employ in order to make sure your programs compile as true ILE?

Activation Group Types

If you set the DFTACTGRP parm to *NO (I want to be ILE), then another parm will miraculously appear on the compile command: the ACTGRP parm, which lets you set the type/name of the activation group that will be associated with this program. That is, this is where you tell the compile what activation group the program will run in and will be started (unless it already exists) when the program is kicked off. Let's take some time and carefully go through each option.

Just so you know, one of the most important things to notice about each group is how it is ended. With OPM, the environment died when the program did (INLR on), but ILE is not that clear-cut because it wants to give you more control over what happens. In other words, ILE trusts you to make the right decision for your app. Oh, that's so sweet. And yet, sad, oh so sad.

*NEW

If *NEW is specified, then a new activation group will be created for this program when it is run. The name of that activation group will be assigned by the system and will be something weird and freaky.

As a result, if two people call the same program with a *NEW activation group, two differently named activation groups will be started.

If you specify *NEW on every compile, then every program will run in its own activation group and you will have essentially an OPM system. That is probably not what you want, but there are definitely times when *NEW is the right option.

On the positive side, this type of activation group is automatically ended when the program associated with this group ends. Thus, the cleanup is automatic and timely.

On the negative side, if you use *NEW for every program, then you will end up with a ton of activation groups that do not share, and you will be no farther along than if you were OPM.

*NEW is not available for service programs. Because they are always called from somewhere else and so, are not really "new."

"Name"

If a name is entered, one that you have made up, then this name will be used on the activation group. It is basically the same as *NEW except that you are specifying the name rather than letting the system do it, so it might be more intuitive to you. Or it may just be one more thing you have to think about.

Like *NEW, if you specify a specific name on every compile, then you will have essentially an OPM configuration.

The difference is in the end. Named activation groups will persist even after the program has ended. The theory is that if a program whose compile was pointed at this activation group starts up again, it can then grab that activation group and save the overhead of starting one up, so it makes sense if a program ends and restarts pretty regularly. The only way to get rid of one of these is to run a RCLACTGRP (Reclaim Activation Group) command. If you use this for a program that is used frequently, you might want to set up the RCLACTGRP for that name as part of the daily or weekly process. You really probably don't want it to live forever.

One additional characteristic of the named activation group is that any global variables you are using in that program will also be visible (that is, usable) by programs in other named activation groups. Whether you think "hey, that is something handy" or "good grief, why did they allow that?" is up to you and says a lot about your personality. It could be either good or bad; just be aware that it can happen. Of course, if you have perfect ILE modules, you shouldn't have any global variables.

*CALLER

In this case, the program compiled with this will use the activation group of the program that calls it.

Obviously, it makes no sense for *CALLER to be used on the first program in a sequence, but after that it makes lots of sense.

You will find that *CALLER is one of the more popular activation groups that you will use. If you are calling a series of programs in sequence, you might as well run all those programs together, you know, sharing resources and making like you are all friends and everything.

And since it does not really create its own activation group but just gloms you on to an existing one (either a *NEW or named), you don't have to worry about ending it.

But *CALLER should only be used if the program you want to run was called by another program that set up an activation group first. If *CALLER is the first program in the sequence, then the program involved will end up running in the default activation group—something you don't want.

And be careful with *CALLER with service programs. The idea of a service program is that it is called from a number of other programs (hopefully a large number), and the result of setting it up as *CALLER is to get a number of versions of it running in different activation groups, which wastes space and resources. You might be better off to set up your service programs to run in a single, named activation group even though you would have to run a RCLACTGRP regularly. It's something to think about.

QILE

This is *not* the default activation group. The default activation group does not really have a name, it just sort of always exists, and in ILE we do not want to use it.

QILE is simply a name that IBM has assigned (hence the "Q") to a named activation group, so that if you do not specify a name or *NEW or *CALLER, the program will fall back onto the QILE named activation group. In most compile commands, it is the default value assigned to the ACTGRP parm.

Using QILE still makes the program ILE (that is, determined via the DFTACTGRP parm being *NO, not based on the value in the ACTGRP parm). When a QILE group ends, you must use RCLACTGRP to do the reclaim (because it is really a "named" activation group). It won't happen on its own as with *NEW.

Generally, using QILE is frowned upon by the cool kids. The main problem is that it is not very discriminating. That is, you might be using it, but it is also possible that some third-party software you are running might be using it, too. Now if you do a RCLACTGRP on QILE (after all, it is a named activation group) to recover your resources, you will also affect other applications that you might not want to have messed with.

The most important thing I want to remind you of is that you do not specify the activation group you want to use when you run the program. You assign it when you do your compile, so it will be the same every time the program runs until you recompile again. Don't get confused by that.

What Happens When an Activation Group Closes?

So, we have some activation groups where the group goes away when the last program in that group sequence ends, and some activation groups which will live until you use the RCLACTGRP command. In addition, an activation group will go away if every program in that group fails.

But what actually happens when an activation group closes (because what happens will have a direct bearing on how we use them)?

1. First, any files that are being used in the activation group will be closed.

2. Second, any file overrides associated with those files will also disappear.

3. Third, storage (both static and allocated) being tied up by that function will be cleared.

4. Fourth, commitment control will end. That is, database changes will be committed if you are under commitment control (otherwise the changes will take place as they happen).

I don't know about you, but all this is very exciting for me. But then I'm a real thrill seeker.

RCLACTGRP

This is the command you will need to use to reclaim an activation group that does not end on its own.

As we said earlier, any activation group created with a user-defined name ("named") or by using QILE will need to be deactivated manually by the RCLACTGRP command. It will not happen automatically.

This is a very simple command, just the name of the activation group you want to reclaim, plus an option for *NORMAL and *ABNORMAL.

*NORMAL does things in a civilized manner: committing any pending changes and sending a polite close notification message to any attached host systems.

*ABNORMAL just gets you the heck out of Dodge, and if someone gets hurt in the process, that's their problem. It rolls back any uncommitted changes and sends a rather nasty and abrupt message to any attached host systems.

The command should only be used when the activation group is not in use.

There is an option for the activation group name to use, *ELIGIBLE, in which case the command will close all activation groups not currently running a job. Using this is not a good idea and should be avoided as it can result in your closing groups that you did not mean to (and which you have no control over, such as third-party groups).

As a parting shot, if you are used to using RCLRSC, stop it. Just stop it right now! It doesn't work well in the ILE world, and you should be reclaiming resources by controlling your activation groups.

So, How Should Activation Groups Be Used?

Oh, I know what you want.

You want me to tell you exactly how to use the activation groups. What to use and when. Yeah, that sounds like a win-win for me. It will be almost like being at home with my family. They love to get advice from me.

But, I suppose there are some things I could say.

First, let's consider the two values *NEW and named.

> We said before that the difference between them was that *NEW assigns the name automatically, and named leaves that assignment up to you. But there is one other difference, too.
>
> If you use *NEW, then the activation group ends when the last program in that group ends. It polices its own existence very nicely. That is because IBM assigns the name and so feels a certain responsibility for it.
>
> But if you use named, then you have to do a RCLACTGRP to get it to stop. You name it, you reclaim it. Oh, yeah.
>
> What seems to be important here is: how often is the stinkin' job going to run? If it runs once every time the moon occults Arcturus, (one of my favorite stars), then I would think that it makes sense to have this run under *NEW so that cleanup occurs automatically when it is done. Chances are it is not going to run twice in a day, so you don't lose anything by using *NEW and letting the system name the activation group.
>
> On the other hand, if it is going to run repeatedly all day, then it makes sense to have an activation group just sitting out there waiting for the program to show up. In this case, make it named. But just remember to do a RCLACTGRP at the end of the day or whenever this job is likely to be done.

What does matter is the use of the *CALLER activation group. Anytime you have a situation where you have one program calling others in a group and you want to share resources (including overrides), the first program should be either *NEW or named, and the others should be *CALLER. Which option you use (*NEW or named) will depend on how you feel about being the one who cleans up the activation groups.

And what about QILE?

While you could use it to run your programs, it is probably the worst option to use simply because everybody might be using it, and you could very easily end up in a reclaim situation or an override situation that is not in the best interests of your application. The smart money here is on *NEW/named and *CALLER.

As I said earlier, the cool kids do not recommend using QILE, but the truth is I have seen references that go both ways.

One source that I consulted thought QILE was fine even though it required the reclaim.

Another source thought it was the worst option, and the author became visibly agitated when it appeared someone was going to use it. So much for the experts.

If it matters, IBM does not recommend QILE, and instead suggests the use of named activation groups. IBM make a good point in that activation groups were designed to represent applications, and so using a generic one is not exactly what they had in mind. Although the way they have marketed the i is not exactly what I had in mind (I would consider using the blonde, British girl from the Viagra commercials as their spokesperson), so you can decide. Plus, there is a difference between IBM technical advice and marketing advice.

In the end, the general rule of thumb is to start the first program in a sequence (like the C of an MVC) in a *NEW or named activation group, depending on whether you want to do the cleanup or have it done for you and how likely it is that the job will be rerun (and so can take advantage of an activation group that is just sitting out there waiting).

And most things that are called from that first program should be *CALLER.

And Service Programs?

The exception to this is service programs. Remember, service programs can be potentially called from a large number of other programs. So if you have a service program that is called by many apps and you use *CALLER for it, it could result in a copy of it being in many different activation groups.

But by naming the activation group of the service program when it is called, that activation group could stay open and be available to those many calls. The connection to the calling programs is still intact, as that is set up through the EXPORT keyword and the binding language entries. You would have to remember, however, that if you did this, then the static and global variables of the service program are going to be available to other environments, something that could be either good or bad. Or a non-issue. Plus, of course, you would have to clean up after it yourself. You should never let the need to clean up determine your choice of activation group types. Just remember to not forget it. Setting up the RCLACTGRP in a CL program that runs automatically once a day or whatever is probably the best way.

Bottom Line

But most important of all, pay attention to what needs to be done, if anything, to end an activation group. Don't just assume it will happen because as we have seen in some cases, it doesn't. And also pay attention to your programs, and to setting INLR on if you want the activation group to end.

Yeah, that's the bitch of ILE: it gives you flexibility, but it forces you to take ownership and make some decisions. Welcome to the new millennium. Glad I could help simplify things.

WRKJOB: Work with Job Command

Just a final note about this command, as you may have not thought about it.

With this command you can see the activation groups that are involved with your job. Specifically, option 11 shows you the programs in the job and the activation group they are running in. Option 18 then shows you a list of the activation groups involved.

Now It's Your Turn

Before you go any further, I think it would be a good idea to stop and think just a bit about how you see activation groups playing out and how you would use them.

If you are already using ILE, how are you using the various types of activation groups? Do you see yourself making any changes to that approach?

If you are not using ILE yet, where do you see yourself starting to incorporate it? And as you do that, how will you use activation groups to help make your programs more efficient and self-contained?

What Ya Shoulda Learned

See, I told ya that activation groups were easy. Short chapter. Nonetheless, you should have learned a couple of things.

First, how activation groups define a startup environment and why they are an essential part of the ILE environment.

And how that is also related to the end of the application and the cleanup that is kicked off.

Understand the difference between *NEW and named activation groups, particularly with respect to what each requires in terms of cleanup activities.

Know when to use *CALLER (i.e., after you have already established an activation group via *NEW, named, or QILE).

Understand the limitations and weaknesses of using the QILE default.

Chapter 18

Service Program Compile Stuff

When we talked about service programs in chapter 10, we kept it very simple. But is simple really where you live? I don't think so.

As you might guess, service programs are not a one-size-fits-all kind of thing, and where there is flexibility, there is often complexity. It's not a lot, but there are a few additional things you should know in order to fully understand and set up your service programs for maximum efficiency.

So let's take a look at what those things are before we go any further.

Binding

Let's start by quickly reminding ourselves what binding is and how it fits into the ILE environment.

Binding is nothing new; it has been around for a long time. It is the process of relating two programs together (the calling and the called programs) so that when you access one from the other, much of the overhead is already taken care of and the whole "call" thing goes quicker.

Of course, you are not forced to do binding. BOPs (Big Ol' Programs) do not worry about binding. You do everything in one program. There are no calls, no binding, no worries. There is also, probably, no way that you can reliably enhance or modify this thing after a few years go by.

But anytime you are calling one program from another, you are using binding. This, of course, is exactly what happens in a modular environment, and the basic thrust of ILE is in that direction. There are two flavors that this binding comes in: *dynamic* and *static*.

Dynamic sounds better, doesn't it? Everything that is dynamic is better than something that is static. But that is not always true, and it happens that for us, static is better than dynamic.

Dynamic Binding

This happens when neither the calling nor the called program knows anything about the other. It's like a big surprise birthday party.

That is, you don't do any kind of pre-compile binding, you just compile each program separately, and then call one from the other. Suddenly, when the call occurs, the two programs become aware of each other and form a connection. All of the overhead responsible for the "call" happens at this point, and so if this is a connection that happens many times while the app is running, it can become excessive and contribute to slow response time.

It is nice, because you don't have to plan ahead for this. It's also nice because since the bind happens when the programs run, we can modify them independently of each other. That is, I can change the called program and not have to redo the compile/bind of the calling program. But it's bad because it can really slow things down if the connection happens repeatedly. Dynamic binding is old-school.

And how do you get dynamic binding? Remember? Just compile the calling and the called program separately. The call between the two will then function not knowing a thing about the other program.

Static Binding

Static binding is the opposite. It is planned and prepared for ahead of time, with much of the work being done at compile time.

In order to set up static binding, you need to follow a two-step process. You start by creating modules (*MODULE) for all the programs involved (CRTRPGMOD or PDM option 15), and then tie them together to form a program with CRTPGM where you list the modules involved.

The advantage here is that you get a lot of the overhead out of the way when you do the compile, and so you have a very fast connect.

The disadvantage is that you have to think ahead and take preemptive action. That's harder for some folks than others. It's also a problem because now, since we bound them together when we compiled them, if either program changes, we need to recreate the changed modules and rebind them together.

And how do you get static binding set up? Simple, just compile both the calling and the called programs as modules (CRTRPGMOD, PDM option 15), and then issue the CRTPGM command to tie the two together.

Now I want to be clear here. This is not ILE. This is the way it has always been. But in the ILE world, static binding is preferred over dynamic binding. I wish they had called it "good binding" and "bad binding"; it would be easier to remember then, but nobody asked me what I thought. Story of my life.

What Does This Have to Do with Service Programs?

Service programs make use of binding, but the situation is a bit more robust than the chocolate-vanilla situation just described.

To start with, let's remember that a sub-procedure cannot exist on its own: it must be embedded in a service program or a regular program. And if it is in a regular program, you cannot call the sub-procedure by itself; you have to call that program as a whole and then somehow get into the sub-procedure. Only a service program can house a sub-procedure and let you call it separately from the rest of the sub-procedures in the service program. And only the service program uses the H-spec, NOMAIN, which removes the main cycle processing from that program.

In other words, service programs are a bit different from "normal" programs. And how they handle binding is a little different as well. To see this, let's review how you create a service program block (the service program and the calling program).

You start by converting your service program source to a module.

> Despite what you might think, this is a required step. Even if you choose all the defaults, you cannot create a service program unless that service program first exists as a *MODULE. Bottom line: you need to do this. Keep in mind, this is the "compile" per se, and so if you want to debug or anything, you need to specify it in the command or with an H-spec.

```
CRTRPGMOD MODULE('service program ID')
```

Then, you turn that module into a service program.

```
CRTSRVPGM SRVPGM('service program ID')
          EXPORT(*SRCFILE or *ALL)
```

> That is fairly simple, and we will talk later (chapter 21) about the difference between *SRCFILE and *ALL in the EXPORT parm. For the moment, let's use *ALL even though that is not the default.

The next step is to convert the calling program to a module.

```
CRTRPGMOD MODULE('calling program ID')
```

This can be done before or after you do the CRTSRVPGM. What is important here is that before the next step you have a service program (the output of the CRTSRVPGM) and a program module for the calling program (the output of CRTRPGMOD for the calling program).

The final step is to then create the final, bound program that combines both the calling program and the service program.

I generally name this program the same as the calling program (since we have only created that as a module so far), but you don't have to do it that way (you can name this program whatever you want).

```
CRTPGM PGM('calling program name' or 'other name')
       MODULE('calling program module name')
       BNDSRVPGM('service prog module name' /
           'library'                          /
           '*DEFER or *IMMED')
```

Now, what is interesting is the last parm, BNDSRVPGM. It actually consists of three pieces.

The first is the name of the service program module that is being bound in.

The second is the library that this service program module lives in. Prior to 7.3, this had to be a physical file in a library. But with 7.3, it became possible to include a stream file as the source of the source.

The third is the one that is interesting because the available values are either *IMMED or *DEFER. And it is the choice here that makes all the difference in how your service program works.

If you specify *IMMED, then the two programs (your calling program and your service program) are bound together at the time that the compile is done. This is static binding in that now your calling program and service program modules are bound together, and if you change the service program, you are going to have to not only recreate the service program but do the CRTPGM command again to bring in the new source for the changed service program. But it is really fast.

If you specify *DEFER, then the bind is delayed until you call that service program from the calling program. This is not quite as efficient because that overhead work gets done when you do the call, but it also means that since the service program source is not bound in at compile time, I can change the service program and not have to create the calling program all over again. If the service program you have changed is used by a large number of calling programs, this can save you a great deal of time.

It is not obvious from the command, but the default if not entered is *DEFER.

Which one should you choose? It depends on what you want. Do you have a service program that is used by a large number of other programs and which may be likely to change? Then using *DEFER is probably a good option. If, however, you don't think the service program is likely to change and/or it is not called from that many places and you'd like to reap the extra efficiency, then *IMMED might be a better choice.

One final thing I should mention is that you might very well have multiple service programs bound to a single calling program (for example, if the calling program calls multiple sub-procedures from multiple service programs). This can be handled quite simply because you can enter multiple BNDSRVPGM parm sets. It is also a good time to bring in binding directories, which we will discuss in the next chapter.

What Happens When You Call a Service Program?

OK, we now have a handle on binding service programs and what some of the pros and cons might be in using them.

In a few minutes, we will look at some of the types of problems, er I mean situations that you can run into when working with service programs.

But before we do that, I want to take a closer look at exactly what happens when a program calls a sub-procedure in a service program.

We know from chapter 10 that the call occurs when we issue a CALLP with the object being the name of the sub-procedure that we want to access. There is no information in that call about the name of the service program that contains that sub-procedure, so how does the system find it?

That should be an easy-to-answer question because we saw a page or two ago that when we do the CRTPGM and bind the calling and service programs together, we actually specify the service program name(s).

So now we have two pieces of information: the sub-procedure name from the CALLP (or rather, actually from the PR D-spec EXTPGM parm), and the service program name(s) from the CRTPGM command (either via the BNDSRVPGM or the BNDDIR parm).

The logical thing to think at this point is that the i starts with the first service program listed in the CRTPGM and begins searching through till it finds a sub-procedure whose name matches the one from the calling program's PR D-spec. But life is rarely as simple as we envision it.

The i does indeed search, but it does not go through the service programs. Instead, it searches through a list that is associated with the service program. Where does this list come from? Hang on. For the moment, just know that it looks through the "list," finds an entry that matches the sub-procedure name from the calling program PR D-spec, and then notices what sequential number that sub-procedure name is in the list. Let's say it is the third one down.

The i then goes out to the service program already identified and finds the sub-procedure with the same sequence number, in this case the third one in the service program, and with complete disregard for what the name of this sub-procedure might actually be, executes it because the position in the service program matches the position in the list.

One thing you might be wondering about here is where in the service program does the system look? Does it look at the list of PRs or at the actual procedures in the program? Normally these will be in the same order, but not necessarily. As it turns out, the system goes through the actual source of the program and ignores the PRs in trying to determine which sub-procedure is called.

The other thing you might be wondering is: why does IBM do this? Why do they look at a list and then use a relative position in that list rather than just looking for the sub-procedure in the service program? And the answer is, efficiency. It is much faster to look in a short list, then determine the relative position in that list (like the index of an array), and then find that position in a service program than it is to search through a service program looking for a name match. This makes sense, but it does leave some room for problems if you are not careful. More on that later.

Anyway, the next question is: where does the list come from? Well, if you compile your service program (CRTSRVPGM) with the EXPORT (Export Source Member) keyword set to *SRCFILE, then the system will look for a binding language source member to use as that list. If one does not exist, there will be a compile error. The spot where this source file is located is then given by the SRCFILE and SRCMBR keywords. We will talk about binding language in chapter 20, but for now just know that you have to set up your binding language source file before you compile your service program, if you are using it.

But if you set EXPORT to *ALL, then the system will, during the compile, look at the service program and create its own behind-the-scenes list that shows the order of the sub-procedures in that service program.

And this is the list, whether created by you via binding language (see chapter 20) or auto-created by the system, that will be used to find the position of a sub-procedure in that service program. It does not throw this list out into a source file so that you can see it, but it creates an object list just the same.

And don't worry about the binding language references above. We will cover that in chapter 20.

What Can Go Wrong

Of course, any time you have a lot of flexibility and options, things can go wrong. I suppose that is not the best way to sell service programs, but sometimes bad things happen to good things.

So what do you need to watch out for in terms of service programs?

Calling the Wrong Sub-Procedure

Yes, it may be hard to believe, but you can actually call the wrong sub-procedure in a service program. That is, you might have sub-procedures A and B in the service program, and you mean to call A, but you end up kicking off B instead.

The primary reason for this is because of the "finding things by relative list position" thing. If we picked them up by name instead of their spot on a list, this wouldn't occur. But we don't, and so it can.

The good news is that it only happens in a very specific circumstance, and there are a number of things you can do to minimize the chances of this ever happening. We'll discuss this in detail in chapter 20.

Signature Violations

The second thing is what is known as a *signature violation*. I won't go into all the details here. See chapter 21 for the whole ugly story. We will just say that the service program signature is similar to a level check except that it is quite a bit different. But you'll see when we get there.

Other than that, it's pretty bulletproof. And very handy, so don't decide you don't want to do service programs because you might have one of the two problems mentioned earlier. That would be very short-sighted indeed.

What Ya Shoulda Learned

The main emphasis here is on binding.

We start with the classic definitions of static and dynamic binding and look at how they relate to even OPM programs.

The next step takes us back through the compile process for a service program and its calling program because they are treated a little differently from regular programs.

As part of this compile review, we saw that we have a number of parms in the compile commands that exert a great effect on the objects. Specifically, we have *SRCFILE and *ALL on the EXPORT parm of the CRTSRVPGM, which we will talk about in chapter 20, and the *DEFER and *IMMED values on the BNDSRVPGM parm of the CRTPGM command.

We talked about the *DEFER and *IMMED values here and saw that using *IMMED causes the calling program and service program to be bound at compile time the way a normal bind works. *DEFER, on the other hand, doesn't actually bind until the run occurs. Both methods have their pros and cons, and you should be able to describe what those benefits/weaknesses are. Can you?

We then went on with a blow by blow description of the sequence of events when a program calls a sub-procedure in a service program.

Finally, we named the two things that can happen to cause problems when you are accessing a service program. Can you tell me what those two problems are? We promised more details on them in a subsequent chapter.

And that's about it. But time wanes, and we must move on. There are two things that you keep running into when you talk about service programs: binding directories and binding language. Let's dive into them next and see what all the fuss is about.

Chapter 19

Binding Directories

Starting to feel just a bit woozy?

I can dig it. We have covered a lot of material, and there might have even been small sections that were not that exciting. But don't despair. We are almost through with the ~~hard~~ boring ILE stuff. MVC is much ~~easier~~ more exciting.

We are going to keep our attention on service programs at this point because there are a couple more things that should be discussed. And we are going to start with binding directories.

At this point, I want to say something very important. Are you ready? I always like to warn people when something important is going to be said. Generally, it tends to be a bit of a surprise for most people. When I say it, at least. But, here we go. Over the next two chapters we are going to talk about two things: *binding directories* and *binding language*. What is important to know is that they are not really related. A binding directory is *not* a place where a bunch of binding language objects are stored. They share the word "binding," but that is about all they share. But I can't say anything more because it will spoil the surprise.

> Binding directories involve the calling program and are solely designed to make it easier to write out the compile command for that calling program.

> Binding language involves the service program and the sub-procedures that are exported from it.

OK. I feel better now having warned you. Ready to continue? We are going to start with the binding directories.

Binding Directories

The first thing I should probably say is that binding directories are not required.

You can do service programs and all that without them, and, in fact, we have done service programs and all that and haven't used them (see chapter 9). But, as we shall see, they can come in really handy once you have more than one service program, and my guess is eventually you will.

To understand where binding directories come into play, let's return to our compile scenario for the program that calls a sub-procedure from a service program. And specifically, let's remember that when we call the service program, we actually call the sub-procedure that we want to use, not the service program per se. So the question immediately surfaces as to how the system finds that sub-procedure. How does it know what service program to look into? In other words, how do we bind that service program to the calling program during the compile when we only know the sub-procedure name?

And the answer to that, as we saw in the last chapter, is when you do the CRTPGM on the calling program, you enter the name of the service program you want to bind to—that is, the one that contains the sub-procedure you are accessing. You do this in the BNDSRVPGM parameter of the CRTPGM command. And that's it; no need for binding directories or any of that pretty boy stuff. When the system is ready to call a sub-procedure, it looks at the list of service programs in this BNDSRVPGM parm, starting with the first one entered, and looks for the sub-procedure we are trying to call. It gets picked up and executed, and the system just a keeps on a rollin'.

But what happens if you are accessing multiple sub-procedures from multiple service programs? Yes, you can put a plus sign in the BNDSRVPGM parm and get several slots in which to type service program IDs, but that could wear a bit thin if you had many service programs or if you were the type of person who makes typos. Remember, you would have to put all of them in every time you did a recompile of the calling program. Maybe that wouldn't happen very often. Maybe it would.

The purpose of the binding directory is simply to allow you to create a "list" of service programs that should be bound to this calling program and then allow you to key in that binding directory name (in the BNDDIR parm of the CRTPGM command) rather than a list of service programs (in the BNDSRVPGM parm). You end up entering less data with the compile (or H-spec), and it uses the binding directory as an intermediary in finding the name of the service program. CRTPGM is the only command that has a spot for binding directory. It is not in CRTRPGMOD or CRTBNDRPG.

The directory contains a list of the service programs that have specifically been added to the directory. It does not carry a copy of the program object (or source) itself, so there is no code or object duplication.

In addition to service programs, you can also just list modules, the output of CRTRPGMOD for programs that you want to bind into the calling program. We generally think of binding directories for service programs, but they do modules, too.

What is important to remember is that even though the binding directory is described here as a list, it is an object (*BNDDIR), not just a source file, and it is set up and maintained through a series of system commands that we will see in a minute. Binding directories are an object set up via system commands.

Big Directories or Small?

One thing you might be thinking right now is, should I just put all my service programs in one big binding directory, or should I have several smaller ones?

I have no clear answer on that. If you use a big directory, then even though a thousand service programs are listed there, the system will only pick up and bind the ones that you are actually accessing from your calling program. So you won't have a size penalty.

On the other hand, if you have different parts of your system that are really different from each other and there is no overlap, then several directories might make a lot of sense from a separation point of view. There is room in the CRTPGM command for multiple binding directories, so you are limited only by your own common sense. I know. It's a thin layer of protection, isn't it?

Using an H-spec

Of course, even with the use of binding directories, it can get a little tedious
filling out your compile command by hand. Fortunately, there is an H-spec
that you can incorporate right in your program to take care of that for you.

```
H  BNDDIR('name')
```

or

```
ctl-opt  BNDDIR('name');
```

Binding Directory Commands

A binding directory is not a source file list, but an object created and maintained
by a set of commands.

First, the CRTBNDDIR (Create Binding Directory) command:

```
CRTBNDDIR BNDDIR (bnddir-name)
```

As you might expect, it creates the directory. This is it, sort of like the CRTLIB
command, with no extra parms. Although now that I think of it, CRTLIB has a
few extra parms, so never mind. It creates an object with a type *BNDDIR in a
library. You don't create this object with a compile, just with this command.

Second, the ADDBNDDIRE (Add Entries to the Binding Directory) command:

```
ADDBNDDIRE OBJ((obj1 obj-type1) (obj2 obj-type2) ...)
```

This adds service programs or other modules to a directory once it is set up.
Only the name is added here, not the object. That is, it adds the name of a
service program to your *BNDDIR object, but it does not include a copy of the
service program object as well. The *SRVPGM object is picked up when you
run the program that has this binding directory attached to it.

There is also a POSITION parm that lets you decide, if you are setting up a
series of binding directories, where this one goes with respect to the others.

The default value is *LAST, but there is also *FIRST, *REPLACE, *BEFORE, and *AFTER. For the *BEFORE and *AFTER parms, you can then specify the name of the binding directory you are making reference to.

Third, the RMVBNDDIRE (Remove Binding Directory) command:

```
RMVBNDDIRE OBJ((obj1 obj-type1) (obj2 obj-type2) ...)
```

This removes a binding directory from the object.

Fourth, the WRKBNDDIR (Work with Binding Directory) command:

```
WRKBNDDIR BNDDIR(bnddir-name, *ALL)
```

This provides you with a work command that, by using *ALL as the binding directory name, lets you see what binding directories are out there.

Fifth, the WRKBNDDIRE (Work with Binding Directory Entries) command:

```
WRKBNDDIRE BNDDIR(bnddir-name)
```

The second "work with" command requires you to know the name of the directory you want to work with. But it takes you right into the functions you want to do, whereas with WRKBNDDIR you need two steps.

Depending on what information you have (whether or not you have the name), you can choose the command that is most useful.

To Binding Directory or Not

And the answer is, it's up to you. They are not required; you can easily (sort of) just key the list of service programs you are binding your calling program to in the CRTPGM command every time you compile. And so maybe it depends on how often you change your calling programs. In a perfect world, that might not happen that often. On the other hand, the world, for most of us, is far from perfect.

All in all, I think it's useful, especially if you use an H-spec to tie it in. It saves time, prevents keying errors, is easy to set up—there's no real downside. Seems like a useful tool to me. But it's up to you.

What Ya Shoulda Learned

Pretty straightforward here.

First, you should know what binding directories are used for. Go on, go back and look it up, but put it into your own words. Please use proper English and *no* profanity!

Second, you should know that the binding directory is an object, not a source file. What is the object type?

Third, what happens if you don't use a binding directory? What data has to be placed on what parm on what command, so that the system knows where to find the sub-procedure that you call from that module?

Fourth, you should know where on the compile command (which command and what parm) the binding directory information can be entered.

Fifth, what is the H-spec that you can use to put the binding directory information into the compile command?

And finally, you should remember the commands you use to set up the binding directory and maintain its entries.

Chapter 20

ILE Binding Language

OK. All checked out on binding directories (chapter 19)?

Good. Remember, their only function is to make it easier for you to fill out the compile command (CRTPGM) for a program accessing service programs by giving you a pre-created object (not source) that contains the names of all the sub-procedures you are accessing. Now we will move on to something with a similar name but a different function.

Binding language is not difficult, but it is multi-faceted. That is, binding directories did only one thing, but binding language provides a number of capabilities that will affect how you do service programs, and a good working knowledge of it is required for strong gums and healthy teeth. Hmmm, you know, I might have to check that last thing. I mean it can't hurt, right?

Ready?

What Is Binding Language?

We will start with a simple question: what is binding language?

Actually, it is not a language at all but rather a pretty limited set of statements that help the service programs function.

These statements are not runnable from the command line but must be placed in a source member, preferably in QSRVSRC (you may have to create that). This source member will then be picked up and compiled as part of the CRTSRVPGM.

The member name you *must* use is the name of the service program.

The reason you might as well use QSRVSRC as your source file is that this is the default name used in the RTVBNDSRC command, which we will talk about in a few minutes. It is probably also the default value in the CRTSRVPGM command, but I don't remember offhand.

The source type that should be assigned to this member is BND.

I want to be sure to mention that binding language is not necessary to creating and using service programs. Again, we did one in chapter 9 and did not use binding language. On the other hand, we shall see when we talk about signatures that using it does make things easier, so you might want to partake.

What Is EXPORT?

Before we go on, let's say something about the word EXPORT that is used on the beginning P-spec of a sub-procedure in a service program.

EXPORT basically relates to the ability to use (call) a sub-procedure from a program outside of the service program it is in. I know that sounds kind of weird, but the way service programs have been implemented by IBM it is not a given that you can use a sub-procedure outside of the service program it is in. That is, it's not a given that you can call a sub-procedure in a service program from another program outside of that service program.

> That is, when you put a sub-procedure into a service program you can, by default, call (use) that sub-procedure only in that service program. Do you see what I am saying there? Cause I would probably miss it. I am saying that when I put a sub-procedure in a service program and don't do anything else, I can only call that sub-procedure from other sub-procedures in that specific service program. I can't call it from an external point.

> Why would you want to do that (only call it from within the service program it is in)? Maybe it accesses data from one or more files that is then used in a second sub-procedure in the service program to determine if the customer should be allowed to order. Or maybe it is something that you don't want other programs to be able to kick off, for security reasons. How do I know why you might do this?

What is important is that unless you put the EXPORT keyword on the beginning P-spec of a given sub-procedure, you can only use that sub-procedure in the service program it belongs to. You will remember in chapter 10 we did in fact use that keyword and so were able to call that sub-procedure externally.

I just didn't want you to be confused because we will use the word EXPORT a lot in this chapter and the next.

And remember, EXPORT does not go on the PR or PI D-spec. It goes only on the beginning P-spec.

The Binding Language Commands

OK, now let's look at how you would set up the source file that contains binding language statements. We don't know if or why we would use it yet, but let's start with the simple task of building it.

Every binding language source file will have three different types of commands in it. All three must be present for the whole thing to work.

STRPGMEXP—starting the program export list

EXPORT—the name of the module you want to export

ENDPGMEXP—ending the program export list

STRPGMEXP—Start Program Export

This is the first command in the binding language source member, and it kicks off the processing of the sub-procedures listed via the EXPORT command. Here is what it looks like, with the parameters associated with it.

```
STRPGMEXP  PGMLVL(*CURRENT/*PRV)
           LVLCHK(*YES/*NO)
           SIGNATURE(*GEN/hex value/char value)
```

The PGMLVL parm indicates whether the program level is to be the current list or a previous list.

> A given binding language source member may contain more than one STRPGMEXP-ENDPGMEXP structure. There must be one, but only one, that uses the *CURRENT parm, and this indicates the most recent list of exportable sub-procedures. The others will be *PRV.

> The idea behind a STRPGMEXP structure that uses *PRV was to allow you to hold on to old listings (old signatures) and have the calling program check not just against the current signature but old ones as well. Don't worry now, this will make more sense in the next chapter.

For the moment, we will just use *CURRENT.

The LVLCHK parm indicates whether we will use the signature that is generated (however that might happen) to edit against the service program, similar to what we would do with a program level check and a file. You generally want this set to *YES, although we will discuss signatures more in the next chapter.

The SIGNATURE parm tells the system whether to generate a signature automatically or to use a hexadecimal or character value that is supplied with the command. Again, more on this in the next chapter. What is important now is to remember that you can modify what type of signature you use here in the binding language.

EXPORT—Export

This is *not* the EXPORT keyword on the beginning P-spec of a sub-procedure. But it does relate to exporting. This command defines the sub-procedure name that is to be exported from this particular service program.

```
EXPORT SYMBOL(sub-procedure-name)
```

Only one sub-procedure name can be specified on each EXPORT command. Thus you may have a bunch of them in your binding source member if the service program has a large number of sub-procedures.

You can either enclose the above procedure name in quotes or not. If you do not, it will automatically be converted to upper case. If you do use quotes, then it will keep whatever mixed-case syntax that you specify. Since this name must match the name of the procedure in the service program (including case), it is not a good idea to be casual about this. For RPG you would probably not want to bother with quotes, just in case you end up mixing cases when you type in the name.

When creating your EXPORT statements, you can't just throw them in there willy-nilly. They must be in the order of the sub-procedures in the service program they apply to. Failure to do this could result in your calling the wrong sub-procedure.

ENDPGMEXP—End Program Export

This ends the list of procedures to be exported from a service program and is the last statement in the binding language source member.

There are no parms for this command.

A typical example of a binding language source member would be:

```
STRPGMEXP

EXPORT(edit_vendno)
EXPORT(edit_buyer_code)
EXPORT(return_vname)
EXPORT(return_YTD_PO)

ENDPGMEXP
```

Don't forget that you could, if you want, have several of these structures. One of them must have the PGMLVL parm set to *CURRENT (which is the default), and the others must be set to *PRV. As we will see when we talk about signatures, we do not have to use *PRV structures. They are optional, and you may decide you want no part of that freakiness.

Plus, each service program that you create (type SRVPGM) should have a corresponding binding language source file (type BND). That is, if you use binding language. Remember, it's not mandatory.

RTVBNDSRC Command

Before we move on, we should take a quick look at this command.

So far, we have sort of been thinking that we would create the binding language source file (that is, the stuff above) by manually keying in the data, and there is nothing wrong with that.

If you want something a little more automatic, however, you can use the RTVBNDSRC command to create the binding language source for a given module or service program.

The command creates a member in the QSRVSRC file for the particular service program you run the command over. At first glance, you might think that this command should allow you to span several service programs, but that is not the way that binding language works. Each binding language list relates to just one service program.

The command can be run for either add or replace mode, so it can be used to create as well as update the member on an ongoing basis. If you did run it in an update mode, please remember that you would still have to recompile the service program to take your source changes and roll them into the object.

Triggering Binding Language Use

So far we have talked about what binding language is and what it looks like but not how it gets turned on. After all, we didn't use it in chapter 10, and so it's not automatic.

The key is the EXPORT parm in the CRTSRVPGM command. It has two values.

*SRCFILE

This is the command default. In this case, the compile goes to look for a source file with a name equal to the service program name in the QSRVSRC source file. This is what kicks off using the binding language that you have put in that source file as what determines what sub-procedures are allowed to be exported. And, if it doesn't find the properly named file, the compile will fail.

If you don't use this parm, then even if you have a binding language source file set up, the CRTSRVPGM doesn't use it.

*ALL

This option does not use the binding language source, even if it exists. Instead the compile looks at the service program itself and makes a list of the sub-procedures from that source that have the EXPORT keyword on their beginning P-spec. And that is the whole point of this: to get a list of the sub-procedures that are in a service program. Otherwise, we might not bother. Might not—because binding language does other things as well.

What Binding Language Doesn't Do

Not to start on a negative note, but I thought we would begin by looking at a couple of things that binding language doesn't do.

Binding Language Is Not Needed for Export

I know I have seen articles that say that for certain types of exports you need to use binding language. Specifically, for cases where you are calling a service program sub-procedure from a program outside of the service program module.

But that's not what my testing shows. Just for the record here, when I am using service programs I try to be good and follow all the rules. So I don't spend my days doing weird things. Seems like a waste of time. But for this book I did try weird things to see how far the rules can be bent. I see no evidence that you have to use binding language for certain types of exports.

Binding Language Doesn't Prevent the Wrong Sub-Procedure from Being Called

OK, this relates to what we said in chapter 19 about the fact that it is possible, in a service program, to call the wrong sub-procedure. And, again, I have seen articles that imply that using binding language prevents this from happening, and I think that is a bit of an overstatement. Now, this will take a few minutes, but stay with me.

Suppose you have a service program that has more than one sub-procedure. Let's say it has two. And let's say that they are Procedure1 and Procedure2, listed in the service program in that order. Feel free to follow along at home with this one using a service program you have written. By this time, it shouldn't be any big deal at all to write one.

Start by creating a binding language source for that service program, with the sub-procedures listed with Procedure1 first and Procedure2 second. Save that in QSVRSRC.

Next, just to make sure we are kosher, let's compile the service program in the procedure 1-2 configuration using the CRTRPGMOD and CRTSRVPGM combo with the EXPORT parm set to *SRCFILE (that is, we will be using binding language). Be sure to do the CRTRPGMOD so that you can get into debug.

Then compile your calling program, set to call Procedure2, with CRTRPGMOD (again set up for debug), and then CRTPGM to tie everything together.

Set a breakpoint in the calling program where you call the sub-procedure and start the program. Use **F22** to jump into your service program, and you should jump in at the start of Procedure2. So far, so good.

Now go into the source for the service program and move Procedure1 so that it is after Procedure2. Go ahead, I will wait. And then, recompile it (first as a module: CRTRPGMODW with debug, and then CRTSRVPGM, again using *SRCFILE). But don't recompile the calling program. We want a way to be able to change the service program but not have to recompile the calling program. You have to recompile the service program, of course, because when the program runs, the IBM i doesn't run the source but the object. Am I being too elementary?

Now, call this service program from a calling program that is calling Procedure2. Put the calling program in debug and use **F22** to jump from calling to called (the service program). What sub-procedure is accessed, Procedure1 or Procedure2?

And the answer is `Procedure1`. Even though `Procedure2` is now the first sub-procedure in the service program, the compile with `*SRCFILE` has used the binding language list in QSRVSRC, and we have picked up the second sub-procedure (`Procedure1`).

Now go in, and just do the CRTSRVPGM using `*ALL` as the EXPORT parm. Then redo the CRTPGM so that you pick up the new service program, and repeat your test. Which sub-procedure is picked up? That's right. This time you pick up `Procedure2`. `*ALL` has generated a new list of all modules with the EXPORT keyword on the P-spec.

Now at this point, binding language aficionados will say, "but you need to change the binder source when you switch the order of the sub-procedures," and they are right. If we had changed the binding language source file when we swapped the sub-procedures and compiled the service program using `*SRCFILE`, then we would have ended up calling the right sub-procedure.

But you can also argue that if you hadn't used `*SRCFILE`, that is, if you hadn't used binding language, you wouldn't have run into this.

And because of that, right now you are probably thinking, "I ain't using no binding language," but it may not be that simple. You will want to hold off making a decision until we go through signatures in the next chapter.

Does This Really Happen?

Of course, any normal person at this point will say, "but who is going to move their sub-procedures around in a service program? Is this really going to happen in the real world?"

Let's skip the fact that I might rearrange things in a service program so that like modules are near each other (a total waste of time, but one that sounds like the kind of thing I would do).

Rearrangement doesn't happen, but often it occurs when you add or delete sub-procedures from a service program. That will push a given sub-procedure up or down in the list position and so is where you might run into this.

For this reason, it is recommended that you add new items to the bottom of your service program. But that in itself doesn't fix things. You still have to recompile and rebind, and so you still have the situation described above.

Besides, if you add or delete sub-procedures, then you run into signature violations, and that will catch you before you can run the wrong sub-procedure. But that is a topic for the next chapter.

That doesn't sound real positive, does it? I was just rereading this as part of the edit. But service programs are definitely worth doing. Just keep things as simple as you can.

What Ya Shoulda Learned

As in the previous chapter, our recap is pretty straightforward.

First, you should be able to describe the difference between (or what each one does) both binding language and binding directories.

Second, you should know where both of these entities are kept. That is, are they a command that creates an object, or a source file that contains instructions, or what?

Third, can you remember some of the source/command verbiage that you would have to use?

Fourth, do you remember how each one is used? That is, what its purpose is?

And finally, were you able to stay awake during the discussion of how binding language, if not used correctly, can result in the wrong sub-procedure being called? Granted, it is not the normal situation, and it won't happen every day, but it could happen, so be careful.

Chapter 21

Service Program Signatures

Finally, we've reached the last topic related to service programs that we are going to talk about. And you thought we would never get here.

Signatures are one of the more controversial features that IBM has built into service programs.

They are only avoidable if you use binding language, which is where binding language rises from its quiet fields to confound the counsels of the great and the wise. Or something like that.

Let's start by talking about what signatures are.

Signatures

The signature on a service program functions a little bit like the level check does on a normal program. That is, the level check warns you if any of the files have changed since you last compiled that program. Similarly, the signature tells you if the sub-procedure list in the service program has changed since it was bound to the program you are trying to run. And by changed, I mean whether sub-procedures have been added or deleted. Logic changes are OK, as is a reordering of the list (although that can then lead to picking up the wrong one, so I don't recommend it).

Of course, "warns" is a relative term. What the level check does is to blow up when you violate it. If you consider that a warning, then I guess you are all set. Signature violations will give you the same type of warning, namely a system failure when you call the service program and the signatures on the calling and the called program don't match.

The signature is a 16-character "thing" that is assigned to the service program and is also attached to the programs calling it during the CRTPGM command. It is created when the service program is created (CRTSRVPGM). It is assigned to the calling programs when they are compiled.

It is meaningful in that its value represents the current configuration of the service program. That is, what sub-procedures are in it. And it changes as the service program changes—but only in some circumstances:

- It does not change if you change the logic in your sub-procedure.

- It does not change if you modify the type or length of the subfields passed into the sub-procedure.

- It does not change if you change the order of the sub-procedures in the service program. And by this, I mean both the order of the actual sub-procedures as well as the order of the PR specs at the top of the program. (Note: Although this situation does not generate a signature violation, it may cause you to pick up the wrong sub-procedure.)

- But it does change if you add or subtract a sub-procedure from the service program.

Fortunately, when the signature changes, you can do the same thing as you would for a bound program logic change: either an UPDPGM on the calling program to pick up the new signature, or else rebind the calling program to the service program to get that signature.

Maybe the real problem with signatures is their shotgun nature. That is, if I change the logic in a sub-procedure in the service program, I really only have to redo those programs that call that sub-procedure. If I have a service program that has 10 sub-procedures and has 100 calling programs, maybe only six of them will use the sub-procedure that has changed, and so I only have to mess with those six.

But if the signature changes, that changes at the service program level, and so now all 100 calling programs have to be rebound. It can get to be quite a mess. So it would be nice not to have to do that, nice to find a way to mitigate the disruption the signature can cause.

And that is where binding language comes into play.

Quick Review

OK, let's pause here and quickly review what we have learned so far. Remember, binding language and binding directories are both involved in the binding process, but they are really completely different things.

Binding Directories

A *binding directory* is an object, associated with the calling program, created by system commands that you run from a command line, that lists the service programs being called by that program. It is not involved with service program signatures in any way.

Binding Language

Binding language is a source file of system commands, not an object, associated with the service program, which is used to set up the list of sub-procedures that you are using in your calling program. The source file is included as a parameter on the CRTPGM for the calling program.

There are three commands involved: STRPGMEXP, EXPORT, and ENDPGMEXP. They create a list of sub-procedures that can be exported from their service program. By "exported," we mean "used" by programs external to the service program itself.

One thing that is really important is that if you are using binding language to access a sub-procedure, you have to be really careful to keep the order the same. That is, even though the sub-procedure name is specified in the binding language source file, the system will actually call the sub-procedure based on its relative position in the service program source. This means that the order of your EXPORT statements must be exactly the same as the order of the sub-procedures in the service program. If they are not, then you will end up calling the wrong sub-procedure, as it ignores the names and just goes off the relative position in the EXPORT list. So be careful adding new sub-procedures to a service program. It's best to just add them to the end rather than trying to group like sub-procedures near each other in the service program.

You can either create the binding language source file manually, or else run the RTVBNDSRC command for either new or update status and have it create the source file. This source file will be given the same name as the service program it represents and be placed in QSRVSRC. A given source file relates to one and only one service program. The source type for this thing is BND.

Signature Violations

OK, let's talk a bit about signature violations.

Remember that when a service program is compiled (CRTSRVPGM), a 16-digit code is generated that is related to the list of sub-procedures in that service program.

And we saw that when this signature was generated it was stored in both the service program and also in each program that calls this service program.

The problem occurs if we do a compile of the service program (CRTSRVPGM) and generate a new signature and do not tie that into a calling program. When that program then calls the service program, the system responds just as it does with a level check and blows up.

Fortunately, the only time a new signature is generated is if a new sub-procedure is added or deleted from the service program. Any other type of change to the service program will keep the same signature when it is compiled.

But rare or not, we still need to deal with it. Remember, the goal is to be able to change the service program and not have to do a single thing, regardless of how simple, to the programs that call that service program.

Fortunately, there are a number of options for dealing with signatures in a civilized way.

Not Using Binding Language

Unfortunately, this is not one of them.

That is, you don't have to use binding language, but if you don't there is no way around the service program signature issues. Signatures are required, and you have to deal with them.

You can still use service programs, of course. You just have to manage any signature changes by doing the UPDPGM or calling program rebind for all programs that call the service program whose signature changes.

And you might decide that is OK. I don't want you to think that you have to use binding language. You might decide that rather than introduce binding language and have to fool around with maintaining that, you will just keep your service program signatures in sync. And by being disciplined, you can do this. Especially if your number of service programs is small.

Or you might find that to be too much work and decide to use binding language. The official line is to use binding language because the "official line" always has you use whatever tools might be available with the amount of work they involve being considered unimportant.

I am really not trying to slant this one way or another. It's up to you. And you might start with one method and then switch to another as the years go by and your service programs start to pile up.

The rest of the options listed here are based on using binding language.

Turn Off Signature Checks

Within the STRPGMEXP command of the binding language source, there is a parm LVLCHK, which can be set as either *YES or *NO. *YES is the default; if you specify it, the system will do the signature check when you call a service program. If you specify *NO, then a zero signature will be generated, and the signature level check will not be performed.

One thing to note is if you opt for LVLCHK *NO, then the next parm, SIGNATURE, must be set to *GEN so it gens the zero signature. You can't set the signature to a certain value if you are going to ignore it.

Of course, this solution requires that you use binding language, but at least you don't have to update it. To be honest, I am not sure that this is the way to go. I mean, would you turn off level checking? Probably not. It's a pain, but it's a good thing. And I think the answer with signatures is not to turn them off but to find a way to live with them in peace and harmony.

Use Both *CURR and *PRV Binding Language Lists

This is one that was popular for a while but not so much now.

Another parameter on the STRPGMEXP command is PGMLVL. If this is set to *CURR, then the system knows this is the current sub-procedure configuration for the service program. Ones that are set to *PRV are recognized as configurations that are no longer valid but have been used by programs in the past. This way, you can add your sub-procedure but not have to update your calling program because the signature that was in effect before (the *PRV one) is still out there in the binding language and so can be accessed.

Obviously, this solution also uses binding language. And not only is it used, but once it is set up, it has to be maintained. That is, when the signature changes (when you add or remove sub-procedures from a service program), you have to take the current set of EXPORT commands, change the PGMLVL parm on the STRPGMEXP command from *CURRENT to *PRV, and then put the new set of STRPGMEXP commands representing the new signature out there set to *CURRENT. Not a big deal, but it does require some fooling around. And you can use the RTVBNDSRC command in the *ADD mode, but you still have to change the current *CURRENT to *PRV.

The real problem comes when you get a dozen or more of these *PRV command sets out in your source. It gets kind of confusing and just feels sloppy, at least to me. Not my favorite, but it does work.

Use a Set Signature

The method that seems to be the most popular today is to use binding language but to set the SIGNATURE parm in the compile command to a set value.

That is, if the value of this parm is *GEN (which is the default), then the system will calculate a signature during the compile. If you specify an actual hexadecimal or string value, then this value will be used for the signature. The idea here is to use a signature value that is not going to change, so that once tied in a program, it will always agree with the signature value in the program. That is, the signature never changes even though the program might.

I can live with this. Of course it also requires that you use binding language, and the source you set up would have to be entered manually and updated manually (as you add or remove sub-procedures). And it does sort of short-circuit the original point of the signature, just as the first option at the top of the page does. But, you didn't ask for them (IBM) to put signatures in there in the first case, so what do you care?

The Bottom Line

All in all, if you are going in for service programs and want to avoid recompiles and UPDPGM, you will probably have to embrace binding language. But that's good. Right? It's neat. Figure out the easiest way for you to roll with it and go.

In the end, service programs provide an extraordinary way to link two modules together for speed and efficiency. But at the same time, there is a price to be paid.

What Ya Shoulda Learned

I'm not sure that "learned" is the proper word to use here. Obviously, you have learned some things: how signatures are set up, what options you have for dealing with them, and so on.

But the main thing you want to get out of this chapter is "how are you going to deal with signatures?" going forward.

You might start out by not using binding language, and just keep track of your service programs as they change and do any rebinding with calling programs yourself. Of course, to begin with, you probably are going to have a fair amount of change in your service programs as they grow and you add more sub-procedures. Just remember to not worry about trying to group sub-procedures in a particular way in the service program. That is just asking for trouble. Always add new sub-procedures at the end of the service program, and use the EXPORT keyword.

This might get old after a while (maintaining everything manually), and you might want to add binding language to assist. Although to be honest, I am not sure that assist is the right word here. In my opinion, there just is no one, right, simplest way to deal with signatures.

And so what you shoulda learned in this chapter is that you are going to have to sit down and give this some good, old-fashioned thought. What do you want to achieve, and what is the best way for you to do this?

Good luck.

Chapter 22

ILE for CL

I really feel uncomfortable about this chapter.

I mean the whole book has been about RPG. And now I am going to bring CL into this? The younger, second cousin of RPG? Next thing you know, I'll be talking about C. But I don't know what else to do. I mean, I have to cover it. Right?

But what do I do with this? It's not RPG /Free or ILE RPG, so it doesn't fit into any of the sections I have set up. Should I set this up in a section of its own? I don't think so. A chapter is bad enough. Let's just get this over with.

Naturally, there is an ILE version of CL. And it is very similar to RPG ILE in that there is a different source file, different compile commands, and even a few language changes. But there is no /Free version of CL. CL is CL, and that is that.

ILE CL is interesting in that very few people seem interested in it. It hasn't drawn nearly the attention that ILE RPG has, and probably only a small percentage of shops have moved their code over to it. But that doesn't mean you can't or shouldn't.

Let's take a moment to look it over and see what is required and what the benefits might be.

Do You Need CLLE?

Hmmm, that depends. Go to the elves, and they will tell you both no and yes. I can call an ILE program from an OPM CL program by using the CALL command. And I can use CALL within an ILE program itself. No problem there, so the initial answer is: no, you don't *need* CLLE.

What I can't do is call a sub-procedure in a service program from OPM CL using the CALL. To do that, I need to use the new CALLPRC (Call Bound Procedure) command. And to do that, I need to use a CL that is ILE. So you tell me. Do you need ILE CL?

And not only does the CL have to be compiled as ILE (more on that in a minute), but it must exist in QCLLESRC as the editor prevents you from using the CALLPRC command if your source file is QCLSRC.

Soooo, the basic question is: will you be calling sub-procedures from a CL?

If you go into ILE the way you should, you are going to build up a nice gackle of service program sub-procedures. And eventually, you will want to take advantage of these modules with a CL. So why not just plan for it right off the bat?

And the CALLPRC is not the only reason you might want to go CLLE. For example, suppose you are using an OPNQRYF (Open Query File) command in your CL. Your RPG program is running as ILE, which means it is running in some activation group. But where is your CL running? If you are still using OPM for your CL, then it is running in the default activation group, which is a different scope of control from your ILE RPG program. Hence, you cannot see the open data path of the OPNQRYF in your RPG program. The same thing will be true of any overrides you might issue in your CL.

Of course, you could define your OPNQRYF so that the OPNSCOPE parameter of the OPNQRYF has a value of *JOB rather than *ACTGRPDFN. This will allow other programs in that job to see the data path regardless of what activation group they are using, but it also makes a lot of sense to just bite the bullet and move all your CL to CLLE.

Obviously, this has implications beyond the RPG-CL connection, and the scope issues also affect straight RPG programs where some of the programs in an application are ILE and some are not. You can work out these issues if you are clever enough, but seriously, dude, just make everything in an app ILE. It's so much simpler for everyone.

Going to CLLE

So if you are going to move from OPM CL to ILE CL, what is involved? Fortunately, it is pretty simple.

Separate QCLSRC and QCLLESRC Files?

One thing you may be tempted to do—I have seen this in a couple of places—is to create a QCLLESRC and put new CLs in there, ones that may (or may not) use actual ILE functionality. Then you would leave everything else in QCLSRC.

The problem now is that every time you need to look for a CL (and many times if you are new or are a consultant, you are looking based on the description because you don't just know the name of the CL you are looking for), now you have to look in two places. Split your source code between several libraries (never a good idea), and suddenly you may have quite a few spots to review.

I would just convert everything to CLLE and be done with it. Doing that doesn't take that long, is not very dangerous, and is good for your blood pressure.

Converting CL to CLLE

This is no big deal. Just copy the CL over to the new source file and change the source type to CLLE.

You should probably then compile it for ILE, but that would not be required. If you do compile, make sure that the DFTACTGRP parm is set to *NO. There's no sense in setting it up in QCLLESRC just to run as OPM.

CL Compile Commands

In QCLSRC, the default compile command is CRTCLPGM (Create CL Program). This creates an OPM version of the CL.

In QCLLESRC, the default compile command is CRTBNDCL (Create Bound CL Program), which is analogous to CRTBNDRPG for the QRPGLESRC side. The DFTACTGRP parm will probably default to *YES, so you will have to be sure to change it to *NO to go ILE. This can also be used in the CL source file.

Or you can use CRTCLMOD (Create CL Module) and CRTPGM. These cannot be used if the source type on your CL is CL. It has to be CLLE.

OK, this may be confusing, so let's pay attention.

> You can use CALL in the CLLE version to call an ILE RPG program when the CL and the RPGLE programs are compiled using CRTBNDxxx.

> If you set up the call as CALLPRC, then you cannot use a CL program that is in QCLSRC; it must be a CLLE program in QCLLESRC.

> Also, if you use the CALLPRC, then both the CL and the RPGLE program must be compiled as *MODULE using the CRTxxxMOD command. And the CRTPGM command must include both the CLLE and RPGLE modules. It isn't enough just to create two modules and put each in a separate CRTPGM command; they have to be bound together.

> Not that anyone cares, but you can also use CALL to do the same thing when calling an RPGLE program from a CL. That is, with CALL you can either set things up as *MODULEs (CRTxxxMOD) and do a CRTPGM, or you can compile both things as CRTBNDxxx and call it good.

> But, if you want to call a sub-procedure from a service program, you need to use CALLPRC. That means both the CL and the service program must be bound together using *MODULEs and CRTPGM.

> OK, I think that covers it.

RTVSRC

One final word. I have seen a number of posts related to people not wanting to use QCLLESRC because once you convert a CL to CLLE, the RTVSRC command no longer works.

I don't honestly believe I have ever had to retrieve source code from the object, and if that is a major issue for you, then you have other problems. The ability to take advantage of the efficiency and modularity improvements offered by ILE CL more than make up for any problems with RTVSRC.

Calling an RPG Program from a CLLE Program

Let's start at the beginning. Suppose you want to call an RPGLE program from a CLLE. What is different?

Well, not that much really.

If you have a CL, that is, if it lives in QCLSRC, then you can call an ILE RPG program just by using the CALL.

And, you can do the same thing if the CL is ILE in QCLLESRC. That is, call an ILE RPG program by using the CALL opcode.

There are differences if you are trying to call just a sub-procedure (like in a service program), but we will get to that in a few minutes.

Calling a CL Program from an RPG Program

So far, we have talked about calling an RPG program from a CL program. But what if we want to go the other direction?

That is, suppose you want to call a CLLE program *from* an RPGLE program in the ILE environment. Fortunately, it is very simple: identical, in fact, to how you call one RPGLE program from another. Again please note—earlier we said that you could call an RPGLE program from a CL with a CL CALL, but now we are talking about the converse. Or inverse. I get them confused. What is important is that we are talking about calling CLLE from RPGLE.

The RPG ILE Program

The calling RPGLE program would be set up with the following PR D-spec:

```
D   CLPRGMID          PR                 EXTPGM('CLPGMID')
D     PARM1                       5
D     PARM2                      10  0
```

If you want to get a little bit fancier and have the RPG program call a CL from a module that is bound into a service program or another module, then you have to set up your PR D-spec as follows:

```
D   CLPRGMID          PR                 EXTPROC(*CL:
      'CLPGMID')
D     PARM1                       5
D     PARM2                      10  0
```

Remember, this is to call a CL from within a sub-procedure in an RPG program.

The CL Program (CL or CLLE)

In both cases, then, you would simply use a CALLP within the RPG program to call the CL:

```
CALLP CLPGMID(PARM1:PARM2);
```

The CL is set up just as normal, with whatever parms are attached to it. There are no D-specs in a CLLE. and so nothing special has to be done for the CL.

Now It's Your Turn

I really had to fight with myself to put in this **Now It's Your Turn** section. Once you get near the end of a book, you just start thinking, "Write more? Are you kidding me?" But after a little thought, I think you should really try this. Remember, you are calling a CLLE from an ILE program. Work through it.

Calling an RPG Sub-Procedure from a CL

The last case involves calling a sub-procedure (like in a service program) from a CL.

To do this, you must use the CALLPRC command in the CL.

This command is not available for a CL in QCLSRC, only for one in QCLLESRC (that is, only for ILE CLs).

It can be used to call a sub-procedure that is in a service program or embedded in a regular RPG program. Please note that if you are calling an ILE (or OPM) program, you should just use the CALL operator, as usual.

The syntax of the CALLPRC is fairly simple.

```
CALLPRC 'procedure' PARM('parm1', 'parm2')
                RTNVAL('field1')
```

There is a limit to the number of parms you can send, but the number is so totally huge (300) that it shouldn't be a problem. If you are calling another CL, for example, a CL can only accept 40 parms.

Parm types supported are text, packed, floating point, and logical constants plus any CL variable.

The RTNVAL parm is optional but if used will return a field similar to the return values option we saw in chapter 12. If you use this, you will need to put the length of the field on the PR and PI of the RPG program you are calling, just as we did in chapter 12. The default setting will be RTNVAL(*NONE).

Now It's Your Turn

Once you get your feet wet, you might as well keep going. So take one of the procedures from your test service program and try to call it from a CLLE. This will be more fun than you might think.

What Ya Shoulda Learned

Fortunately, for this chapter, that's a pretty easy set of questions to answer.

Is there an ILE version of CL? Yes.

You can create a QCLLESRC source file to hold your ILE CL programs in and compile them in ILE mode from there. The current QCLSRC is totally OPM, just as QRPGSRC is. Remember, if you create the QCLLESRC, the record length is 112. You will want to do this.

What determines whether a CL is compiled as ILE or as OPM? This is determined by the compile command that is used to create the object. If it is compiled by CRTCLPGM, it is OPM.

If it is compiled by CRTBNDCL, then it may or may not be ILE depending on the value of the DFTACTGRP parm.

If it is compiled by a CRTCLMOD and CRTPGM combo, then it is ILE all the way.

You can call an OPM CL program (QCLSRC) from an ILE RPG program by using CALLP, and it requires no changes in the CL.

You can also call an ILE RPG program from a CL or CLLE program by using CALL in the CL.

To call an ILE RPG procedure from a CL program, you must use CALLPRC, which can only be issued from a QCLLE program, which can only exist in a QCLLESRC source file.

If you use the CALLPRC command, then the modules involved in the call must be set up as *MODULEs and bound together into a program via CRTPGM.

MVC

Finally. We made it! I knew we would. Never lost hope. MVC is the civilized way to take your /Free and ILE knowledge and build apps that are worthy of your name.

Chapter 23

Design Patterns

You would probably have to be living under a rock today to not have heard of MVC. You might not know what it is, but I am sure you have heard of it. And I am sure there are many of you who have not only heard about it but are starting to use it in your new applications. Unfortunately, there are a number of misconceptions about MVC that still seem to exist.

First, that it is hard or very technical. It isn't.

Second, that it is some weird, freaky, kinky thing that probably uses OO and some crazy language. It doesn't.

And third, that repeated exposure to it causes anemia and a skin condition similar to but separate from psoriasis. That is the most ridiculous one of all, especially since the early results of all the current studies show only the slightest chance of that occurring. But, as I have said before, people will believe anything.

Let's take a quick look at what MVC really is.

A Few Basic Facts

First, let's step back a bit. Start by answering this: how do you go about coding a program?

In the olden days, which for many of us is right now, people built programs by just coding. They would take a deep breath and start at the beginning, go on to the end, and then, hopefully, stop. The result would be a big ol' program (BOP). When it was done, then they could see what the structure of the program was. But going in, you have only the foggiest picture of what that structure is going to look like.

Of course, by this point in the book, we know that what we should be doing is writing small modules that fit together efficiently to produce a completed app. But by themselves, writing small modules may not be enough. Because you still end up with a bunch of code entities, and you are still stuck with the question of how to put them together. And if you do that poorly, you end up with a spaghetti of small modules to navigate. How do you avoid that?

The sad but true fact is that even if you are doing /Free and all that jazz, you may still have no idea what the final structure of your program, and by extension your application, is going to look like when you start.

To get a clearer picture, up front and ongoing, of what your app structure is going to look like, you need to be using *design patterns*.

Design Patterns

Design patterns are a development strategy: reusable templates of software applications.

And the key word there is "applications." Design patterns are not program models, although they do provide some help in that arena. They are *application models*, templates for how you should structure and build your application, what modules the app should have, and how those modules should be interconnected—that sort of thing.

In most cases, the pattern is not specific enough that you can just change a few things and all of a sudden you have an application (although in Web frameworks, it can be close sometimes), but it provides the overall structure for the app. In essence, the pattern defines the architecture or structure of an application. Instead of you figuring out where the control statements or business logic will go and how the system will determine what is next, the design pattern does it for you.

It's not a revolutionary idea. In one sense, all of us have been using design patterns all our coding lives when we use one program as a model for another one. But design patterns take it one step further and provide not just the structure for a program but for an application. Plus, while it is possible that copying one program to create a second is just a way of duplicating a mess, design patterns are well thought-out and organized.

Design patterns are something fairly new in our (the IBM i) arena, but they have been in use on the Web side for quite some time. In fact, that is what most Web language frameworks are based on (a particular design pattern, or several design patterns). When you use a Web framework, you select the design pattern you are going to use, and that automatically generates much of the standard code that you need to make the app work. And it is time for the i world to get on board.

Characteristics of a Design Pattern

Let's take a little closer look at what a design pattern is and its characteristics.

Module Oriented

First and foremost, a design pattern is built by taking modules and binding them together into an app, not by building one monolithic program.

Fortunately, this is right up ILE's alley. And, ILE is therefore uniquely suited to design patterns (and therefore, MVC).

OO or Not OO

Second, because the design pattern is oriented around small code modules, it is ideal for OO, but—it is not just for OO, and you can apply it to RPG just as well as to PHP or one of the other cool languages. What I really mean here is not that design patterns only work with an OO language, but that they help you to focus your thinking in the same way OO does.

As I have said before, RPG and other procedural languages point you toward thinking about the process. This is not a bad idea, but sometimes it does tend toward BOPs as the method of delivery. OO thinking pushes you toward thinking about the elements first and the delivery second. I'm not sure if that is the best way to put that, but it helps you think about developing modules first and then linking them together second. And design patterns do start with modules; they can't really have a BOP design pattern.

Eliminates Decisions

Third, using a design pattern eliminates many of the decisions you would normally have to make.

Things like how your application will be structured, what code elements will go in what modules, how control will flow, and so on. By letting the design pattern specify this, it makes it much more likely that someone else's inventory application will look a great deal like your accounts payable application.

In the end, it will be easier to understand something you have never seen before because not only are all the modules truly modular, but the structures will be essentially identical as well.

In short, design patterns are reusable structures that are not implemented directly but are used as a "pattern." They may be designed to solve a particular type of programming question or to represent a particular "problem." They are not frameworks, but a framework may provide an implementation skeleton for one or more design patterns.

Design patterns are a means of thinking about a particular business or communications problem in a way that helps you organize your thoughts on how you will actually solve that problem.

There Is More Than One (Design Pattern)

More than one? To be honest, there are dozens or maybe hundreds of design patterns that have been identified.

Each pattern is oriented around a particular type of app or problem, and the idea is to pick the one that most nearly approximates what you want to accomplish. Only some of the design patterns will really apply to the solution of a business problem. Many of them relate to messaging or problems that are specific to object-oriented languages and other more technical issues.

Design patterns were really put on the map by the Gang of Four (Erich Gamma, Richard Helm, Ralph Johnson, and John Vlissides) when they published their now famous tome *Design Patterns: Elements of Reusable Object-Oriented Software* (Addison-Wesley, 1994). They outline 23 different patterns organized into three basic groups.

Today the number of design patterns has expanded greatly, and there are roughly four different groups into which these fall.

Creational Patterns

These are patterns that, yes, you guessed it, create something.

Examples would be the Builder, Factory Method, Lazy Initialization, and other similar patterns. They result in some type of object or thing being created.

The Lazy Initialization pattern, for example, is a way of delaying the actual creation or value assignment of an object until it is really needed rather than up front when the app starts. Obviously, this is related to OO, as are many of the design patterns.

Structural Patterns

As you might expect, structural patterns define a structure that the app should follow. Another way to put that is that they define relationships between separate components.

Examples of this would be the Adapter, Flyweight, and Decorator patterns.

Most of these are also OO related, like the Decorator pattern that allows you to add functionality to a class at run time. You could always use subclasses to do this, but that can lead to an explosion in the number of subclasses defined. The Decorator pattern provides an alternative to that.

Behavioral Patterns

These patterns are communication oriented, linking modules together and increasing the efficiency of the interaction.

Examples include the Chain of Responsibility, Interpreter, and the Protocol Stack pattern.

The Protocol Stack defines a multi-layer communication hierarchy that handles the transfer of data between different objects or modules.

Concurrency Patterns

These are for tasks that use multi-threading.

Examples are Active Objects, Leaders/Followers, and my personal favorite, the Disruptor.

The Disruptor ensures that every piece of data is owned by one and only one thread, thereby reducing write contention in the app.

Architectural Patterns

Yes, I realize this is the fifth of four basic groups. It came along sort of after the fact, as business users became more involved in design patterns. This is the one that we are really interested in because this is where MVC and its variants belongs. And this is also where the patterns tend to be oriented more toward business than software only. Although Architectural Patterns is not considered one of the traditional "big four" patterns, many people consider it a valid category.

Other examples of this pattern are Data Discovery, Message Exchange Patterns, and Change Data Capture.

Change Data Capture is really a set of design patterns (that is true of many of the previous examples) that identifies and tracks data elements that have been changed to ensure that the proper action can be taken with respect to those elements.

Anti-Patterns

Design patterns are so popular that they have even inspired anti-patterns: application patterns that should not be followed because they are dangerous and anti-productive.

Oooo. That's right: they are the bad boys of the pattern world. Rebellious. Anti-social. Yet strangely alluring. Drawing the unwary into a life of screwing up things for the rest of us. Beware, these *are* the patterns your mother warned you about. Unfortunately, many of them are probably pretty familiar to a lot of IBM i developers.

Anyway, I owe the following list of anti-patterns to Paul Watt, whose blog post (*www.codeproject.com/Articles/791302/Software-Design-Patterns*) highlighted the idea of anti-patterns. I have redone them somewhat, but the essence of the original list remains.

The Big Box Pattern

This one does it all. Everything you could possibly want is in this one pattern. Can you spell BOP? How convenient. No searching around for just the right one, you've already got it in place. You just have to figure out how to make it work for what you want to do.

Hopefully, you will not need to make a change in it. Good luck doing so without breaking it for all the other things it does.

Patterns should have a purpose, and only one purpose. If there is more than one purpose to a pattern, stop, drop, and roll. It's your only hope.

The Optimization Gambit

Another way to mess things up with design patterns is by putting the focus on optimizing a single part of the pattern.

This is something that is easy to do. There are always certain things that a person will naturally think are more important than others and that need to be given a front row seat when it comes to optimizing. The ability to think broadly and give up some efficiency here in order to gain a greater efficiency overall is very hard to achieve. Although I do feel it is a particular strength of mine, along with the ability to always look at the negative side of things. So, if you ever want the worst-outcome option, let me know. But it will be very efficiently presented.

But we know from the work of giants like Leonid Kantorovich (who was instrumental in sealing the Kryptonian city of Kandor in that bell jar) and T. C. Koopmans (who played bass for Willie Nelson for almost 15 years before succumbing to a tragic chewing gum overdose), linear programming mathematics tells us that a local optimum always leads to a less than optimal global solution. It is only by balancing various local sub-optimal solutions that you can truly get your most efficient overall solution.

In other words, leave the patterns alone; don't try to improve on them by optimizing.

The Spray Paint Solution

This is related to the Big Box pattern, and for a while (15 or 20 minutes), I thought it was the same. But the more I thought, the more I realized that this pattern is more oriented toward hoping that a change to a given design parameter will act equally across all the situations covered by this pattern.

It is a broad brush approach to changing things. Make a change in one place and let it roll out over a lot of situations. Sounds appealing, doesn't it?

The main problem here is that by trying to cover too many bases, this option becomes increasingly hard to reuse in new situations.

The Complexity Algorithm

The last anti-pattern I will mention is the use of complexity or system tricks to shorten up and "simplify" a pattern.

Usually, a pattern is not written to minimize the amount of code that is written. It is written to provide visibility in terms of what is being done. Since the pattern is being used over and over again in multiple solutions, minimizing the code length is not important. What is important is knowing what is being done.

Have you ever run into an RPG routine or section of code that used some old, obscure, or technically complex algorithm for the purpose of reducing the number of lines of code? Of course you have. And how has that generally worked out for you?

To be effective, design patterns must be straightforward. They should not be convoluted or involve esoteric components.

What's It All About, Alfie?

So, what's the bottom line?

First, design patterns provide not just a model for a program but a model for your application.

Second, the model they define is logical, consistent, and properly structured from a modular point of view.

Third, MVC is an example of a design pattern, and the one that is most likely to be used in a business situation.

So, where do we go from here?

Well, we will continue in the next chapter to zero in on MVC, so please try to control your excitement.

What Ya Shoulda Learned

I know.

You were expecting more.

I don't know what you were expecting, but I know you were expecting more.

The truth is, MVC is just a design pattern, and design patterns are not that hard to understand. The proof of the pudding, though, is in the use. Stay tuned.

Chapter 24

MVC and Its Variants

As we noted in the last chapter, MVC (Model-View-Controller) is a design pattern.

Unlike many of the design patterns that have been defined, it is not uniquely oriented to OO, but can easily be used with procedural languages as well.

Nor is it related to some sort of programming or communication issue. Instead, it is uniquely suited to the types of applications we run in the business world: applications where we access data, display it somewhere, make changes to it, take it back in, edit it in various ways, and write it back out to the spot it originally came from.

Now before I go any further, I want to make one thing clear. When I use the term "MVC" I am using it in a generic, not specific sense. That is, in a specific sense, MVC is a very specific design pattern that has very specific requirements and attributes.

It is actually part of a family that is loosely called "MVC." This family consists of MVC plus MVP (Model-View-Presenter), MVA (Model-View-Adapter), MVVM (Model-View-ViewModel), HMVC (Hierarchical Model-View-Controller), and others. Each of these has very specific properties; the particular format I will be using is probably more MVP than MVC.

For more information about MVC specifics, I suggest Martin Fowler's excellent article "GUI Architectures" on his website (*www.martinfowler.com/eaaDev/uiArchs.html*).

What Is MVC?

At a practical level, MVC is a pattern consisting of a number of separate modules of the following types:

The *Model* is somewhat misnamed in my opinion, but it's too late to do anything about that now. Essentially the model is the business rules, the logic, that you want to apply in your application. It may or may not contain the access code to get to the data.

View is pretty self-explanatory; it is the code required to display the information that we have accessed or the user wants to enter.

Controller is the code that ties the other two together, acting as the traffic cop that tells the logic flow when to go to the appropriate module.

Generally, you will have multiple model and view modules. That is, it's quite probable that you will have a number of screens in this function, and each one would be a separate view module. Similarly, you could easily have several models, each one oriented around retrieving or processing a specific type of data. Usually, however, there is only one controller module, although that is a guideline, not a rule. (Although now that I am editing this, I can't imagine you needing two controller segments. Maybe it should be a rule.)

What is a rule is that whatever you code up, it should fit into one, and only one, of these categories (model, view, or controller). And it should be true to the spirit of ILE: each module should have basically one and only one logical idea behind it.

After that, it is a bit of a judgment call.

For example, some people feel very strongly that you need to separate out your data access logic from the model code. And in some ways that makes sense, particularly if there is much chance that you will change the database or platform that you are on. If you separate the data access, it makes the app much more portable. For us on the IBM i, that is probably not going to happen (unless you switch from DDS to DB2), and so for simplicity I believe in keeping the data access code in with the logic statements in the model. But that's just me. And most normal people.

Other people get fixated on the relationship between the model and the view.

In theory, the controller should be the intermediary between the model and the view, but the fact that MVC is always shown as a triangle lets some people build connections between the logic and the display.

There is a version of MVC called MVP—Model-View-Presenter—that is specifically designed to not allow communication between the model and the view. Everything has to go through the controller. I sort of prefer this.

There is also MVA—Model-View-Adapter, which to me seems identical to MVP, although I would never suggest that to a partisan of either.

There is also the MVVM—Model-View-ViewModel, which allows the unthinkable to happen, for the model and the view to communicate with each other via slightly different types of view modules.

I hate to be blunt about this, but I really find it very hard to care. I guess I am more in favor of not allowing the logic (model) and the display (view) to talk to each other, but if it happens I am not going to consider my life a failure. I've got a lot of other reasons besides that. No, we are going to look at a middle-of-the-road implementation of MVC and get on with our lives.

Why MVC Is Important

OK, MVC breaks things into specific pieces. Big hairy deal. Like the whole world is about to explode, and they changed the cast for the third Fantastic Four movie, and Peter Jackson just won't stop making crummy movies that rewrite the two greatest books ever written, and you think I care about MVC? Hey, pal, I got real things to worry about.

But the truth is, we should care at least a little about MVC. And I'll tell you why.

I do not believe in the wholesale rewriting of applications to make them "modern." Or at least, I don't believe in rewriting the whole thing in terms of some other language, such as Java. And yet, RPG is incapable of producing those cute little GUI screens that are so in today. What's a body to do?

What I am in favor of is taking the BOPs that are out there for an application and breaking them down into model, controller, and view modules. Then I would redo the model and controller RPG code using /Free and ILE. And I would then be free to redo the view portion in whatever Web language is the most exciting at the time.

And so, for me, MVC is a requirement for any modernization.

But it goes beyond modernization. MVC is a requirement to get your programs set so that they are maintainable into the future.

I mean, forget modernization. You don't need to do that to have your RPG programs continue to function just as they are today. And you can add additional functionality to them to make them even more valuable. But doing that to many BOPs is easier said than done, and when you are done, the program will undoubtedly look even worse than it did before. Going to MVC simplifies and cleans up these programs.

Quite simply, MVC is the next iteration in i program structure. It is replacing the more or less single program app structure with the MVC format. That should be the basis of any modernization that you do.

Everybody Loves MVC, but ...

At this point, you may be tempted to go out to the Web, google MVC, and see what you get.

I guarantee it will be a ton. MVC is very widely used, extremely well known, and very effective.

And yet, most of the articles that you see will probably be some variation of "MVC is great, but this is what's wrong with it."

The reason for that is that most of the articles on MVC are written by Web language people. And things on the Web are more complicated than things in the i world. There are a lot of issues and situations that are standard for them, which just don't come up for us. As a result, there are a lot more things that can "go wrong" with the relatively simple MVC design pattern. Things like inversion of control and dependency injection. Some of the implementations of MVC, like MVVM, tend to be slow and difficult to implement (don't even get Dave Bush started). And, since MVC is a design pattern, it does not really force you to do anything. So you can use MVC and still write very complex and disjointed programs. Or have a high degree of data coupling. Or intermix functionality, so that view logic is somehow embedded in the model or model logic shows up in the controller.

OK, so MVC isn't perfect. If you are determined to screw it up, you will. Common sense and basic programming disciplines are still necessary.

But, MVC does provide a framework to allow you to write applications with a couple of very important characteristics.

First, MVC does force you to be modular, and in an RPG world that is still heavily involved with BOPs, that is an important fact.

Second, it makes a pretty strong effort to separate business logic from the view process from the program flow (control) actions. Yes, you can mess that up, but if you are paying even just a little attention, that shouldn't happen.

Third, it provides the only way to have flexibility to change your view method and maybe even your database, without having to go through a major rewrite.

And those are the things that I want us to focus on as we develop an example of a /Free-based, ILE-using MVC design pattern application: specifically, modularity and separation of function, two of the keys to developing truly modern applications.

What Ya Shoulda Learned

You should know how to spell MVC.

And you should know what it stands for: Model (business logic), View (the display of the data), Controller (application flow control).

The real thing you need to know is how to create an MVC application rather than doing a BOP. And that is what we will look at next.

Chapter 25

MVC Example

Okie dokie. Time to get down and get dirty with a very simple application of the MVC/MVP design pattern.

This is an application that I did for one of my clients. It was designed to accept inventory into a consignment warehouse without going through all the freakiness of normal receiving. Prior to this, my client had been doing it in receiving and then backing out the GL transactions. You can imagine how excited they were when I gave them this app. Yeah, as I remember it, they didn't start using it for four months. Some people just love backing out GL entries. I don't work with them anymore.

I did it for them as a single program. I know, I know. But it was a while ago. It only had one screen that you enter data on, and no subfiles. So it makes a pretty simple example.

On the following pages, I have broken up the original app into three programs: a control module that controls the whole thing, a view module that displays the screen, and a single model module that checks the value of the vendor number entered to ensure it is valid.

The original app had about a dozen data elements on the screen, including warehouse, location, quantity, a couple of really weird control flags, and other stuff. For this example, I have stripped it down to just one field, a product number. I want to keep things as simple as possible.

Anyway, here it is. Ready?

Data and Display Files

Before we get started doing our MVC programs, we have a couple of things to do.

Data File

First, you will need to create a file that we can use in the model program to verify the product number against. In my model program, I am calling this file MSPMP100. This is just a product master type file. You can call yours anything you want, just be sure to mentally convert my MSPMP100 to your filename when you are reading this chapter. Or else use MSPMP100 for your file. I don't really care.

This should be a normal, old keyed file with only one field, the product number. I will be using a field called PRDNO, 10-digit, alphanumeric, with no special attributes. PRDNO will be the key for this file.

I would create this file in the library where the MVC programs are going to be, but that is up to you. Doing it this way just keeps the library list simple.

Display File: DWS0260FM

The second thing you need to create is the display file that will be used by the view program.

This will be a simple screen, with only one field on it—you guessed it, the PRDNO field, which will be 10 digits, input capable.

Oh, you will also need a MSG field somewhere on the screen to display any returned messages. I am making this 70 digits and alphanumeric, but I guess that is up to you.

I am calling this DWS0260FM, but again, you can name it anything you want as long as you can do the mental translation.

Create these two modules first, as we will refer to them within the programs below. These simple tasks will get your hands dirty and make it easier for you to dig into what's to come.

Model

To a great extent, it doesn't matter where we start here. So we will go in alphabetical order: M, then V, then C.

The purpose of the "model" is to handle database interactions and other business logic foolishness. This is where the work is done, so we would expect to find relatively small, concentrated modules like the one below.

```
H*****************************************************************
H** DWS0260M1 - Model Program 1
H*****************************************************************
H DFTACTGRP(*NO) ACTGRP(*NEW)
F*****************************************************************
FMSPMP100  UF A E           K DISK
F*
F*****************************************************************
D DWS0260M1      PR
D   M1_PRODUCT                 10
D   M1_MSG                     70
D   M1_ERROR_FLG                1
D DWS0260M1      PI
D   M1_PRODUCT                 10
D   M1_MSG                     70
D   M1_ERROR_FLG                1
D*****************************************************************
 /Free

   CHAIN(E) (M1_PRODUCT) MSPMP100;
   IF NOT %FOUND;
      M1_ERROR_FLG = 'Y';
      M1_MSG       = 'THIS AINT NO VALID PRODUCT';
   ELSE
        M1_ERROR_FLG = 'N';
        M1_MSG       = *BLANKS;
   ENDIF;
   *INLR = '1';

 /end-Free
```

Now, as is our custom, let's take this thing apart so we are sure we understand it. As before, we will show the snippet and then under that the description.

```
H************************************************************
H** DWS0260M1 - Model Program 1
H************************************************************
H DFTACTGRP(*NO) ACTGRP(*NEW)
F************************************************************
FMSPMP100  UF A E          K DISK
F*
F************************************************************
```

First, the H- and F-specs. We have the H-spec if you need that to make your program ILE, then a rather pedestrian F-spec for the one file we will be using in this model. Nothing special here, folks, so let's move along. And I am using an F-spec for those people who are not able to do the /Free control statements. But if you can use them, then feel free to do so.

```
D DWS0260M1       PR
D    M1_PRODUCT              10
D    M1_MSG                  70
D    M1_ERROR_FLG             1
D DWS0260M1       PI
D    M1_PRODUCT              10
D    M1_MSG                  70
D    M1_ERROR_FLG             1
D************************************************************
```

Next, come the D-specs. Remember what the model is: it's a program that is called from the control module, and so, being the "called," program, it has both a PR (prototype) and a PI (program interface) D-spec. This consists of three parameters: a 10-character alphanumeric product number, and then a message field, and an error flag that is set to Y if an error is found.

Because the M1_PRODUCT field value comes from the view display file, I could have passed the entire display record over instead of just one field. This would have made the models look more standardized but would have also increased the size of the parms being passed. In addition, if we had decided later that we needed another parm from the screen to do the editing on the PRODUCT, then it would have been there and we wouldn't have needed to add another parm to the prototype. At the same time, however, that sort of violates our one module-one logical idea model, and I am not sure I like that. You make the call. Either way you go, if you add another field to be edited here you are still going to have to change the program to add in that logic. Just passing the entire display record in dioes not eliminate the need for a modification here.

The model is called from the control program, and we will see that in due time.

```
/Free

CHAIN(E) (M1_PRODUCT) MSPMP100;
IF NOT %FOUND;
     M1_ERROR_FLG = 'Y';
     M1_MSG       = 'THIS AINT NO VALID PRODUCT';
ELSE
     M1_ERROR_FLG = 'N';
     M1_PRODUCT   = *BLANKS;
     M1_MSG       = *BLANKS;
ENDIF;


*INLR = '1';

/end-Free
```

Finally, the logic. It's fairly straightforward. We use the product number that came in through the PI data structure and read the MSPMP100 file. Then if the record is not found, we set a message value and send this information back to the control program. If we find it, then we just return to the calling program, no message required. In all of this, I am not bothering to set the cursor position. This would be unnecessary code that would glop everything else up. Besides, the screen only has one field, but normally you would want to set the cursor position.

View

The next module we want to look at is the view. It's a little longer, but that isn't a big deal.

```
H***************************************************************
*****
H* OBJECT ID: DWS0260V1
H* TEXT:       MVC View Program
H***************************************************************
FDWS0260FM CF    E                      WORKSTN INFDS(WORK_INFDS)
F*
F***************************************************************
D/TITLE INPUT SPECIFICATIONS
D
D DWS0260R01    E DS
EXTNAME(DWS0260FM:DWS026001)
D*
D WORK_INFDS      DS
D   FILLER1                    368
D   FKEY                         1
D
D DWS0260V1      PR
D   V1_FKEY                      1
D   V1_DWS0260                        LIKEDS(DWS0260R1)
D   V1_MSG                      70
D DWS0260V1      PI
D   V1_FKEY                      1
D   V1_DWS0260                        LIKEDS(DWS0260R1)
D   V1_MSG                      70
D*
D***************************************************************
  /FREE

    MSG = V1_MSG;
    DWS0260R1 = V1_DWS0260;


    WRITE DWS026001;
    READ  DWS026001;
```

```
    V1_FKEY = FKEY;
    V1_DWS0260 = DWS0260R1;


    *INLR = '1';


  /end-Free
***************** End of data *********************************
```

```
H**************************************************************
*****
H* OBJECT ID: DWS0260V1
H* TEXT:      MVC View Program
H**************************************************************
*****
FDWS0260FM CF   E                     WORKSTN INFDS(WORK_INFDS)
F*
F**************************************************************
```

First, we have the F-specs, but the only file here is the workstation file for the DDS display that we are supporting.

```
D/TITLE INPUT SPECIFICATIONS
D
D  DWS0260R01    E DS                       EXTNAME(DWS0260FM:DWS026001)
D*
D WORK_INFDS     DS
D   FILLER1                  368
D   FKEY                       1
D
D DWS0260V1      PR
D   V1_FKEY                    1
D   V1_DWS0260                            LIKEDS(DWS0260R1)
D   V1_MSG                    70
D DWS0260V1      PI
D   V1_FKEY                    1
D   V1_DWS0260                            LIKEDS(DWS0260R1)
D   V1_MSG                    70
D*
D**********************************************************************
```

Then the D-specs. Since the view module is called from the control module, you will immediately recognize the prototype (PR) and program interface (PI) structures. The only thing that is different here is the V1_DWS0260 parm, which is actually the layout of the display file (because we need to pass the screen data back and forth to and from the various modules).

You cannot define a DS within a PR or PI (it assumes everything is a standalone field), so we need to attach the LIKEDS keyword and refer to a separate data structure, the DWS0260R01.

And, to avoid having to list all the display fields under the DWS0260R01 data structure, I am using the EXTNAME keyword to specify a filename (DWS0260FM) and a record format within that file (DWS026001).

It seems complicated when you first look at it, especially the introduction of the DWS0260R01, but once you think about it for a couple of weeks it doesn't seem so bad (actually you just lose interest and give up, but what the hey).

```
/FREE

    MSG = V1_MSG;
    DWS0260R1 = V1_DWS0260;


    WRITE DWS026001;
    READ  DWS026001;


    V1_FKEY = FKEY;
    V1_DWS0260 = DWS0260R1;


    *INLR = '1';

/end-Free
```

Finally, the logic itself. And, again, it is pretty simple.

First, I set the fields in the DWS026001 workstation record from the values passed in via the prototype.

> You might think at this point, "wouldn't the MSG field be covered by this—after all it is in the workstation record?" And the answer is, no, I don't think so. The workstation record is kind of weird, having both an input and output format (designated by a system-defined I- and O-spec). The MSG field is part of the O-spec but not the I-spec (because you don't make this an input-capable field), and the one that seems to be picked up and passed is the input format. Hence, MSG is not part of that and needs to be addressed separately.

Then we do the write and read combo to display the appropriate results on screen. Mostly we are interested in the MSG field in case there are any errors and the appropriate fields on the screen if they need correction.

Finally, I get the function key that was used on the read and put it in the prototype data structures for return to the control program, along with any data that has been entered on the screen.

Controller

The last step is to look at the control module. This is what will actually be called when you want to access this function. It contains calls to the model and view programs that are required to make this all work.

```
F***************************************************************
*****
F** DWS0260C1 - Controller Program
F**
H DFTACTGRP(*no) ACTGRP(*NEW)
F***************************************************************
*****
FDWS0260FM CF    E              WORKSTN PREFIX(V1_)
F                                       INFDS(Work_INFDS)
F*
DDWS0260R1       E DS                   EXTNAME(DWS0260FM:DWS026001)
D                                       PREFIX(V1_)
D*
D WORK_INFDS      DS
D   FILLER1                   368
D   FKEY                        1
D*
DDWS0260M1       PR                     EXTPGM('DWS0260M1')
D   V1_PRODUCT                 10
D   V1_MSG                     70
D   M1_ERROR_FLG                1
D
D DWS0260V1       PR                     EXTPGM('DWS0260V1')
D   V1_FKEY                     1
D   V1_DWS0260                          likeds(dws0260r1)
D   V1_MSG                     70
D
D V1_MSG          S          70
D M1_ERROR_FLG    S           1
D V1_FKEY         S           1
D V1_DWS0260      DS                     likeds(dws0260r1)
D
D   F03           C                      CONST(X'33')
```

```
D    F07            C                          CONST(X'37')
D    F12            C                          CONST(X'3C')
D    ENTER          C                          CONST(X'F1')
D**
 /Free

  M1_ERROR_FLG = 'N';
  V1_FKEY      = ' ';
  CALLP DWS0260V1 (V1_FKEY:
                   V1_DWS0260:
                   V1_MSG);


  DOW V1_FKEY <> F03;

       SELECT;

          WHEN V1_FKEY = F03;

          WHEN V1_FKEY = F07;
                V1_PRODUCT = *BLANKS;
                V1_MSG     = *BLANKS;
                CALLP DWS0260V1 (V1_FKEY:
                                 V1_DWS0260:
                                 V1_MSG);


           WHEN V1_FKEY = ENTER;

                CALLP DWS0260M1 (V1_DWS0260.V1_PRODUCT:
                                 V1_MSG:
                                 M1_ERROR_FLG);
  IF M1_ERROR_FLG = 'N';
                   V1_MSG = 'Product Added.';
                   V1_PRODUCT = *BLANKS;
             ENDIF;
                CALLP DWS0260V1 (V1_FKEY:
                                 V1_DWS0260:
                                 V1_MSG);
```

Continued

```
        OTHER;

    ENDSL;

  ENDDO;

  *INLR = '1';

/end-Free
```

Now, let's rip that baby apart.

```
F**********************************************************************
*****
F** DWS0260C1 - Controller Program
F**
H DFTACTGRP(*no) ACTGRP(*NEW)
F**********************************************************************
*****
FDWS0260FM CF    E              WORKSTN PREFIX(V1_)
F
INFDS(Work_INFDS)
F*
```

Nothing major here, just the display file.

Oh, yeah, the display file. But we have the view module to handle the displays, and the reason for this whole thing is to separate display from logic from data manipulation. So, why is the display file here in the control module? You might have expected there to be nothing in the F-specs for this program.

We will get to why it is there in a moment.

```
DDWS0260R1             E DS
EXTNAME(DWS0260FM:DWS026001)
D                                              PREFIX(V1_)
D*
D WORK_INFDS           DS
D    FILLER1                     368
D    FKEY                          1
D*
DDWS0260M1             PR                      EXTPGM('DWS0260M1')
D    V1_PRODUCT                   10
D    V1_MSG                       70
D    M1_ERROR_FLG                  1
D
D DWS0260V1            PR                      EXTPGM('DWS0260V1')
D    V1_FKEY                       1
D    V1_DWS0260                             likeds(dws0260r1)
D    V1_MSG                       70
D
D V1_MSG              S           70
D M1_ERROR_FLG        S            1
D V1_FKEY             S            1
D V1_DWS0260          DS                       likeds(dws0260r1)
D
D    F03              C                        CONST(X'33')
D    F07              C                        CONST(X'37')
D    F12              C                        CONST(X'3C')
D    ENTER            C                        CONST(X'F1')
D**
```

The first thing we run into is a data structure for the workstation record.

And that is followed closely by the INFDS structure that we will use to determine what function key has been used.

Then we have the prototype for the model module. We have named this program DWS0260M1. If we had another model that we were calling, we could call that DWS0260M2 and include a PR for that. Below the PR are the actual definitions for the M1 parms because the PR D-spec does not really define those fields to the program. And do you remember the reason for that? That's right: because.

This is followed by the prototype for the view module, DWS0260V1.

We then define the fields from both of the prototypes that are required. (Remember, the PR does not really define the fields, so if they are not in an F-spec or another D-spec, they need to be defined.)

Finally, we have the constants that we are using in the SELECT statement to review against the function key used in the read.

```
/Free

  M1_ERROR_FLG = 'N';
  V1_FKEY      = ' ';
  CALLP DWS0260V1 (V1_FKEY:
                   V1_DWS0260:
                   V1_MSG);


  DOW V1_FKEY <> F03;

      SELECT;

        WHEN V1_FKEY = F03;

        WHEN V1_FKEY = F07;
             V1_PRODUCT = *BLANKS;
             V1_MSG     = *BLANKS;
             CALLP DWS0260V1 (V1_FKEY:
                              V1_DWS0260:
                              V1_MSG);


        WHEN V1_FKEY = ENTER;
             CALLP DWS0260M1 (V1_DWS0260.V1_PRODUCT:
                              V1_MSG:
                              M1_ERROR_FLG);
             IF M1_ERROR_FLG = 'N';
                V1_MSG = 'Product Added.';
                V1_PRODUCT = *BLANKS;
             ENDIF;
             CALLP DWS0260V1 (V1_FKEY:
```

```
                              V1_DWS0260:
                              V1_MSG);


            OTHER;

        ENDSL;

    ENDDO;

    *INLR = '1';

/end-Free
```

We are now ready for the logic per se.

Start by doing a couple of basic initializations (V1_Error_Flag and V1_MSG), then call the view program to display the initial screen. Then check the value of the FKEY to see what function key was used.

If it is **F3**, then we exit the SELECT.

If it is **F12**, then we initialize the screen values and call the view program to clean off the screen.

The only other option I am using here is the **Enter** key. If that is selected, then that is the branch that processes the data entered on the screen. Since there is only one field on the screen, this is rather limited in what it does.

First, it calls the DWS0260M1 model program that will validate the product number.

Upon return from that program, we check the value of the error flag. If it is N, that is, the product number is OK, then I set the message to indicate that the record has been added. It hasn't of course, as we do not do a write anywhere in this example, but we will come to that later.

Then we call the view program, DWS0260V1, to redisplay the screen.

And that's it. Pretty simple, really.

What Ya Shoulda Learned

It's pretty obvious, actually.

Granted, this is very simple, but simple is a good place to start, and this is a very simple example of an MVC program.

The essence of MVC is to keep 'em separated. Separate the display logic from the business rules from the control structure. Nowhere is this separation more pronounced than with the data. Take a look at the structure. Everything has been done to reduce data coupling as much as possible. For example, the application file appears only in the model program. Even the decision to pass in only the field value being modified, rather than the whole display data structure, helps to insulate this program from changes to the app. If you decide to add a field later and need to enter and edit the vendor classification, it will not affect the model that handles the product master information.

In a perfect world, the one that I dream will exist when the Overlords return, we would limit the display data structure to the view program. Unfortunately, that is not the way our world works now, and something has to tie the various pieces of this application together.

Chapter 26

Turning Up the ILE in MVC

OK, so where do we stand now?

What we have looked at in the previous chapter is a simple application structured using MVC. Actually, it's probably actually MVA or MVP, but that's not my problem.

There is really only one thing wrong with it: it's not very ILE, is it? And it sort of assumes that RPG is the only player in town, which certainly isn't true.

It is written in a modular fashion using /Free, but it is not as ILE as it could be. It has no service programs and no sub-procedures—only straight programs that could just as easily be OPM.

Surprised? The fact is, you could have been doing MVC all along. It's not a new idea. The problem is, in its present form (that is, the way I did it in the previous chapter), it would suffer from many of the problems that OPM programs normally have. Yes, it would be modular, but it would not be efficient. And it would not scale well if you applied this same MVC architecture to an application that had more traffic.

But worst of all, it used very few of the things that you learned in this book. And if you do not make use of what you have learned, what was the point? Although, you did buy the book, and I did get paid, soooo ....

No, no, the point is that after all this effort, you need to use some of the things you have learned to write an application that is not only MVC but also ILE as well. Now to fix this, I could rewrite my application using everything we have learned. But to be honest, that would be a fair amount of work for me, and I already know how to do it. So here is what I am going to do: I am going to let you do the rewrite and call it a learning experience for you. Whadda ya think?

So, what can we do to make this application truly representative of what we have learned in this book?

In General

First off, there are some things that you can do in general to the programs we have looked at to take advantage of what we have learned.

Control Statements

First and foremost, if you are at a level that supports the control statements, start using them. Replace your H-, F-, D-, and P-specs with the appropriate control statements.

Why? Because we need to move forward and leave the last vestiges of old positional RPG behind.

And you need to get used to seeing the control statements and being able to recognize in an instant what they are saying, just as you do today with the logic control statements. The only way to do that is to use them.

The end result should be to code /Free throughout and say goodbye, once and for all, to positional code.

Remove Delimiters

Second, if you are at a level where you can, remove the /Free, /end-Free delimiters. I have included them only because some people may not be there yet, but if you are, then take them out.

Activation Groups

What are you going to do about activation groups? You never had to think this about with OPM, but now you do. So, as you define your MVC application, how will you do your activation groups?

The obvious solution is that for the module and the view, you will use *CALLER. But what about the controller? Will you let this be a named or system assigned group? The answer depends on how long you want it to live.

And how do you set the activation group? Remember, it is set in the compile command.

Binding Directories

Again, you will have to make decisions here. Probably not at first. If you have just one or two service programs, it's not a big deal. But, as the number of service programs you have increases, you may want to buy into this. Or not. it's up to you. But I would like you to at least think about it.

Binding Language

Same thing here. When you get a service program or two, think about this. And the signatures.

And maybe that is the essence of ILE. It is not really about how you will write a single program, except for being modular and using sub-procedures. It is more about how the application as a whole is structured and connected. How are things compiled? What activation groups tie everything together? What about binding directories and binding language? How will Frodo ever get into Mordor? Was Harry Potter bored after he destroyed He Who Must Not Be Named? Is it even realistic to think that Hermione, who was pretty hot, could get interested in someone who has to be one of the most boring people in the world? So many questions that need to be answered.

Model

We will start with the model because it is my favorite. How do we redo that in a more ILE format? Think carefully, and then raise your hand when you have an answer.

Service Programs

That's right: service programs. What we need to do is rewrite this model program as a more general service program. There will only be one sub-procedure, the one to validate the product number. As I see it, as we expanded the fields involved in this display, we would add additional service programs. One for the vendor stuff, for example, another for something else. And, if there are two fields that need to be validated against the Product or Vendor Master, then we get into having multiple sub-procedures in that particular service program. I mean seriously, do I have to think of everything?

Of course, you could always add the other sub-procedures to this one service program. So, you could add a sub-procedure for verifying the vendor number. In practice, I would definitely put that sort of thing in a separate, vendor master-oriented service program, but in this case I will take either one as a serious attempt on your part to learn this stuff and would not reduce the grade you will be getting.

And that was actually your cue to develop that. The service program, that is.

Go on. Git. If you have learned anything at this point, you should be able to do that. If you can't, then either you need to reread this book, or I need to rewrite it. Guess which of those two options will actually occur?

I/O-Oriented Service Program

One thing that I have seen some people suggest over the years is to insulate yourself from a potential database change by using separate I/O sub-procedures that are called by the sub-procedures used in the model.

That is, at this point I am sort of assuming you will use the RPG I/O as your database medium. If at some point you decide to switch to DB2, for example, all of your model programs would have to change to take out the RPG I/O logic and install either embedded SQL or the DB2 SQL Procedural Language. So, you would write a set of data access sub-procedures and call those from the service programs used in the model.

I know that sounds like extra code, and it is. And extra work, and it is. But it also gives you the ability to quickly swap out a new I/O method without affecting the edit logic. I'm not a big fan of this personally. If you were truly in a Web environment where you had to port your app on different platforms and using who knows how many different databases, it might be worth it, but in the IBM i world I think you are pretty much going to be RPG I/O or DB2. You should probably decide at the start of your modernization project which database environment you will use and then not look back. But remember that the I/O sub-procedures method is an option.

DB2 SQL/PL (Procedural Language)

And speaking of options, this is another one.

This book is about RPG, so we have sort of restricted ourselves to that. But when you look at developing the models, the use of a data-centric language like DB2 SQL/PL over a procedure-centric language like RPG is a serious option.

PL is a standalone declarative language (unlike embedded SQL that is inserted into an RPG program) that allows you to do control structures as well as bring the full power of DB2 data access into the picture. Using this, it would be quite practical—some people would say "quite sensible"—to do your model program entirely in PL.

If you are interested in this, I would suggest perusing the IBM Redbook *SQL Procedures, Triggers, and Functions on DB2 for IBM i.*

I have honestly not made up my mind yet about PL, not that anyone is waiting for me to do so. I admit, on one hand, it is an intriguing idea. But I have always had a certain morbid fear of two-page-long SELECTs. Your program can get pretty confusing pretty fast, and it looks positively awful. But, as Dan Lovell has reminded me on several occasions, that is more a result of bad coding practices, and you can make the same kind of mess in RPG. Although /Free is a lot easier on the eye than SQL.

But my prejudices aside (I am working on that, by the way), PL versus RPG is a real option.

View

And now the view.

There is not much we can do to the RPG, but what if we put a PHP or Java module in here? You could, you know.

By moving all the display logic to a single module, it would be easy to replace that module with something written in a more Web-friendly language. For example, one of the advantages of ILE is that you can call a Java module from the RPG directly.

Or, you could use PHP, Ruby, or even just HTML or JavaScript. This is not as trivial as it may sound, however. For one thing, if you are using PHP or Ruby, those are server-side languages. As a result, you don't really call the PHP script and run it on the i. Instead, you would need to open up a browser session and let the PHP script run on a server. Now you would probably do this via something like Zend Server running in your box, but you get the idea.

Historically, that has been an issue for MVC for the last few years—namely the difficulty in mating up RPG with other, especially server-side, languages. And that is probably one reason that some sites have opted to redo their systems either in Java or directly in PHP or another Web-oriented language. We will discuss that more in the next chapter. There are a number of options available, and work is being done constantly to make this process more seamless and less mysterious. I think the advantages of using your properly structured RPG code along with a true Web language are worth fighting for.

Controller

Finally, the controller.

I suppose you could take all the logic under the **Enter** key branch of the SELECT and put it in a sub-procedure embedded in this program. It's not something I would do now with the small bit of logic that is there. However, as you add other fields that need to be edited, the code could become unwieldy, and putting it in a sub-procedure might be a good way to do that. I am a firm believer that people can only take in and process so much information at one time, and too large of a code section just becomes too big to handle. But maybe that is a limitation I have rather than humans in general. Certainly doing something like that has as many negatives as positives.

The main thing I would look at here is whether you want to do this in RPG at all.

That is, the main job of the controller is to call the view and the models. Now we know that the view is probably going to be in a scripting language. And the model with probably be RPG or PL. So what it boils down to is, what language should we write the controller in so that it can easily call both Web and native i languages and pass data back and forth? Will it be easier to do that from RPG (PL, great as it is, is not a candidate for this task) or a powerful scripting language like PHP or Java?

Many factors are involved in answering this question, and we will continue that discussion in the next chapter.

Chapter 27

RPG and the Web

Before I begin, I want to acknowledge my deep indebtedness to Alan Seiden, Aaron Bartell, and Dan Lovell for their help with the details of this chapter.

As I said before, in this book, we have sort of been making the assumption that RPG is the only game in town. And, as I also said before, that is not true.

Fact is, probably no one is doing straight RPG development anymore. For better or worse, the days of green-screen applications are over. And since RPG does not have a native Web interface, the days of pure RPG development, regardless of how ILE or /Free it is, are over, too.

Currently, there seem to be four main scenarios for how the IBM i is involved in developing new systems.

Abandonment

I think, based solely on my limited personal experience, a fairly significant number of companies are abandoning the i (and therefore RPG) completely.

Often this is done in concert with a switch to SAP or Oracle, which is generally conceded to be the best way to rid your company of excess cash. If neither of these two products are involved, then it is usually a switch to some Windows Server solution and the adoption of .NET or something similar.

Either way, the end result is we all go out to the end of the driveway and wave goodbye as another shop drives away because the efforts to update the i were too little and too late. My experience has also been that most of the people who have to work with these new systems are not very happy about this, but the ones who made the decision are not the ones who have to do the work, so it all works out OK.

Full RPG Replacement

The second scenario that seems common is to keep the i but completely replace the RPG systems with something else that you have written, often Java-based.

I find this interesting, and frankly it is an option that I don't really understand very well. I have been in several shops doing this, and it seems to take forever and involve a much larger group of people than are on the RPG side. Plus, while moving things to production in RPG is not all that big a deal, moving things to production on the Java side seems to be something that requires a lot more thought and care. I am not a Java programmer, so I probably shouldn't be giving even a cursory opinion, but a number of people I know and respect who do have a solid hold on both Java and RPG seem to indicate it is a much more cumbersome way to approach business problems.

But, none of that matters because this strategy does work and, as I said, I have seen a number of shops go this direction.

DB2/PL Replacement

No, I do not mean replacing DB2 and its associated Procedural Language (PL), but rather using them to replace RPG. This is the whole "data-centric" approach.

I have somewhat of a checkered history with the whole SQL/DB2 thing. Part of it is that I just don't see the point of going to DB2 to just read the product master and verify that the input parameter is a real product number.

On the other hand, I have to admit that the adherents of the SQL/DB2 approach are right. Just as Polish is the international language of love (well, if you are in Warsaw), SQL is the international language of data. Over the past four years, I have been in about five different types of shops in terms of platforms and languages. And they all had one thing in common. Yep, SQL in one form or another. In this day of a thousand languages, the one thing you can be sure your new hire will know is SQL.

So, lately, I have been looking a little more closely at the whole question and in particular how you can use DB2 PL on the i to replace the RPG code that you have. I know this flies in the face of me not wanting to lose my RPG investment but—sometimes you have to be able to give a little. I at least want to understand what DB2 PL can do better.

And for the model role, DB2 PL works fine. Heavy lifting of data is what it is designed to do. I probably wouldn't use it for the controller, although if you wrap up a Web script up like a stored procedure, PL can call it, but I would still prefer to use RPG.

Multi-language Rewrite

The final option is to use a variety of Web languages along with RPG, picking the languages based on their strengths and how they fit into the particular tasks we are being asked to do.

I have to admit that I kind of like this approach.

For one thing, it keeps your RPG around where it makes sense, and I just can't see the benefit of throwing away this very valuable investment.

Second, it allows you to pull in the language that is best for solving the specific problem you have. And this seems to be the direction that we are headed in. That is, moving away from a monolithic language that does everything, whether it be RPG or Java or whatever, and toward using a number of languages tuned to do specific tasks.

Finally, it tends to adopt an open source approach. Open source is an interesting topic. Over the last 10 years it has gone from being a very primitive, almost scary concept to being the primary initiative for innovation and change. The best news is there are some very interesting things going on in the open source world right now related to RPG and its relationship with other, more Web-oriented languages. So that's cool.

That said, what does that all mean for RPG?

RPG and Other Languages

We will proceed based on the assumption that you are going to choose Door Number 4 (otherwise you probably wouldn't have bought this book) and will potentially be interfacing RPG with other, more Web-happy languages.

Just exactly how does that work? Like most good things, it's complicated.

RPG has always had the ability to call CL.

And by using ILE and the prototyped call, you can add C and Java to the list of things you can easily call directly from RPG (which is a good reason, despite all the semi-negative things I said about Java above, for using it in concert with RPG). Using these languages, you could pretty easily take your MVC program from the previous chapter and modify it to use Java, for example, to perform the view portion.

But when we are talking about an open source approach, we are generally looking at languages like HTML5, some version of JavaScript, PHP, Ruby, maybe Python, whatever. And the question then becomes, how does RPG interface with these guys?

There are two ways that we can go here: either RPG can call the other language, let's say PHP, or PHP can call RPG.

Since we are talking about an MVC application, and all of the calls in MVC originate from the controller, then what we are really talking about here is what language the controller will be written in.

I think you know my preference: write the controller in RPG because I think the code is cleaner and more straightforward than doing it in a Web language, but since I am currently in fourth place (out of six) in my fantasy football league, you may not want to just blindly follow me. (To be fair, I ended up in third place in my fantasy baseball league, although we have one fewer person in that one.)

So, going with the odds from Vegas, let's start with the other option: calling RPG from scripts (which means we would write the controller in Java or PHP or Ruby or something).

Calling RPG from Web Languages

We could choose anything, but I am most familiar with PHP, and it does come alphabetically before Ruby, so let's start there. Suppose we write the controller in PHP.

PHP is a good option. Support for it would probably come from the Zend Server that would run right on your i. PHP has plenty of logic syntax in it, so you could easily write the controller using it. I honestly don't think it is as straightforward and pretty as /Free, but what can you do?

From your PHP controller script, you can not only access RPG but also DB2 databases on the i (including ones that are set up using DDS). In terms of what PHP can do on the Web, it is fully functional, supporting XML and JSON, SOAP and REST, curl and other HTTP functionality, and so on.

The actual process of calling an RPG program (or CL or COBOL) from a PHP script is done via the PHP Toolkit that is available from Zend. It's pretty simple to use, and as I said previously provides access to both programs and databases.

Calling Web Languages from RPG

The other side of the coin, of course, is to write the controller in RPG, and that is what I sort of would rather do. Unfortunately, of the two options, it is probably harder to call Web languages from RPG than the other way around. But that is changing.

Let's start again with PHP. We have several options here, most of which we won't want to use.

The first is to use the QP2SHELL approach to call PASE. From there, you can kick off your PHP script that could, for example, be a link to the screen you want to show. Sounds OK, eh? There is one disadvantage, which could be pretty serious, and that is you can't send any data back to the RPG program. So this method would be pretty limited. Plus, it's not the fastest thing in the world.

Another option is to use UNIX pipes. There are a couple of flavors of this out there: one by Tony Cairns from IBM called Popen, and another from Scott Klement called UNIXCMD. The good news on this is that it does allow you to send data back to RPG from the PHP program. The downside is that it is slow, and what Alan Seiden describes as "hacky," which scares the heck out of me.

Apparently you can also use data queues. This is much faster, but again, Alan describes this as "hacky," too. Besides I've never cared much for data queues anyway. But it might be worth investigating.

Fortunately, there is one more thing to consider, and it is new and part of the open source initiatives that we were talking about. Specifically, it is the VLANG-RPG initiative. You can find more information about this at *https://bitbucket.org/inext/vlang-rpg*. Essentially, VLANG is an RPG service program that handles the call to PHP. PHP therefore functions like a slave to the RPG.

One of the advantages of VLANG-RPG is that even though it only functions with PHP right now, it is possible to use it with any scripting language that uses EVAL script functionality. This would include Ruby, Python, Node.js, and others. Undoubtedly more will be forthcoming on this topic in the near future, and googling it is probably your best bet. Check the YIPS site as well, for more information (*http://yips.idevcloud.com/wiki/*).

The Bottom Line

OK, anyone want to draw a conclusion? Or maybe I should say summarize.

We know we want to design our applications, as much as possible, using the modular programs in general and the MVC design pattern in particular.

And we know that means we will have a controller, model, and view, perhaps several models and views.

The model we will write in RPG (or PL). You could do it Java or PHP or whatever, but why? Why throw out that investment? Yes, you may have to redo the RPG section to be more modular, but that is much easier than redoing it in Java. Why is it that in the IBM i world we can't bring in two RPG programmers to modularize apps, but we can create a new sub-department, create a manager position, and hire half a dozen Java guys? I don't get it.

For the most part, the view will be in some scripting language (e.g., HTML5, JavaScript, PHP). Which you choose probably depends on what skill sets you have in house and what kinds of things the screen is doing (e.g., does it need JavaScript effects?).

And that leaves the controller, which could be written in either RPG, a script language, or Java. I know that I have poo-pooed the use of Java, but that was mostly related to its use in whole hog replacement of RPG. I have no problem with a limited use of Java, although it wouldn't be my first choice, either, because then you get into all the Java baggage. And Java does infect everything else. Suddenly everybody wants to do everything with Java, and then the whole multi-language thing is out the window. As I have said, I would probably prefer to write the controller in RPG and then use the VLANG-RPG facility to do the connection. But there are other options, and I am hardly an expert in the use of that function.

I know what you're thinking.

"So just tell us how to use VLANG-RPG to do this."

And maybe I should. But the whole discussion of interfacing RPG to the Web is a complex one. One that depends heavily on what you actually want to accomplish and what skill sets you currently have to work with. And one that is still evolving. But maybe this is enough for now.

Chapter 28

What's Really Important

It's amazing how hard it can be to keep track of that.

What's really important, that is.

You start out with good intentions, and all of a sudden you are distracted by all this stuff, and you sort of start to lose focus. Eventually you end up getting all hot and bothered with details about something that is not important at all. And the next thing you know, the Hundred Years War has started.

So let's end by reminding ourselves what really is important.

The Bottom Line

In the end, it's all about modernization. There are many options, and I have no idea what you are going to do.

As we saw in the last chapter, it is unlikely that you will do everything in RPG green screen. And so, some people will probably say that there is no point to this book at all. After all, the future is Web languages.

And maybe that is true. But to me, I see no reason to give up on RPG, a language that is still growing and is specifically designed to handle business—no, organizational—issues. Because in the end, it doesn't matter whether you are running a foundry, a metal stamping plant, a medical instruments company, a retail products distribution company, or a hospital that needs to track patients and lab results.

Yes, you can do this stuff using just Web languages. But I do not believe that you can develop those apps faster than you can develop RPG data control and access apps. And so, in my opinion, RPG still has a place and still has value.

And if that is true, then it is just as valid to say, "I am going to code the best possible RPG," as it is to say, "I am going to code the best possible PHP (or HTML5 or JavaScript or whatever)."

The question then becomes, what does it mean to "code the best possible RPG?"

The end goal here is not to use MVC.

Or ILE.

Or even /Free.

They are just tools, although they are tools I think you should definitely be using.

No, the end goal is to produce software that is easy and quick to write, easy to understand (either by someone else or by you two years from now), and easy to completely test (especially automatically).

The end goal is to produce software that is as bug-free as possible and is easy to enhance as the years go by.

The question is, how do you do that? And what tools give you a leg up on that task?

Write Modular Code

If you are only going to do one thing to move toward modernization, then it should be writing modular code.

Stop developing applications using BOPs. Stop writing 2,000-line programs that have dozens of subroutines and data coupling up the wazoo.

Instead, start writing modular code.

Oh, I know. You are not writing code anymore. You are maintaining code. So sell management on the benefits of rewriting those horribly big applications as modular, perhaps even MVC. Everyone complains about the BOPs, but nobody really does anything about it. Until they start switching to Java. Then they do it. You don't have to start with the biggest one, but start somewhere. And I do realize how very hard it can be to convince management to do something like that. But I have tremendous faith in you. You can do it!! Can you spell the word "hero?"

And as you redo (or write new things), start thinking about your application not as a process first, which lends itself to coding large programs, but as a set of objects.

Think about what those objects are.

Think about the work that they will do or have done to them.

Think about the natural boundaries between those objects.

Finally, think about how the various objects can be related to each other without being subsumed by a larger entity.

Yes, it's true. You will end up with more programs than if you did just one big one. But complexity is the enemy here, not the number of programs you have.

By writing small modules, you are giving yourself the best chance to make the application easy to test, easy to understand, and easy to modify without screwing up the world.

Write Simple Code

We all know them.

Some might even be reading this book.

And while I envy their technical prowess, I always pray that I will never have to look at one of their programs.

These are the programmers who use esoteric and obscure methods to accomplish what needs to be done. They do in three lines what it takes me 8. Their code runs in .00056 seconds while mine labors along at .0023 seconds. They remember things from the System/38 world that I never even knew about.

When they have moved on or even go on vacation, other folks are afraid to touch their code. And when they do, it takes twice as long to figure out what has been done, and you (OK, me) are twice as likely to introduce a bug when you try to modify it.

Most of them do it without realizing it.

I believe there is nothing more dangerous in today's IT environment than complexity. There is no such thing as something that is "too simple." And so, the ability to write simple code is a real asset. True, simple is a hard concept to define. Most of us know it when we see it, however. Is it patently clear what you are trying to do? Can I look over the code and see the flow? Does it make sense to me?

How do you code *simple*?

First, don't use any techniques that are not in general use anymore. I don't care how things were done 20 years ago.

Second, use BIFs as much as possible as a lingua franca for how things are done today. But use them cautiously. Don't make your BIFs so complex that you need to bring in a top litigator and his staff to unravel them. In that case, it's better to have several steps so that you can easily see what is going on.

Third, think really, really hard before you create one of those heavily indented IF statements. Use a SELECT instead. Or break it up into several, logically separate IFs. And think hard again before setting up a condition as a negative, especially if there are other conditions involved and you will end up switching the connector operators.

Fourth, as much as possible, use a limited set of RPG commands and operations. Yes, sometimes you have to bring in something you don't use very often, but if you can use a limited set 90 percent of the time, doing so will go a long way to making your code easy to understand.

Fifth, as much as possible, use common code structures. People need to see code as a segment, rather than as individual commands. Using common structures helps you do that.

Sixth, and maybe most importantly, control your data. Reduce data coupling. Use local variables. So very important.

Code /Free

Needless to say, I think coding /Free is pretty important.

To be honest, I can't think of a single reason why you wouldn't, other than nostalgia to go on with positional RPG.

With its non-inverted, English language-like phraseology (without being as very verbose as COBOL), /Free makes an excellent medium for expressing your thoughts in terms of code.

Oh, I know. Some places won't let you code /Free. If I hear one more out-of-touch shop say, "we don't use /Free because not everybody knows it," I will explode. Well then, get everyone to learn it, bunky. It doesn't take that long, and if you are smart enough to code in RPG positional, you are more than smart enough to code in /Free.

Code /Free and never look back! Can I have an "amen"?!

Use ILE, Especially Sub-Procedures and Service Programs

So many people look at ILE just in terms of efficiency. Write in ILE, and your calls will be quicker.

Yeah, that's true, and that is a good reason to use ILE. But again, when you have a POWER8 and your application is not being used 10,000 times a day, is that really a big deal?

The real value of ILE is threefold:

First, the ability to use sub-procedures instead of subroutines.

Not only do sub-procedures allow you to write modular code, but you can call that code either from within the program where it resides or externally.

But what I love about sub-procedures are the local variables. I just think it is so important to use those and so reduce the amount of data coupling in your programs. I honestly believe that runaway data coupling is the root cause of the majority of the bugs that are introduced into code when it is originally designed and subsequently enhanced.

Plus, using sub-procedures sets you up to learn Web languages where classes and other functions act much like sub-procedures and where local variables are the norm.

Second, service programs.

They may not be perfect for every situation, but in most instances they are the preferred method of binding two modules together.

They facilitate the use of reusable code and are very efficient.

But most of all for me, they force you to use sub-procedures as your primary module, and I think you know how I feel about them.

Third, interfacing with other languages.

Finally, ILE makes it easier to interface with other languages in the IBM i stable.

Languages like Java or C. And in today's world where you may have your business rules in RPG but the display logic in something else, that ends up being pretty important.

And the best thing about ILE is that it's not hard. Yes, there are some weird situations out there, but most of it is very simple and intuitive. It's also very modern in its structure. I don't see that as icing or a Joe Cool factor. Modern is what gives RPG validity in a world dominated by Web languages.

Grab the ring the next time it comes around, and get going.

Embrace Design Patterns

It doesn't have to be MVC. But it will probably be one of the family of MVC patterns. Although you owe it to yourself to check out some of the more prominent patterns and see what else might be useful in the business world.

But you should begin to think about using a standard application design.

Perhaps you are already doing this. And if you are just copying from a sample BOP that you have, that doesn't count. I am talking about a modular pattern here—something amenable to ILE and /Free.

Previously, we talked about using standard commands and operators, a limited set to make it easy to see what was going on. But the same is true from an architectural point of view. Having all of your apps conform to three or four standard patterns gives you an app set that is much easier to understand than one where every function is built differently.

Keep Up to Date with What Is New

If we learned anything from chapter 27, it is that we don't know everything yet that is possible here.

I would have not guessed it, coming from a planet that had so many snakes, but Yoda was right: "Hard to read, always in motion is the future," and that is exactly where we are right now. There are new things coming out in the open source world between RPG and the Web almost continuously.

Keep track of the changes, and don't ignore new initiatives. Too often the i world has ignored or delayed new initiatives (/Free, ILE, MVC), and the result is that many shops have moved away from the i to other, less desirable situations.

Ignorance may be bliss, but knowledge is power.

Why?

Why do all of this? Why change the way we have made a living for the last 20 or 30 years?

Frankly, you probably don't need to do it to keep your current job, or you would have done it already.

And if you lose that job, there seem to be plenty of moderately low-paying RPG programmer jobs out there. I have heard from half a dozen headhunters how hard it is to find RPG talent. They say this before they offer me a rate that is humiliatingly lower than what the guy who just changed my transmission oil gets. Not that there's anything wrong with changing transmission oil. Glad someone knows how to do it. It's just that, well, you know ...

But there are two reasons that I think are valid for doing all of this, and I alluded to them at the beginning of the book.

First, for personal growth. Unless you are within spitting distance of retirement, growing professionally is probably a good idea. The days of knowing only one language and one set of tools is over, and you never know when you will either get the opportunity or have to switch to something else. The techniques we have talked about in this book are applicable to more than RPG, and it might be a good idea to get in the habit.

Second, as I said earlier, I believe RPG is fighting for its life right now. Yes, it is still used in lots of shops. But do you know how many RPG shops I've seen go to .NET or Java or goodness knows what else in the last few years? No, seriously, do you know? Because I didn't keep track, and I'm curious.

But I know it was quite a few. And every time a longtime IBM i person retires, they are probably going to be replaced by someone who doesn't know RPG or the i. Do you really want them to see positional code and programs the size of Rhode Island?

So, who cares?

I guess I do. I didn't think much of RPG when I first met it. But it's grown on me over the years. And I don't like smart-mouthed Web kids smirking when I say that it is a powerful and vibrant language (that really happened about two months ago). I want them to know the RPG that I know: smart, sophisticated, and still very much in prime time.

Advertising the new RPG is not the job of IBM. They'd just screw it up anyway. It is the job of all of us who use it every day. It is up to us to use the modern techniques we have been given, to work and function like true professionals who are always learning and changing, to show the world the IBM i and RPG that we know.

And that's about it. I can't think of anything more to say. So I guess I will just stop. Thanks for tuning in.

And if anyone says, "it's about time," I will find you.

Index